AN ENDURING PASSION

AN ENDURING PASSION

My Ryder Cup Years

SAM TORRANCE

MAINSTREAM
PUBLISHING

EDINBURGH AND LONDON

First published in Great Britain in 2010 by
MAINSTREAM PUBLISHING COMPANY
(EDINBURGH) LTD
7 Albany Street
Edinburgh EH1 3UG

ISBN 9781845966294

This book is a work of non-fiction based on the life, experiences
and recollections of the author. In some cases, names of people have been changed
to protect the privacy of others. The authors have stated to the publishers that,
except in such minor respects not affecting the substantial accuracy of the work,
the contents of this book are true

A catalogue record for this book is available
from the British Library

Typeset in Giovanni and Trajan Pro

Printed in Great Britain by
Clays Ltd St Ives plc

1 3 5 7 9 10 8 6 4 2

Carpe diem.

Acknowledgements

Mark Baldwin, for his skilful writing.

Sarah Wooldridge and Vicky Cuming at IMG.

Bill Campbell, Graeme Blaikie, Alex Hepworth and Emily MacKenzie at Mainstream Publishing for their help with this project.

Ken Schofield, for being a great leader and a good friend.

All my Ryder Cup teammates over the years.

My past captains: John Jacobs, Tony Jacklin, Bernard Gallacher and Mark James.

All the staff at the European Tour, especially Mark MacDiarmid.

Mum and Dad, for always being there.

Suzanne, Daniel, Phoebe and Anouska for their love and support.

The authors would also like to acknowledge the valuable reference material provided by the book *Sam: The Autobiography of Sam Torrance* (BBC Books, London, 2003).

CONTENTS

THE RYDER CUP AND ME

It was my privilege and honour to captain a winning European Ryder Cup team at The Belfry in the glorious late September of 2002. Eight years have now passed since that defining moment of my golfing life, but the memories and the emotion of that week live on within me. More sobering is the realisation that it is now 25 years – a quarter of a century, for goodness' sake – since I sank the putt that ensured Europe's historic triumph in 1985.

That was also at The Belfry, of course, on the steeply tiered 18th green, and it meant that the Americans had been beaten in Ryder Cup combat for the first time in 28 years. Since 1985, the Cup has changed hands five times; in the twelve matches between 1985 and 2008, the match result has been Europe seven wins, United States four wins, plus one tied match.

The task, and the challenge, facing Colin Montgomerie and Corey Pavin at Celtic Manor in October 2010 is the same as has faced 46 previous Ryder Cup captains in 37 matches: to lead with skill and dignity and to combine a finely tuned tactical cunning with a proper appreciation of what it means to the elite golfers who play in the event and for whom you are responsible. And, if you can, to win.

The Ryder Cup has become one of the biggest sporting events in the world. It all began in 1927 at the Worcester Country Club in Massachusetts, and although various Great Britain and Great Britain and Ireland teams enjoyed notable successes in 1929, 1933 and 1957, it was not often an even contest until the Americans agreed to take on a full European team, from 1979.

In the following chapters, my own Ryder Cup story is charted from my debut as a player, at Walton Heath in 1981, until my captaincy in 2002. That's twenty-two years of virtually unbroken involvement, and, without doubt, my eight appearances as a player and then my vice captaincy role under Mark James at Brookline in 1999 gave me an understanding of the Ryder Cup that was to prove invaluable in 2002.

What is largely forgotten, however, is that I had tried for more than ten years as a professional to get into the Ryder Cup in the first place. I was close to qualifying on several occasions and wondered if I would ever get the opportunity to play. But those years of striving also made me even more determined to become, one day, a Ryder Cup golfer. It made it much more special to me when, finally, and at the age of 28, I made the team.

Almost three decades on from my debut, I can look back and see how the Ryder Cup has defined me as a golfer and as a person. It has dominated my career, and I will admit that at times I have been consumed by it. Not in a bad way, because it has been more like a love affair that has stood the test of time. To have been involved in ten Ryder Cups – to have lived the moments and seen grown men cry – has been the greatest privilege and thrill of my sporting career.

That is why I wanted to do this book: so that I could record my own recollections and try to give an insight into what it is like being a Ryder Cup player and, ultimately, a Ryder Cup captain. My love of team golf – and, for me, this has also included the Dunhill Cup, the Hennessy Cup and the World Cup – means that I've always been fascinated with its demands and its nuances.

Yet it is the Ryder Cup that towers above everything else, and it is the job of Ryder Cup captaincy that makes the greatest demands of all. What did I learn from the captains I played under and against? What did my experiences as a player give me when I was appointed Ryder Cup vice captain, and then captain itself? What decisions did I make at The Belfry in 2002 that were directly influenced by those first-hand and hard-won experiences?

I hope the rest of this book will provide answers to those questions and reveal the magic of the Ryder Cup for those of us players who have been inside the ropes as well as those spectators watching from outside of them.

Not for one minute, moreover, as players, do we forget that every shot is being watched in golf club bars and lounges, in pubs and in private homes by the golf-loving public of Europe and America. As members of the European team, we appreciate that there are thousands and thousands of people watching on their television screens and willing our every shot to finish up well or go in the hole.

We appreciate it fully, and, of course, we all know friends and family who are supporting us as well. At all the Ryder Cups I have been involved in, and, I dare say, the ones I haven't, I can say without equivocation that every European player has felt this huge support – and understood how much the result of the match means to our supporters. For my part, I have often drawn on that knowledge out there on the course.

From chapters one to eleven, Mark Baldwin's narrative provides the backcloth for my own reminiscences, comments, analysis and opinions of the ten Ryder Cups that provided me with the greatest moments and experiences of my golfing life.

Sinking the winning putt in 1985 at The Belfry gave me a fame that I still find hard to believe. People still want to talk to me about it or want to tell me they were there or why it was also such an important thing in their own lives. Sometimes people get quite emotional about it – almost as emotional as I got at the time, or still do when I think back to how I felt at that moment.

Blood, sweat and tears are all relevant words when I think about my own Ryder Cup career: the blood that seeped through my sock from the septic toe that forced me to pull out in 1993 after playing just one foursomes match; the sweat of trying to make the European team – especially before my debut appearance – and of the Ryder Cup competition itself; and also the tears that I have shed unashamedly, both in sadness and in joy, throughout my entire association with this great and unique event.

But it has all been worth it and more. For me, indeed, the Ryder Cup has become an enduring passion. I have loved every minute of those ten matches for the excitement, the camaraderie and the opportunity to stand up there on the tee and try to beat the Americans.

When I first became a Ryder Cup golfer, it was widely thought almost impossible to beat the best of the United States. Perhaps no team, from either side, has been as powerful or as intimidating as the 1981 Americans. Yet look at what happened both at Oakland Hills in 2004 and then at The K Club in Ireland in 2006. Those European teams, under Bernhard Langer and Ian Woosnam respectively, absolutely annihilated their opponents – despite the presence in the American ranks of Tiger Woods, who is perhaps destined to be the greatest golfer of all time, let alone of this modern era.

And, only two decades on from our breakthrough victory of 1985, the most remarkable aspect of those crushing wins was that, from a European perspective, they were no surprise at all. One of the great legacies of the Ryder Cup, since it became US v Europe, has been a true contest between two sides who know, if all goes their way, that they can achieve anything.

Moreover, as the great American fightback of 2008 under Paul Azinger's inspired captaincy showed – without the presence of Woods in his team at Valhalla – it is still very much a contest. The 2010 event at Celtic Manor promises to be as classic and as close a confrontation as those witnessed since 1983 at Palm Beach Gardens, at The Belfry, at Muirfield Village, at Kiawah Island, at Oak Hill, at Valderrama and at Brookline.

What Azinger's captaincy confirmed, above all, was the results you can achieve when you put the emphasis on getting the little things right in the build-up and in the match itself. For me, that is imperative, and I think Pavin's approach will be right out of the Azinger school.

Yet being a home captain, as Azinger was, allows you to do so much more in terms of course set-up. And he did an especially fantastic job of that. He created a birdie-fest on the last day at Valhalla with the easiest of pin positions, and he told his players to go out there and shoot for as many birdies as they could get.

I understand Kenny Perry, for instance, made nine birdies in his singles match. Anthony Kim made a whole bunch of them to beat Sergio

García. In fact, all the Americans did. And Azinger sent them out to give it a rip. Look at Boo Weekley, playing to the crowd by galloping down the first fairway after his drive and pretending his golf club, between his legs, was a horse! Brilliant.

I am not sure that the European team, that Sunday, really knew the course had been set up to be so easy by Azinger. The Americans were thinking *easy, easy, easy* when they went out ready to go for every pin and for every shot, and perhaps we were thinking *tough, tough, tough*.

John Daly would have loved to be in that American line-up on singles day in Valhalla, and I always thought that the various American teams of the 1990s missed a big trick by not selecting him – especially for matches in Europe, where he is hugely popular. Sometimes, in my time, the Americans could appear a bit aloof, even to their own crowds, but that certainly wasn't the case at Valhalla, and full marks go to Azinger for helping to create a real rapport between his team and their supporters.

I remember, in 1987, Jack Nicklaus actually remarking how the American fans at Muirfield Village seemed to have more of a rapport with the European players than with his own team. Well, Jack, that was something we had deliberately tried to establish all week.

It is in the following chapters, however, that each of the Ryder Cups I was involved in is looked at in fuller detail. For now, I just want to underline how much being captain of the Europe team in 2002 meant to me as someone who, as a player, had witnessed at first hand the complete transformation of the event from, well, non-event to must-see sporting theatre.

I made my Ryder Cup debut seven years before my son Daniel was born, and yet in 2002 I was able to share with him – then a golf-mad fourteen year old – some extraordinary moments out there on the course at The Belfry. It made me so glad that he too had experienced just a little of what this event is about.

My wife, Suzanne, and I also put so much thought into all the gifts and presents, for both teams, that a home captain is traditionally expected to provide. And we did so because I wanted all my players, in particular, to realise – if they didn't know it before – just how special

15

it was to be a part of a Ryder Cup. I wanted to pass on to them how special I felt it all was.

I wanted everything to be better than perfect during my captaincy at The Belfry, and I wanted to win. The job of captain consumed me, but even with all my previous experience as a player and as a vice captain, I could not have predicted how incredible the reality of doing that job would actually be.

Everything else I have ever done in golf – including winning forty-four individual events worldwide as a professional and captaining Scotland to victory in the last of my eight Dunhill Cups – pales into insignificance compared with the thrill of winning the Ryder Cup as European captain.

I have never won a major championship, but I don't think even that could have come close. That's what the Ryder Cup means to me.

CHAPTER ONE

1981 WALTON HEATH

It had been a long time coming when Sam Torrance finally stepped onto the first tee at Walton Heath, in Surrey, to become – at last – a Ryder Cup golfer. It was Friday, 18 September 1981; he had just turned 28 and had been a professional player for 11 years. It was, in the end, however, more than worth the wait.

The Ryder Cup was all that Torrance had anticipated, and the matches he played at Walton Heath in 1981 were to be the first passionate stirrings of what became – over the next 21 years – a love affair that brought him the most memorable moments of his golfing life.

I cannot remember very much detail about walking to the tee for my debut match, playing with Howard Clark in a fourball game against Johnny Miller and Tom Kite on the first afternoon. I wouldn't even be able to tell you if it was Howard or me who hit off first. I think I was in such a state of total concentration – and fear of what I had to do – that I shut everything else out of my mind. It was just a case of putting your tee peg into the turf when it was your turn to drive, placing your ball on it, going through your pre-shot routine and, if possible, getting the ball off the tee and somewhere down the fairway.

I remember going out onto the course to watch during the first session of matches that morning, which were foursomes, but from lunchtime onwards it's all a bit of a blur. Actually, 'fear' is the best word to describe my state of mind on that day. I was representing Europe in the Ryder Cup, and it was everything and more – far, far more – than I'd ever dreamed it would be. But it was also utterly terrifying – although you also knew you had to try to turn that to your advantage because, if you were feeling the fear, then you knew that your opponent and every other player was feeling it too. I suppose that is what gets you through it: turning it to your advantage, if you can.

Twelve years earlier, in 1969, a sixteen-year-old Torrance had been transfixed by the Ryder Cup at Royal Birkdale that ended in a 16–16 tie with the United States retaining the trophy as holders. Watching on television, he had felt the magic of the Ryder Cup for the first time and, in particular, was astonished by the famous gesture from Jack Nicklaus to Tony Jacklin in the anchor singles match.

With Brian Huggett halving the penultimate singles game against Billy Casper, the Great Britain team knew that Jacklin, all square with Nicklaus playing the last hole, needed to win his match to bring the Cup back home for the first time since Dai Rees's team had triumphed at Lindrick in 1957.

Nicklaus asked Jacklin how he felt as they walked down the fairway after their drives. When he replied that he felt terrible, or words to that effect, Nicklaus merely laughed and said that he did too, if that was any consolation. The pair also decided that it didn't get any better than the situation they were in, with their respective team's hopes resting on their actions and with the eyes of much of the golfing world on what was going to happen next.

What did happen is that both were on the green in two, and both missed lengthy putts for birdie. Jacklin's putt came to rest only two or three feet from the cup, but Nicklaus charged his birdie attempt fully five feet past. The thousands clamouring for a view around the green made not a sound as Nicklaus, hunched familiarly over his ball, courageously made the one back for par. It was then that Nicklaus did something that was to reverberate around the globe and enter Ryder Cup legend, summing up the spirit of the event and that of the game of golf itself. He bent down to pick up Jacklin's ball marker, and he conceded his opponent's par putt.

Their match was halved, and the whole match was tied. The Americans, of course, had been assured of retaining the Cup once Nicklaus had holed for his four, but it was still some gesture for him to take out of the equation the possibility of Jacklin missing. Under all that pressure, even Jacklin – the winner of that summer's Open Championship, just along the coast at Royal Lytham, and Europe's best player – might have messed up, and then the United States would have won the match outright. Nicklaus, however, merely told Jacklin as they shook hands that he didn't think he was going to miss it, but that he certainly didn't want him to have the chance to do so either.

I could not believe what I saw when Jack conceded that putt to Tony. Would I have done that in a similar situation? What was this Ryder Cup where such a thing was possible? Jack Nicklaus, of course, was already a golfing superstar by then, and one of my biggest heroes. For me, though, at that impressionable age, it was amazing to see someone like him give his opponent a putt on the last green, when so much was at stake. It made a huge impression on me.

Obviously, by then I was dreaming of one day soon being a professional golfer myself and one day in the future becoming a Ryder Cup golfer. That Nicklaus concession made me realise just what this great biennial match was about. This was something totally different again from a normal strokeplay tournament. This was another world, another level up. This was 'Wow!' And what happened at Royal Birkdale, in that last match between two such great players, was clearly a very big deal indeed, and something to be remembered for evermore in the history of the game. More than ever, in the wake of watching that 1969 match, I really wanted to be a part of this Ryder Cup myself.

If the young Torrance had fallen quickly in love with the Ryder Cup – and the concept and possibilities raised by team and matchplay golf – then the following year, 1970, was to bring another early lesson that taught him just how serious a business it was to represent your country in this excitingly different format of the game.

The venue this time was Hillside, near Southport, and now it was Torrance himself who was playing. On 15 August 1970, just a week or so before his 17th birthday, he was selected to represent the Scotland boys' team in an international match against the hosts, England. It was his first taste of international team golf, playing foursomes and singles, and although Scotland were well beaten, he has never forgotten an incident near the start of his singles match.

On the second green my opponent putted up to about two feet, and I attempted to knock his ball back to him, conceding it for the par four. But, clumsily, I only succeeded in tapping the ball into the hole instead. To my astonishment, he claimed it as a birdie three, as, technically, I had no right to touch his ball. And, what is more, he was given the three! I went on to win the match by 5&4, but to this day I have never forgotten that incident.

Sure, I was mad at the time because I didn't expect it – and I certainly didn't think it was the right thing to do! But I have never forgotten it because it was another valuable lesson. It was matchplay golf, and it is different. Yes, it was just a boys' international, but it was huge for all of us at the time. In fact, it was the most important day of my life at that point – being selected to play for my country while not yet 17 – and I imagine all the other competitors felt the same. One of my oldest friends, Carl Mason, was actually playing for England in that match.

I lost my foursomes game, partnering Barclay Howard, and then my singles opponent did everything in his power to beat me, and I never forgot that. It taught me that this thing called team golf was serious. If someone could do what he did to me, and if it meant so much to him, then it was important stuff. It was on the completely opposite end of the spectrum from the Nicklaus concession, of course, but in September 1969 and August 1970 I saw two things that spelled out to me just what made team golf so different. Two utterly contrasting lessons, but both equally instructive.

The only other thing I remember about playing in that boys' international was that, the evening before, in a nightclub in Southport, I got dancing with a girl who turned out to be with the leader of one of the local youth gangs. But my teammate David Chillas somehow ended up getting the blame for this – perhaps it was a case of mistaken identity by the locals – and he got a smack in the mouth! I'm not sure if David, a good friend still, even knows the reason why he got punched that night. Sorry, David! But perhaps that was another vital early lesson for me, off the course and on: learn the art of survival!

Growing up as a player at Routenburn Golf Club, near his family home in Largs on the west coast of Scotland, and later in his first job as an assistant professional at Sunningdale, Torrance often played members for an agreed amount of money – both small and, increasingly, large – and it was an experience that, he insists, helped to instil in him an added competitive streak and an ability to soak up pressure.

Lee Trevino always says that the biggest pressure you are under on the golf course is playing for more money than you've got in your pocket, and in my early days at Sunningdale in particular it was a necessity for me to play for money. I got paid £5 a week at that time, and that had to cover my rent and my food and everything. No wonder that I needed to play the members for the fee, which, I seem to recall, was £1.50. But it was the experiences of all those matches as I was growing up, even from very young when I used to play the local priests for a shilling at Routenburn, that I believe stood me in good stead when I began to play team golf. I would even say it helped me when I became a Ryder Cup player.

In the decade it took him to get into the Ryder Cup, though, Torrance also had the considerable benefit of playing in a number of team golf events as a professional. Between turning pro and representing Europe at Walton Heath, he played for Scotland in three Double Diamond Internationals and two World Cups, plus three Hennessy Cup contests featuring Great Britain and Ireland against continental Europe.

The first of these experiences came in the 1973 Double Diamond event at Prince's Golf Club in Kent, where he was called up as a late replacement for an injured Harry Bannerman and found himself under the captaincy of Eric Brown, the eccentric but quite formidable Scot who, in fact, had also been Ryder Cup captain at Royal Birkdale in 1969 – when his aggressive style of leadership had so nearly succeeded in bringing Great Britain an against-all-odds victory.

Eric Brown was my first pro team captain, and what an experience that was! Eric was a great man, but he was not someone you wanted to mess with. And what I remember above all else about that event – after the thrill of getting

21

the call-up and having to pick up Harry Bannerman's car in London and drive myself down to the Kent coast to catch up with the rest of the Scotland team – was Eric telling all of us players that he would do terrible things to us if he saw any putt coming up short. He insisted, in a manner that brooked no argument, that he wanted every putt to get past the hole. That, he said, maximised your chances in matchplay golf of making as many putts as possible. It was fine in theory, but soon I was to find myself coming down the 18th fairway at the end of my singles match against Manuel Ballesteros – Seve's elder brother – and, from about twenty feet, having two putts to win the match.

My win would also have clinched the overall match for Scotland, so it was a fairly important moment in my young life. Then, as I crouched down, lining up the putt, I saw in the crowd around the green the face of Eric Brown and instantly I heard again the words 'Don't ever leave a putt short.' What did I do? I didn't leave it short, but the ball finished four feet past and I missed the return. You can imagine my feelings. It was heartbreaking, but fortunately for me Ronnie Shade was coming up the last in the match after mine and was also about to win his game. That meant, ten minutes or so later, that we were all celebrating a famous Scottish victory and my three-putt had not, after all, cost Scotland dear.

I don't think I ever said anything afterwards to Eric, mainly because the overall joy of the occasion quickly took over, but it was another big lesson learned. In team golf it is not about you and what you are thinking. It is about the team and doing everything you can to ensure that the team wins. In the 1995 Ryder Cup, when Philip Walton was left with those two putts from fifteen feet to clinch the trophy for us on the last green at Oak Hill, I'm very glad he lagged it up and took those two putts to make sure!

The next big stepping stones on the Torrance journey into the elite levels of team golf took place in 1976, when he played not only in the Double Diamond again but also in the World Cup and the Hennessy Cup. Indeed, Torrance was to play in all but the first of the six Hennessy Cup events, which were played between 1974 and 1984 and staged biennially in non-Ryder Cup years.

Representing Scotland in the World Cups of 1976 and 1978 was certainly a big step up for me, in terms of getting used to international competition, but the Hennessy Cup was selected and played in a similar format to the Ryder Cup, so it was really the nearest thing you could get to it. And in my first Hennessy Cup, in 1976, I came up against Seve Ballesteros in the singles – and that was the year in which he had finished runner-up to Johnny Miller at the Open Championship at Royal Birkdale, playing that memorable chip and run between the bunkers at the last hole. Seve may have been still just nineteen, whereas I was almost four years older, but he was already moving into the superstar class and meeting him in that singles match was serious stuff for me.

The Hennessy that year was staged at The Belfry, and by the time we reached the 17th, a long dogleg par five, of course, I was one down. Seve didn't hit the green in two but chipped up stone dead for a birdie four. I was about three yards off the green, after two good hits, and knew that if I chipped in for an eagle three then I would be all square. I duffed it, and the ball only went about a foot in front of me. But I was pumped up, and I then chipped it right into the hole for a four, and a half. I was still one down, but at least the match was still alive.

After picking my ball out of the hole, I was off, head down, to the next tee. I was now really pumped, and all I could think of was getting my ball teed up and launching my best drive. Suddenly, however, after putting my tee in the ground, I was aware that I was completely on my own. There was no one else around. When I looked up, I saw Seve standing about 70 yards away. He was actually on the 18th tee, waiting for me, and I'd mistakenly gone to the 9th tee! You can imagine my embarrassment, but I'm pleased to say I still managed to knock it on in two, take two putts for the four and then watch as Seve three-putted from distance for a five. I had halved the match – and on the green that was to witness my two greatest moments in golf, in 1985 and 2002. What is it about that last hole at The Belfry, I wonder?

Torrance, though, has good reason to remember his World Cup debut in 1976, too, when he was selected to partner Brian Barnes as Scotland's representatives in that year's tournament in Palm Springs, California.

Brian Barnes was a legend and a larger-than-life character as well as an enormously talented golfer. Looking back, to have had Eric Brown as my first high-profile team captain at senior level and Barnesy as my first high-profile partner in a team event – well, what a double that is! In those days, in the mid '70s, Brian was a drinker, and that week in California was quite an eye-opener for me, a youngster representing Scotland for the first time in a World Cup.

Brian was drinking on the course, as well as off it, and he got through quite a few cans of beer while we played. I remember, in the team element of the week, he would put a can in the breast pocket of his golf shirt while he putted, and he often used a can – already half-empty in most instances – to mark the position of his ball on the green! That is not illegal, by the way, although it's not a good idea if another of the players in the group has to putt anywhere near the line that it is standing on. Anyway, on one occasion, I recall Brian crouching over his ball, lining up his putt, when some of the beer sloshed out of the top of the can and down onto the green. So he calmly took the can out of his shirt pocket, had a good slug to get the level of beer down a bit, replaced it in his pocket and got back to his putt.

By the end of the week, Michelob, the beer sponsors of the event, brought out onto the course a buggy with a cool box on the back of it full of their product, packed with ice cubes, and Brian would help himself. Eventually, especially because the weather was pretty warm, I joined in and had a couple of beers myself. It didn't do a huge amount for my game, though, but we came second in the team event and Barnesy finished second in the individual event. So it didn't do him much harm!

A further World Cup appearance came along for Torrance in 1978 – this time with Bernard Gallacher as his Scotland partner – and two more Hennessy Cup selections, in 1978 and 1980, were to come before he made his Ryder Cup bow. There was, too, a third and final Double Diamond International match, in 1977.

I was very disappointed that I didn't get to play in the Ryder Cup until 1981. I felt I had chances of making the 1975, 1977 and 1979 matches, but I couldn't seem to do enough and it was a very frustrating time. I know I was getting all this team golf experience elsewhere, but the Ryder Cup was my goal because it went hand in hand with finishing high up on the qualifying points, or money, list. Becoming a Ryder Cup player meant that you were recognised as being an elite player on the European Tour, and that was what I desperately wanted to be.

Having turned pro in 1970, my first professional tournament victory came in the Under-25 Matchplay Championship at Royal Birkdale in 1972 – another big stepping stone in learning the nuances and psychology of matchplay golf – and by the end of the 1970s I felt I was good enough to qualify for the Ryder Cup. In my autobiography, written seven years ago, I said that 'maybe I wanted it too much; maybe I was not sufficiently disciplined', and, looking back, I would have to say I still feel that now. But, back then, there is no doubt that I beat myself up about my failure to get into the Ryder Cup teams of the late 1970s. It was a case where I was asking myself, 'What is it about this Ryder Cup that means I can't get into it?'

I suppose the blunt fact is that, for whatever reason or reasons, and despite a total of seven professional tournament wins in the 1970s, I was not yet good enough to get myself into the upper echelon of European golf. It hurt, but I can see now that I was progressing and that I had to make that progression – slow as it was – in order to get there.

Torrance's breakthrough arrived in 1980 with what he still considers to be his best tournament victory in a career that has so far brought him 44 professional wins, including a whole clutch of Seniors Tour titles from 2004 onwards.

In the Australian PGA Championship at Royal Melbourne, Torrance held off the challenges from both Seve Ballesteros and Greg Norman to win, saving par from a bunker on the 16th to stay one stroke ahead and then birdieing the 17th to make sure of his victory. Torrance also played the last 36 holes of the event with Ballesteros – already both an Open and Masters champion – but defended his overnight lead going into the final round with skill and tenacity. Photographs showing Torrance's swing sequence during that Australian PGA are mounted in a frame and adorn one of the walls of his den at home, and Torrance says that his father, Bob, believes it shows his golf swing at its absolute best and technically perfect – quite a compliment from Bob.

It was not just the win in Melbourne but the manner of it that gave me a real boost in terms of my self-belief. News of it hardly made the papers at all here, but I knew how well I had played to hold off both Seve and Greg, who were both superstars by then, and when I also won the Irish Open at Portmarnock in the summer of 1981 it clinched my place in the Ryder Cup team for Walton Heath. I was in at last, and I was ready for it. Both in terms of my individual career and in the amount of team golf I had played, I had earned an awful lot of collective experience by the time I lined up with Europe's best against the Americans in 1981.

Yet, just to underline what a remarkable experience the Ryder Cup is, none of all of that was anything like the Ryder Cup! You just can't compare it. Nevertheless, everything I had done, and achieved, leading up to 1981 prepared me for it on one level. And, especially with the team golf, I had learned a lot about having to gel with your partner, about the disciplines of playing for a team and how it is the team that matters above all else.

Coming through moments of real pressure – from playing for money as a kid and as a young assistant club professional to closing out that tournament at Royal Melbourne – had added hugely to my growth as a golfer. I had always believed in myself, and I should have made the Ryder Cup before 1981, but now I couldn't wait for it – especially as it was being played on a course like Walton Heath, which I knew very well and liked a lot. There were just three weeks between the team being finalised and the match itself, and it was very exciting for me to receive my first Ryder Cup bag and shirts. There was nothing like the amount of gear given to every team member now, or even by the time Tony Jacklin took over the captaincy from 1983, but it was still special and it meant an awful lot to me. All the stuff you were given told you that you were now a Ryder Cup player.

The United States team that arrived at Walton Heath in September 1981 was a jaw-dropping array of golfing talent. Nine of the twelve Americans had, by then, amassed no fewer than thirty-six major titles between them; three of them – Tom Watson, Bill Rogers and Larry Nelson – were, respectively, the Masters, Open and US PGA champions of that year. Jack Nicklaus, of course, headed the list of major champions, and he was to go on to win a historic 18th major title at the 1986 Masters.

But there was also Lee Trevino, Ray Floyd, Hale Irwin, Johnny Miller and Jerry Pate.

Of the three Americans who had not at that stage won a major title, both Tom Kite and Ben Crenshaw were later to do so – Crenshaw twice – leaving only Bruce Lietzke, another world-class golfer, as the sole player on that team to finish his career without at least one of the four majors to his name. Indeed, when you add up all the majors that 11 of those 12 men won in their careers, it is a staggering 49.

Although Nick Faldo, Bernhard Langer and Sandy Lyle were to go on to win ten major championships between them in the next decade, none of them had won a major by 1981, and with Seve Ballesteros – the 1979 Open and 1980 Masters champion – overlooked for the team due to his disagreement with the European Tour over appearance fees and his resultant boycotting of a number of events that year, it was an outclassed bunch indeed that turned up in leafy Surrey to do battle with the Americans.

There is no doubt in my mind that the American 1981 Ryder Cup team was the greatest and most powerful team in the competition's long history. Our team in 1987 wasn't too shabby, with its five major champions and a sixth to come in José María Olazábal, but that 1981 United States line-up was just ridiculous. No wonder we lost, and no wonder, on the scoreboard at least, we were hammered.

It was obviously a shame for us that Seve was not playing, but I am not sure if even his inclusion would have had much bearing on the final result. Don't forget, Seve and Antonio Garrido, his fellow Spaniard, had played at The Greenbrier in the 1979 Ryder Cup – when, partly as a result of Nicklaus's counsel, continental European players had been included alongside the British and Irish for the first time in an effort to make the match more competitive – but had failed to stop the Americans winning 17–11 there. This time, the final scoreline was 18½ points to 9½, but, in fact, I believe the European team played rather better than most people have given them credit for in the years since.

Without Seve, and with Tony Jacklin also overlooked as a wild card – Peter Oosterhuis and Mark James were chosen as his two picks by John Jacobs, the

Europe captain, and his fellow selectors Neil Coles and Bernhard Langer, who qualified as such as the leader of the Order of Merit – our team had very little collective experience of Ryder Cup combat, as well as being outmuscled to a very large degree by the powerhouse American company. We had five rookies in myself, Bernhard, Manuel Piñero, José Maria Cañizares and Howard Clark – and only Oosterhuis, with five previous Ryder Cups and many years playing the US Tour, could be said then to possess the sort of long experience to go with a genuine stature in the world game.

After the first day of competition at Walton Heath, however, Europe led by 4½ points to 3½. Langer and Piñero were squeezed out by one hole in the opening foursomes match against Trevino and Nelson, but there were wins for Sandy Lyle and James (against Rogers and Lietzke) and Bernard Gallacher and Des Smyth against the strong pairing of Irwin and Floyd. Indeed, it took a 4&3 win by Watson and Nicklaus against the anticipated best European pairing of Oosterhuis and Faldo to bring the Americans back level at 2–2 after the first morning.

Oosterhuis and Faldo, the classic Ryder Cup partnership of top-class old hand and highly promising young gun, had won four of the five foursomes and fourball matches they had played together during the previous two Cups in 1977 and 1979, and Jacobs can be forgiven for looking to them once again for a precious point or two. Neither player, however, as Torrance himself was to discover at first hand the following day, was on the top of his game in 1981 – although Faldo, with typical grit, was still able to grind out a 2&1 singles victory against Miller before the match ended in American celebrations.

For Torrance, though, before his second-day trials and tribulations, there was the little matter of a first Ryder Cup outing to be negotiated. Sent out after lunch in the opening fourball group, Torrance and Clark found themselves up against the formidable pair of Miller and Kite. The British pair nevertheless gave an excellent account of themselves, and coming up the last hole they still had a chance of a win.

I really enjoyed playing with Howard Clark, a good friend, in several Ryder Cups, and we were a good partnership. Playing with someone like him in my very first match – as it was for Howard too, of course – went a long way towards settling the nerves. We trusted each other, and although you are playing your own ball in that format, you do still need the support of your partner. You need to gel. You can help each other, and you can inspire each other. I recall that we both played well in the match, especially as rookies against experienced opponents, and we got tremendous support from the home crowds. There were almost eleven thousand spectators at that first day, despite showery conditions, and they really got behind us when we went two down quite early on but then fought back to all square.

The quality of the match was such that both teams were to finish with better-ball scores of 65, but on that 18th tee all I could think of was trying to make the birdie that might win us the match. Well, I got it to about twelve feet with my second shot and, with both Kite and Howard out of the hole, Miller putted up from the bottom half of the green and got his four. Now it was down to me, and I hit the perfect putt. Halfway along its line, I would have bet a lot of money that it was in, but somehow the ball horseshoed around the back of the hole and stayed out. I could not believe it, and, before I had left the green, I could feel the tears coming. They were tears of utter frustration as much as anything, but I could not stop the emotion.

This was the Ryder Cup, and this is what it could do. I'd never before felt as emotional on the golf course as that, and to be honest there are tears coming again now as I think back to that moment. We had them beaten. We had a full point, but the ball decided to stay out. I couldn't have hit the putt better, but we had to settle for the half. I suppose that was still a good result, and it helped us into a narrow lead by the end of that first day, but I had wanted that putt to drop so very much. The Ryder Cup had bitten me, right from the start of my involvement in it, and the Ryder Cup had already tested me and tested my character. It's what it does.

Day two, though, was something of a trial for Torrance, even though in the morning fourballs he had Faldo as his partner and after lunch found himself paired with Oosterhuis in the foursomes against the same opponents, Lee Trevino and Jerry Pate.

Again, he felt he played well, but the results were humbling: a real beating of 7&5 with Faldo and then a 2&1 reverse in the afternoon.

Europe, moreover, only gained 1 point on the whole of the second day, with Langer and Piñero winning 2&1 against Floyd and Irwin in the morning fourballs. The peerless Nicklaus and Watson combination won 2 more points, both by comfortable margins, while Nelson and Kite were a third American pair to pick up maximum points on the day.

We were battered, and the less said about my own two matches that day the better, to be honest. The afternoon game was actually quite a close-run affair, but Oosterhuis did not play at his best and on one hole I remember him hitting a six iron from the middle of the fairway that finished up about forty yards left of the green. Oosty, you must realise, was by some distance our most experienced and senior player. I was thinking, 'Hang on, he's the best we've got – what's happening here?'

The other thing that grabbed my attention that day, though, was the performance of Trevino. His partner, Pate, was a terrific striker of the ball and also, of course, himself a major winner. But it was as if Lee would not trust Pate to make any decision for himself. Literally, and I mean literally, he advised him how and where to hit every shot. Every drive, every iron and every putt. For hour after hour, morning and afternoon. It was amazing to see, but Trevino got what he wanted at the end of it all: two more points.

What is also remarkable is how often during Torrance's career the wisecracking figure of Trevino appears. The man called 'Super Mex' was one of the first elite players that a young Sam met in the flesh. In 1972, at Dalmahoy, he and his fellow young Scottish thruster, Ewen Murray, now a long-serving Sky Sports commentator and a leading coach, were given the opportunity of playing eighteen holes with Trevino – who was to go on to win five major titles – and Bob Charles, the New Zealand left-hander who had won the 1963 Open at Royal Lytham.

It was a tremendous chance for me, at the time, to watch two of the world's top players up close, and, although I was a complete unknown to Lee then, I have had the privilege of getting to know him very well over the years that have passed since that day. And I have never forgotten the thrill of playing with him when I was still a lad of 19. It was a chance to learn, and it was an opportunity I tried to take full advantage of in terms of watching how he approached certain shots, how he actually played them and things like his overall course management. Later in my career, he taught me how to play one particular splash shot from a bunker, and it is a real coincidence that in my first Ryder Cup I was to play two team matches and my singles match against Lee Trevino.

Then, in 1985, when we won the Cup for the first time in 28 years, Lee was the American captain – and he was the very first person from the United States team to come up to me and congratulate me on the putt that clinched the Cup for Europe. The 1981 match was Lee's last as a player, and I am so glad I got the chance to go up against him in Ryder Cup competition. I've always got on well with him, and in 1985 he told me that, although he was sad that his American team had lost, he could not have been more pleased that the European who sank the winning putt was me. I thought that was a tremendous thing for someone of Lee Trevino's stature to say to me, and I will never forget it.

On the eve of their singles contest in 1981, however, Trevino was intent on being anything but kind to Torrance. As the shadows lengthened around the Walton Heath clubhouse on that Saturday evening, Europe were trailing by 10½ points to 5½. The 7–1 demolition in foursomes and fourballs earlier in the day had made yet another United States victory seem a virtual certainty.

The Americans needed just another 3½ points from the 12 singles matches to retain the Cup, and 4 points to win it outright for the sixth time in succession. What is more, Trevino was being sent out first in the singles by his captain, Dave Marr, and he was in the mood to get one of those points as quickly as he could.

They were just an awesome team, and, frankly, we were in awe of them. There's no other way of putting it. We still wanted to go out there and give it everything we could to beat them, and we wanted to bloody their noses, but as golfers they were people who operated on a different level from us. On that Saturday night it was obvious that we were going to get beaten, even though mathematically we could still do it, and Trevino came up to me when he saw that we had been drawn together at the top of the singles order and said, 'Sammy, I'm going to beat the moustache off you tomorrow!'

The next morning, as it happened, I came out of the hotel where both teams were staying and saw Lee waiting for a courtesy car to take him to Walton Heath. I had my own car with me, and was going to drive anyway, so I offered him a lift. 'Sure, thanks,' he said. When we drove out of the hotel entrance, I turned left and not right. 'Hey, this ain't the right way to the course,' said Lee. 'I know,' I replied. 'I'm taking you straight to London instead – shall we call it a half?' Well, Trevino loved a jest, and we had a real chuckle at this as I turned the car around. But I knew I could have a joke like that with Lee. And, after he beat me 5&3 in little more than two hours of play, as the United States went on to claim seven of the twelve singles, plus two halved matches, I shaved off my moustache in the locker room so that I could then go up to him at the after-match function and say, 'Look, Lee, you did beat the moustache off me!' He loved that, too.

What is truly wonderful is that, a couple of years ago, on the Seniors Tour, I was in Mexico and I came out of the hotel and, once again, met Lee standing around waiting for a courtesy car. So I went up and said, 'Hey, Lee, want a lift?' And, quick as a flash, a look of mock horror came over his face and he said, 'Hell, no, I remember what happened the last time I took a lift with you!' How lovely that he remembered it too. Great Ryder Cup memories are not just about what happened out there on the course.

1981 RYDER CUP RESULTS: 18–20 SEPTEMBER, WALTON HEATH
Captains: John Jacobs (Europe), Dave Marr (US)

Europe		US	
Morning foursomes			
Bernhard Langer/Manuel Piñero		Lee Trevino/Larry Nelson (1 hole)	1
Sandy Lyle/Mark James (2&1)	1	Bill Rogers/Bruce Lietzke	
Bernard Gallacher/Des Smyth (3&2)	1	Hale Irwin/Raymond Floyd	
Peter Oosterhuis/Nick Faldo		Tom Watson/Jack Nicklaus (4&3)	1
Afternoon fourballs			
Sam Torrance/Howard Clark (halved)		Tom Kite/Johnny Miller (halved)	½
Sandy Lyle/Mark James (3&2)	½	Ben Crenshaw/Jerry Pate	
Des Smyth/José Maria Cañizares (6&5)	1	Bill Rogers/Bruce Lietzke	
Bernard Gallacher/Eamonn Darcy	1	Hale Irwin/Raymond Floyd (2&1)	1
Morning fourballs			
Nick Faldo/Sam Torrance		Lee Trevino/Jerry Pate (7&5)	1
Sandy Lyle/Mark James		Larry Nelson/Tom Kite (1 hole)	1
Bernhard Langer/Manuel Piñero (2&1)	1	Raymond Floyd/Hale Irwin	
José Maria Cañizares/Des Smyth		Jack Nicklaus/Tom Watson (3&2)	1
Afternoon foursomes			
Peter Oosterhuis/Sam Torrance		Lee Trevino/Jerry Pate (2&1)	1
Bernhard Langer/Manuel Piñero		Jack Nicklaus/Tom Watson (3&2)	1
Sandy Lyle/Mark James		Bill Rogers/Raymond Floyd (3&2)	1
Des Smyth/Bernard Gallacher		Tom Kite/Larry Nelson (3&2)	1
Singles			
Sam Torrance		Lee Trevino (5&3)	1
Sandy Lyle		Tom Kite (3&2)	1
Bernard Gallacher (halved)	½	Bill Rogers (halved)	½
Mark James		Larry Nelson (2 holes)	1
Des Smyth		Ben Crenshaw (6&4)	1
Bernhard Langer (halved)	½	Bruce Lietzke (halved)	½
Manuel Piñero (4&2)	1	Jerry Pate	
José Maria Cañizares		Hale Irwin (1 hole)	1
Nick Faldo (2&1)	1	Johnny Miller	
Howard Clark (4&3)	1	Tom Watson	
Peter Oosterhuis		Raymond Floyd (1 hole)	1
Eamonn Darcy		Jack Nicklaus (5&3)	1
Europe	**9½**	**US**	**18½**

SAM'S ANALYSIS: 1981

Europe

Sam Torrance	The rookie gained his first Ryder Cup half-point in the opening fourballs, but this was a real eye-opener. Seen off by Trevino in the singles.
Sandy Lyle	Played superbly throughout the match in his second Ryder Cup appearance, despite winning just 2 points from five games. No one has hit a one iron quite like Sandy.
Bernard Gallacher	An opening point in the foursomes, alongside Des Smyth, and then a brave half in the singles against Open champion Bill Rogers. Battled hard and as tenacious as always.
Mark James	Gave his all in a bid to justify his wild-card selection. Took 2 points alongside Lyle on day one, but nothing from his remaining three outings. His dry wit was always appreciated in the team room.
Des Smyth	The Irishman was another European to be smiling after day one, when he gained a maximum 2 points with partners Gallacher and Cañizares. Again, however, nothing else came his way despite playing in all five matches. These days he basks in being the oldest winner of a European Tour event – a record I want!
Bernhard Langer	The point he gained with Manuel Piñero in the morning fourballs was Europe's only point on day two. But he had two foursomes defeats alongside the Spaniard before the small consolation of a half against Bruce Lietzke in the singles.
Manuel Piñero	Small of stature but a real fighter in matchplay, as he proved in the company of Langer and then in his 4&2 singles win over Jerry Pate.
José Maria Cañizares	By no means a deflating debut, but only 1 point to celebrate out of the three matches he was given. Later in our Ryder Cup careers, I used to call him 'Grandpa'.

Nick Faldo	Already a Ryder Cup veteran at the age of 24, this was his third appearance. But it was an unhappy one until he dug out a singles win over the great Johnny Miller on the last day.
Howard Clark	Perhaps unlucky to be given only one outing on the first two days, partnering me to our half against Miller and Kite. He showed what he can do in matchplay by then beating Tom Watson 4&3 in the singles.
Peter Oosterhuis	The last of his six Ryder Cups, and his worst. Picked as the senior man, he struggled badly with his game and lost all his three matches. But Oosty was a hero of mine, and it was a delight to be able to play with him. The first man to win consecutive Order of Merit titles on the European Tour.
Eamonn Darcy	Played two and lost two, and was probably less than thrilled to find himself up against Jack Nicklaus in the anchor singles. The match, of course, was long over by the time he lost 5&3 to 'the Golden Bear' in what was Jack's last Ryder Cup appearance as a player.
John Jacobs (captain)	He is as nice a man as you could wish to meet and was the supremo of the European Tour before Ken Schofield. We all looked up to him for what he had achieved as a player, coach and administrator, and the huge amount he had done for the growth of European golf. A very gentle man, as Ryder Cup captain he probably did not instil the sort of belief that was needed against such a formidable American team, but it was still an honour to play for him and under him.

United States

Lee Trevino	Took 4 points out of 4, including my scalp in the singles. He was as good as it gets, but I really should have driven him to London instead of Walton Heath on that final morning!
Tom Kite	Unbeaten, with 3½ points from a possible 4. Very steady player, if not at that stage one of the real American superstars. A very impressive ball striker but had a weakness on the greens.

Bill Rogers	Open champion in 1981, he later disappeared from the world stage when he seemed to lose the will to play at the highest level. Lost his first two matches, but then recovered with a win and a half.
Larry Nelson	Continued his astonishing run of success in Ryder Cup play. In 1979, on debut, he had won 5 points from 5. Here it was just 4 out of 4. Got his comeuppance in 1987, though! A formidable opponent.
Ben Crenshaw	Played just once in the first two days, in a fourball match that was lost, but got something out of his debut by winning his singles by a big margin. One of the great putters, and you used to pray that he missed the green!
Bruce Lietzke	The only American from the 1981 team destined never to win a major, the talented Lietzke sat out day two after two losses alongside Rogers but ended up with a consolation half in his singles match against Langer.
Jerry Pate	Coached through his fourball and foursomes wins by his day-two partner Trevino, following an opening loss with Crenshaw, but lost again on his own against Piñero.
Hale Irwin	One of my best friends from the American teams I have played against, and 2 points out of 4 here. A magnificent all-round player.
Johnny Miller	Just one fourball outing for the mercurial Miller, who in truth was out of sorts at Walton Heath – which was perhaps just as well for myself and Clark. Lost his singles.
Tom Watson	Took 3 points out of 3 alongside Jack Nicklaus in the team matches, but then lost his singles game against Howard Clark. One of world golf's greatest ever players.
Ray Floyd	Won two and lost two on the opening two days, but then added a singles point by squeezing out Peter Oosterhuis by one hole. You could not face a tougher man on the golf course. I never got to play against him in Ryder Cups, but I did in money matches.

Jack Nicklaus	An unbeaten last Ryder Cup appearance for the greatest golfer of his era and, perhaps, of all time. Took 4 points from 4. Poor old Eamonn! Jack was 'the King' to me.
Dave Marr (captain)	A delightful and witty man, and a fine player before becoming well known to a younger generation through his insightful television commentary. What a privilege it must have been to captain this particular American Ryder Cup team. I do not wish to be disrespectful, but he might as well have brought an armchair and found himself a nice comfortable corner of the Walton Heath clubhouse! To be able to pair up Nicklaus and Watson, and to be still awash with talent in your three other pairings, is a luxury granted to very few!

CHAPTER TWO

1983 PGA NATIONAL, FLORIDA

It still hurts. It still rankles. Even with all the great Ryder Cup achievements and successes that the European team, and myself personally, have enjoyed in the past quarter-century, it is extraordinary how much I still wish we had won in 1983. I felt we played well enough to do so. I felt we deserved it, but we just could not get over the line at the end. We were all absolutely devastated, but, in the team room afterwards, we all made a pact. All of us together. We now knew we could win this thing, and we pledged there and then that next time it would be us doing the celebrating.

A transformation had come over the European Ryder Cup team since the defeat at Walton Heath. In the two years that had passed since Europe had been trampled underfoot by the greatest American team ever assembled, a new resolve had been found, and the reason for that was the inspiration and planning provided by one man. When the PGA turned to Tony Jacklin and asked him to captain the 1983 Ryder Cup team in Florida, it made probably the best and most far-reaching decision in European golf history.

Jacklin, nevertheless, was initially minded to refuse it. He had been left disillusioned by his own Ryder Cup playing career, spanning seven matches, because he felt he had not been competing on a level playing field with the United States golfers. It was not just the gulf in strength in depth between the Americans and the (then) Great Britain and Ireland teams – although Jacklin had also played, in 1979, in the first all-European selection – but the chronic lack of preparation and support that the teams in his era had received.

Everything had been done on the cheap, especially for the away matches in America, with caddies, wives, girlfriends, personal coaches and adequate support staff not included in the official team lists. Official clothing and equipment was often shoddy and of poor quality. Europe's players felt like the poor relations even before a ball was struck in anger.

Jacklin was also annoyed at having been ignored for the 1981 match. He had finished 12th in that year's Order of Merit, but the selection committee headed by John Jacobs, the captain, had chosen Peter Oosterhuis – who played predominantly on the US Tour – and Mark James, in 11th place on the money list, as their two wild-card picks for Walton Heath. James, when making his own playing debut at The Greenbrier in 1979, had been disciplined for behavioural issues. Jacklin felt sore that his own huge contribution to the Ryder Cup cause had been overlooked, especially when it came down to a straight choice between him and James.

Although shocked to be asked to captain, Jacklin found himself quickly thinking about the possibilities and positives that could arise if he did it – his way – and he began to push the negatives to the back of his mind. Soon, he was requesting a meeting with Ken Schofield, the executive director of the European Tour, and Colin Snape, who headed up the PGA. Slamming his cards down on the table, Jacklin gave them his vision of what competing in the Ryder Cup should be all about for Europe's elite players and his vision of what making a success of the team could do for the whole of European golf.

That was Tony. He was very passionate about everything he did, and he made it very clear that if he was going to do this job he was going to leave nothing to chance. He wanted everyone on the European Ryder Cup team to be treated as special people. Yes, he wanted us to fly over to America on Concorde and to look the part, but he also transformed everything else about being involved in the event. The leather golf bag we all received when we were confirmed in the 1983 team, for instance, is absolutely the most gorgeous-looking golf bag I have ever had! Yes, even better than the ones the players had during my own 2002 captaincy, I have to admit! I've got it on display at home, and I often look at it with affection. It's a bit of a historic item these days, of course, and I suppose that adds to its appeal. But I still remember getting it at the time and the impression it made on me. And all our clothing, both golf wear for on the course and suits, jackets, trousers, shirts and ties for the official functions off it, and all our towels and golf equipment and things like that were of real quality. Our golf shirts were made from a special fabric that would help to absorb the humidity of Florida at that time of year and help to keep us cool. We had extra pairs of golf shoes added to our list of official gear, in case we needed to change into dry shoes, because the course underfoot was expected to be quite sodden in places. Nothing was forgotten. Suddenly, Tony made us all feel a million dollars.

Jacklin also had two more pressing concerns when he took on the job. Firstly, and most importantly, he simply had to get Severiano Ballesteros back on the European team – and enthusiastic about the European cause. Then he needed to address what he perceived to be the handicap of a selection system that, for 1983, meant he was faced with a fait accompli of the top 12 players on the tour's Order of Merit qualifying for the team. There were not even two captain's picks, as there had been in 1981 and 1979, to give Jacklin some form of control over the final make-up and balance of his team.

The first battle he won after meeting Ballesteros in private at the Prince of Wales Hotel in Southport during the 1983 Open Championship. With almost a missionary zeal, Jacklin told Ballesteros that he should look beyond his still festering disagreement with the European Tour over appearance fees, the issue that had led to his absence from the 1981 match. Jacklin said that, together, with Ballesteros providing the on-course leadership, they could achieve great things. Only Jacklin, the biggest name in European golf and himself a double major winner – Ballesteros himself was at that stage the holder of three major titles following his 1979 Open and 1980 and 1983 Masters wins – could have sold the idea of Ryder Cup glory to the great Spaniard. Only he had the stature, belief about how it could be done and the genuine passion to bring Ballesteros back into the fold.

Jacklin's second battle, however, had to wait until after 1983 to be turned in his favour. There was not time enough left to move the goalposts of the selection procedure for Florida, and, although by 1985 he had secured three captain's picks to go with the top nine golfers on the European Tour money list, he was temporarily cheered by what he saw as a format – sixteen fourball and foursomes matches requiring a minimum of eight players, followed by twelve singles – that favoured the Europeans.

With less strength in depth than the Americans, it was in Europe's interests to make the very most of the first two days, and that was why Jacklin, later on in his captaincy reign, rejected United States suggestions that the match should be expanded to include five fourball and five foursomes matches in each session so that more players from each team could see action on the Friday and Saturday of Ryder Cup combat.

For now, though, Jacklin had successfully persuaded Ballesteros to end his short self-imposed exile, and he was not displeased with the team he saw revealing itself as the 1983 summer drew towards a close. He would certainly have picked Manuel Piñero, the diminutive but tough Spanish player who loved matchplay and had showed up well in 1981, and probably Howard Clark as well, but otherwise he was content enough with the 12 the system had bequeathed him. Now it was all about preparation and getting his players ready for the challenge awaiting them in Palm Beach Gardens.

Everything changed under Tony. And, at that time, Tony Jacklin was king. We all so respected him for what he had done and how he was with us. He made us feel important and made us feel that these Americans could indeed be beaten. We had done OK in many respects at Walton Heath, despite the final scoreline, but Tony now added layers and layers of belief on top of that. We also had Seve back.

Jacklin transformed the event for us players and changed how we looked at it and ourselves. He was fantastic in his attention to detail and the way he enthused and encouraged us. For example, he and his wife, Vivien, put a lot of thought into the colour of the outfits we would wear on each day of the match. He wanted us to look good for the television cameras and to be proud of our team 'uniform'. He flew out to Florida and reconnoitred the PGA National course and the facilities and checked the hotel accommodation and ensured we had a team room and that it was serviced with everything we needed there. Tony believed passionately that they were all vital to our chances of success.

He was, without doubt, the best captain I played under, and what he achieved for European golf through the Ryder Cup is just magnificent. I can remember being so excited about the prospect of playing in the 1983 Ryder Cup. By the time we gathered together to fly out on Concorde, we all knew that this was going to be different. We really did believe we were on a mission to win back the Cup, not just to go through the motions of trying to be competitive. As I say, everything under Tony was different, and we wanted to win that trophy so badly.

Torrance was right in the thick of the action, both when the match began with four opening-morning foursomes and a couple of nights earlier, when he and Ian Woosnam somehow found themselves gatecrashing an American team get-together.

We had been invited to a function at the local yacht club, which, we were told, was very near to the hotel where both teams were staying. When Woosie and I came out of the hotel we saw Fuzzy Zoeller giving directions to some of the other American players, who were piling into some courtesy cars. We thought they were all off to the same function as us, so we got in another car and followed them. We did wonder why we had driven for quite a way, but then we stopped outside a magnificent property.

We jumped out and knocked on the door, just ahead of Calvin Peete and some of the other Americans. Who should answer the door but Jack Nicklaus! He did look a bit bemused, and asked us why we were there. We asked him if this was the yacht club, and he said that it wasn't – but it was his house! He invited us in and we ended up having a quick drink and a laugh with the United States team, of which Nicklaus was captain, of course, before getting back on the road to the yacht club. Jack did lead us over to one of the huge picture windows of his house at one stage and pointed out to us the yacht club buildings, which could be clearly seen over the other side of the lake which lay between his property and the club.

Sadly, we didn't pick up any American secrets during our short time at Jack's house, but it was a funny episode – especially to the likes of Woosie and myself, as we both enjoyed the social side of Ryder Cup weeks and always wanted to mix with the opposition when it was possible. To me, that's a big part of the Ryder Cup experience.

When the match began, on 14 October in hot Florida sunshine, Jacklin paired Torrance with José Maria Cañizares and sent them out in the third foursomes game, against Ray Floyd and Bob Gilder. Bernard Gallacher and Sandy Lyle lost the top foursomes, going down 5&4 to Tom Watson and Ben Crenshaw, but then Europe rallied as Nick Faldo and Bernhard Langer closed out Lanny Wadkins and Craig Stadler 4&2 at around the same time as Torrance and Cañizares were celebrating a 4&3 win.

Even though Ballesteros and Paul Way were beaten 2&1 in the final foursomes match of the morning, Europe had begun well and, at 2–2 at lunchtime, could be well pleased with the start. Ballesteros, however, was not happy at being defeated by the combination of Tom Kite and Cal Peete.

I understand that Seve was not initially overwhelmed about Tony's decision to partner him with Paul Way, a rookie who was then just 20 years old. Paul played some tremendous golf in that Ryder Cup and had not disgraced himself in that first match because foursomes is a tricky format for experienced players to deal with, let alone a youngster on his Cup debut. But Seve told Tony that Way was asking for his advice on virtually every shot – what club to play and how to play it. 'I feel like his father,' said Seve. Well, Tony merely replied that, to Way, Seve was like a father, especially on the golf course.

'You have won three majors – to him, you know everything,' said Jacklin. 'Is that such a problem?' Instantly, Seve's attitude changed, and Tony believed that, in that moment, he truly began to understand what the Ryder Cup was and why it was so different and so appealing. It was about the team, about the more experienced helping to bring through the younger players and about meeting the challenge of playing with a partner. Seve and Paul then won two and halved one of their three remaining fourball and foursomes matches, and Tony was richly rewarded for putting them together in a classic master and pupil partnership – and then sticking with them when it did not initially go right.

Way was inspired in that Ryder Cup by the excitement of playing with Seve and because playing with someone like that enabled him to relax in the knowledge that he had the great Ballesteros alongside him to make sure everything would be OK. It was very clever captaincy by Tony, who knew that such a pairing would bring out the best in each of them. We all know what happened when Seve finally got the young José María Olazábal under his wing in 1987: they quickly developed into the greatest Ryder Cup partnership of all time. But perhaps a big part of the success of that great Spanish pairing was the knowledge and experience that Seve learned with Paul Way in 1983.

With only Faldo and Langer losing in the afternoon fourballs, it was a very satisfied Jacklin who surveyed the scoreboard at the end of the first day and saw Europe leading America by 4½ points to 3½.

Ballesteros and Way beat Ray Floyd and Curtis Strange by one hole after a fierce contest, and the rather unlikely fourball pairing of Brian Waites and Ken Brown also triumphed, by 2&1 against Gil Morgan and Fuzzy Zoeller. It was another masterstroke by Jacklin, another hunch that paid off with a handsome point. The halved afternoon fourball match, meanwhile, was between Torrance and Ian Woosnam and an American pairing of Crenshaw and Peete.

I was so up for that match. Having won my opening foursomes in the morning with José Maria Cañizares, and played well, I was right up for going out there and getting another point. I didn't care who I was up against. Crenshaw and Peete were a decent pairing – at that level, you knew that any American pair would be tough – but I was in confident mood during the brief lunch break, and, on the putting green with Woosie as we prepared to go out in the final fourball match, I was very upbeat.

For Woosie, of course, this was his Ryder Cup debut match, and, understandably, even for a player of his huge ability, it was a big moment. There I was, telling Woosie that I felt in great nick and that we could beat anyone, while he was just trying to control his own nerves and concentrate on getting into his golf and getting a decent swing on his first couple of strokes. So, after telling him that we could take out Crenshaw and Peete, I also told him that I would hit off first and bang one down the middle so that a little bit of pressure would be off him and he could really enjoy the thrill of hitting his first shot as a Ryder Cup player.

What happened? My opening tee shot was blocked horribly straight right, and the ball flew miles out of bounds. I couldn't really look at Woosie. But he was more than equal to this little crisis right at the start of our match. He rifled a one iron down the middle, clipped a nine iron to about four feet and holed it for a birdie three. And I was supposed to be the strong man of this partnership! In actual fact, from then on, I reckon I played the best sustained golf of my entire Ryder Cup career. We traded birdies with Crenshaw and Peete as if they were going out of fashion. I remember birdieing eight of the last ten holes myself as the quality of the match touched real heights.

It was dizzying stuff, and, remarkably, the match came down the par-five 18th when we knew we needed yet another birdie to ensure the half and possibly even get a full point if they did not get a four between them. I had a ten-foot putt remaining, and Woosie was just inside me with an eight-footer for birdie. When I holed it, Woosie just said to me, 'Aren't you going to let me do anything?' I reckon we must have been about 12 under par as a team, and I suppose Crenshaw and Peete were about the same, otherwise they wouldn't have held us to a half. It truly was golf of the highest standard and thrilling to be a part of.

The second day brought more exciting and fiercely contested fourball and foursomes play. Europe's challenge was carried forward by the Faldo–Langer and Ballesteros–Way partnerships.

The Englishman and German, both then yet to be major champions, saw off Crenshaw and Peete in the morning fourballs by a 4&2 margin and then downed Kite and Floyd 3&2 in the afternoon foursomes. Ballesteros and Way came away with a half from their morning joust with Morgan and Haas but followed up with a brilliant 2&1 foursomes win over Watson and Gilder.

Waites and Brown, however, lost twice, and Torrance, first with Woosnam again in the second round of fourballs and then once more with Cañizares in the foursomes, suffered two heavy defeats – by 5&4 in the morning to Watson and Gilder, and a thumping 7&5 reverse against Morgan and Wadkins.

Sometimes, in matchplay, a game can just get away from you and there is nothing you can do about it. If your opponents play superbly, for instance, and hole everything they look at on the greens, it doesn't matter if you are playing half-decently yourself. And the margins are so fine, even on occasions when the final winning scoreline makes it look like a really one-sided affair. That's what makes matchplay golf so different and so exciting to play and to watch. You simply never know what is coming next. Literally, anything is possible!

I can remember, in our second fourball match, for instance, being in complete control of one hole midway through the game against Watson and Gilder. Both Woosie and I were on the 9th green in regulation, Gilder was out of it and Watson was in some trouble in the rough some way off the putting surface. We were standing behind the green, watching Tom figure out how best to play his shot, and I said to Woosie, 'He's great at these sort of shots, you know.' And Woosie said to me, 'What the hell are you saying that for?' And then Watson chipped it up, and it rolled right into the cup for a birdie three and ended up winning the hole. Woosie has always held me responsible for that one.

The upshot, after two captivating days of cut and thrust, was a match level at 8–8. The Ryder Cup, at last, was going down to the wire, and Europe's players still believed they could do it. They were, in truth, slightly peeved not be ahead. They had played well, but a few points and half-points had slipped away. Nevertheless, the mood in the European team room on the Saturday night, and again on the Sunday morning before the decisive singles matches, was totally upbeat.

There weren't lots of rousing team talks, or if there were I didn't hear them. I also wasn't part of the upper echelon of the team, of course, and in many ways I never was – even in my later Ryder Cups, when, by virtue of my experience and age if nothing else, I was regarded as one of the senior players. But Tony's management was not about thumping the table. He spoke with all his players, of course, but he did so individually more than anything and it was just the confidence and desire to win he instilled in you that mattered the most. He had Seve as his captain on the course, and in Florida he also had Bernard Gallacher still around as his most senior player in terms of previous Ryder Cup experience, but mostly we were a young team just determined to do our very best and achieve this great dream.

Jacklin's singles order in 1983 was a classic example of his belief – especially with the match still in the balance – that power was needed at the top and experience was most required at the end.

Gordon J. Brand, or Gordon Brand Senior as he was called officially to distinguish him from the other Gordon Brand who was to play in the Ryder Cups of 1987 and 1989, was the only player in all four of Jacklin's captaincy outings whom he did not manage to include in at least one fourball or foursomes match. So Brand was put out fourth behind an intimidating top three and sandwiched between Langer and Sandy Lyle, two of Europe's acknowledged high-quality performers. Gallacher, Brown and Cañizares brought up the rear, with the three young, or younger, thrusters of Way, Torrance and Woosnam immediately above them.

Jacklin's singles line-up was as follows: Ballesteros, Faldo, Langer, Brand, Lyle, Waites, Way, Torrance, Woosnam, Cañizares, Brown, Gallacher. It was so close to achieving the prize, and it reversed an accepted trend up until that point in the event. Before, both teams had by and large put out most of their strongest men last – just in case things should get tight.

The Americans, of course, had nearly always been very much in command going into the singles and so could afford to be a little generous with some early points in the knowledge that some very big guns indeed were firing down the order. But now, with Europe level going into the singles, Jacklin was beginning to think radical thoughts. Nicklaus, the US captain, was the only person slightly taken aback by Jacklin's new-look approach.

You can see Tony's strategy very clearly in that choice of order. Putting Seve, Nick and Bernhard out first was a real statement of intent. Having Cañizares, Brown and Gallacher out last showed that he believed it could, and probably would, all come down to the end games. He put Sandy in between Gordon Brand and Brian Waites, whom he would have considered to be his weaker singles players, and then he had three of his form players in Way, myself and

Woosie coming in at seven, eight and nine, where it all might be decided, if everything went well. And how nearly it all worked out! It is shattering to look back and see how close we were to pulling it off.

Before he announced his singles line-up, on the Saturday evening, Tony had asked us all if we minded where we played in the order. None of us did. That meant it was down to him, after he had taken his little soundings here and there, and the final decision on the exact order was solely his to make. That is absolutely right. When I was captain, also looking at an 8–8 situation going into the singles, that was the decision I wanted to make too, and that was the question I asked all my players. Likewise, none of them had any strong preference, which was perfect for me.

There has been possibly no greater shot played in the entire history of the Ryder Cup than the one struck by Seve Ballesteros at the 18th hole during his singles match against Fuzzy Zoeller. Three up with seven to play, Ballesteros had suddenly and inexplicably lost control of things. Zoeller fought back so well that, with one hole left, he was now one up and a match Europe was banking on to win was slipping away in distressing fashion.

Ballesteros then put his second shot into a bunker, after hooking his tee shot into deep rough, but at least Zoeller, a shorter hitter, could not get up at the par five in two. The Spaniard considered his options and then proceeded to hit the most breathtaking of three woods fully two hundred and forty yards – with the ball missing the front edge of the bunker by millimetres as it skimmed out of the sand – to the side of the green. A chip and a putt later, Ballesteros had won the hole with a par five, and Europe's first half-point, from the 6½ required on that final day, was on the board.

Two more full points then quickly arrived, from Faldo and Langer, and Jacklin's plan was working. Out on the course, the middle and lower order could feel the excitement mounting as they fought to keep a hold on their opponents, and also on their concentration and their golf games.

Going out in match number eight, I knew that I was likely to be in the thick of it. Unfortunately, both Gordon Brand and Brian Waites lost their matches at the 18th after putting up brave performances against Gilder and Peete respectively. Indeed, to this day I do not know what really happened after there was an incident on the last hole of the match between Brand Senior and Gilder. I even spoke to Bob [Gilder] about it when we met up on the Seniors Tour a few years back, and I have still not really got to the bottom of it.

The facts, as I understad them, are these. Bob was one up, standing on the last tee, but obviously Gordon could still get a half, and in the situation out there at the time that would have been huge. Bob then blocked his tee shot, and the ball went a long way right. Gordon's drive was down the left, and into the rough there, and so the two players moved off in completely different directions and Gordon didn't see what happened next. The story goes that Gilder's ball went into a hazard, and he took relief and dropped out. Gordon was also in a bit of trouble, and the upshot, when they got to the green, was that Gilder's ball was marked five feet from the hole. Gordon thought it was there for four, and, because he could only get a six himself, he conceded it. Gilder thus won the match by two holes, but the rumour is that he was there for five – because of the penalty stroke – and therefore would have needed to hole his short putt for a half in six. If he had missed it, Gordon could have won the hole and therefore gained a halved match. Bob might well have holed it, of course, to confirm what would then have been a one-hole victory – but we'll never know!

More worryingly for Europe, there was nothing from the Lyle v Crenshaw match, the fifth in the singles order, which went to the American by 3&2, and with six matches still out on the course the score was 10½ to Europe and 11½ to the United States.

Paul Way, however, put the seal on his own magnificent debut by beating Curtis Strange 2&1. America, though, landed the next blow when Craig Stadler, perspiring profusely in the steamy weather, defeated Woosnam 3&2. Four matches left, with Europe needing 3 more points. And, at this stage, Ken Brown was well up against Ray Floyd in match 11, and Bernard Gallacher was ahead too against Tom Watson in the anchor game.

Torrance had felt in control of his game for long periods, and, although he could see from the scoreboards that Woosnam was up against it, he also knew that Cañizares was in contention for a massive point against Wadkins. Soon, everyone still out there realised that – from Europe's perspective – it was all coming down to 2 points from three matches, as Brown kept up his superb domination of the much-feared Floyd.

What a magnificent performance by Ken Brown to beat Floyd 4&3. That must go down as one of Europe's most remarkable singles wins of all time. You have to hand it to Ken, because Raymond was the man to beat on their side at that time of the Cup's history. He and Wadkins – they were both unbelievably tough. But Floyd was the Godfather of their team, he was like a mafia boss and he was one American you didn't want to play. But Ken beat him, and by a distance. Sadly, though, the other three of us out in those last four games could not get the 2 points that we ended up needing. Or even the 1½ points that would have tied the match, which would have been some sort of consolation even though America would have kept the Cup had it finished 14–14.

Gallacher was losing his early lead against Watson, but the Cañizares–Wadkins match was still nip and tuck and Torrance was hanging on against Kite, despite walking onto the tee at the par-three 17th one hole down.

I had a 25-foot putt on that hole to win it and get back to all square. And, for those few minutes of my life, all I was thinking about and all I was seeing was the ball rolling straight into the cup for the birdie two. I remember being convinced that I was going to hole it. You are totally in the zone and in the moment. You don't think about any possibility other than the one you want. What did I do? I left it four feet short. It is a good job that dear old Eric Brown was not in the gallery! So, now, I suddenly found myself realising that, if I missed that, I was not even going to go up the 18th fairway, let alone be back to all square. I needed that putt just to match Kite's three and not lose the match right there by 2&1. It was one of the most defining moments of my life, because it was not a straightforward putt – that is, if any putt can be called straightforward in such a situation. But I holed it, and it was a great putt. I felt so determined, and I was equal to it. That's why it was a defining moment. And that's why the Ryder Cup determines things like that.

Although still one down, Torrance knew that Europe could still win the Cup – or tie the match – if he could find a birdie four at the last and Kite could only par. Anything could yet happen behind him, even though it was increasingly looking as though Europe might just fall short. Again, he tried to shut out the bigger picture and to channel all his concentration and competitive spirit into his final hole of the 1983 Ryder Cup.

I hit a decent drive but then pulled my second shot left and into a gully. The ball came to rest about 90 yards from the pin, but it was not in a very pleasant place. It was lying in an area of casual water, and I could have claimed relief and got a free drop. But it was also lying on a bit of an upslope, and so I decided that my best chance of hitting the shot I wanted was from that lie. It would have been too risky a gamble to take the drop and find myself in a worse lie in terms of the slope. It was also a perfect distance from the flag for me with my sand wedge. After all the fiddling about preceding my decision not to drop, I knew I was facing the moment that would decide if I could get the win on the hole that might gain me the half that I was so desperate for. What goes through your brain at a time like that? Well, you know your task, and you know what you have to do.

In that situation, there was no issue with the club – it was a full sand wedge. All I had to do was try to make the best contact I could. That is all I was thinking about, to be honest. And, as soon as the ball was in the air, I knew it was good. In fact, it was the shot of my life at that stage of my career. It flew straight at the target and came down no more than three feet from the flag. It was the chance I needed. Kite, meanwhile, had just missed the green with his third shot and then chipped up almost dead – perhaps three and a half feet away, and just outside of my ball.

From somewhere deep inside me, and to this day I don't know why I said it, I looked at his ball and mine as he walked over to mark it and said, 'Good, good?' Oh my God, the look he gave me! What, of course, I was saying with that remark was, 'Will you give me the hole, and therefore the halved match?' I was offering him his five, and suggesting he give me my four in return! It must have been pure Scottish cheek, but the look Tom gave me has stayed with me ever since. It is now almost three decades ago, but I can recall it as if it was just this minute. It was a look that said everything about what the Ryder Cup was about. And why would he ever give that putt to me?

Of course, after what I had said and his reaction, I couldn't now insist he picked up his ball – I had to let him hole it and steel myself to hole mine. But, after he tapped in, there was no way on earth that I would have allowed myself to miss mine. In it went, and I had my half! On 17 and 18 I had been under the most pressure on a golf course that I had ever experienced, at that stage, and I had come through it. Those holes, and that half, were to stand me in good stead in the Ryder Cup battles still to come.

Europe now had to get a point from Cañizares and a half from Gallacher, who was one down with two to play. Cañizares and Wadkins were all square, playing the 18th, and for a nerve-tingling ten minutes or so it seemed as if victory might yet prove possible.

Wadkins was in trouble all the way down the long last hole, but Cañizares could not get his third shot close enough to put his opponent under real pressure, and, with the Spaniard looking certain of a five but not the four he craved, Wadkins produced the defining stroke of his own career – a brilliant sixty-yard wedge over the bunker guarding the front left of the green to leave the ball stone dead. He also had his par five, and the match was halved.

Nicklaus, who was with that match as it came up the 18th, went down on his hands and knees and kissed the spot from where Wadkins had hit his glorious fourth shot.

Without wanting at all for this to sound like sour grapes, because Lanny's shot was spectacular and we did come up just short, I've always had a bit of an issue with Tom Watson for his tactics back down beside the 17th green while all this was going on up ahead in the Wadkins–Cañizares match.

Tom had missed the green to the right with his tee shot on 17, but Bernard Gallacher was also in trouble after duffing a chip and looked as if he would not make his par. But Tom still waited an age before playing his second shot, a chip up to the flag, because he wanted to see what happened up ahead before he committed himself to his own shot. Sensible tactics, in a way, but it also made Bernard wait, and I'm not sure if that was right. As it was, Bernard could not make par and Tom won his match there, by going two up with one to play. I still think Tom should have played more quickly, as, in golf, play is supposed to be continuous and I think you have to have a regard for your opponent in that respect. But, as I say, it is not sour grapes. The Ryder Cup has always thrown up little things like that over the years!

With Gallacher beaten, and Cañizares held to a half by the nerve and skill of Wadkins under extreme pressure, Europe were left a mere half-point short of a tie and an even more despairing single point away from victory itself. Jacklin's 12 warriors were distraught.

We had stood up to the challenge that faced us, and we felt we had played well enough as a team to have won it. In those moments after it was all over, and especially when we were together in the team room, we were inconsolable. In private, there were floods of tears. Seve and Bernhard Langer were both in tears. It might surprise you, but I didn't cry. I know I've always been emotional, but in Florida there were no tears streaming down my cheeks in the sheer frustration and distress of having given absolutely everything but having come up so narrowly short. Indeed, I found myself saying to my teammates that I didn't think it was right to cry in defeat – even though I totally understood those emotions. I said we should keep the crying until we won. I wanted to take all those feelings on to the 1985 match. I just wanted to bottle it all up and pour it all into the next Ryder Cup. I said, 'Let's win it next time,' and then there could be tears.

1983 Ryder Cup Results: 14–16 October, PGA National, Florida
Captains: Tony Jacklin (Europe), Jack Nicklaus (US)

Europe		US	
Morning foursomes			
Bernard Gallacher/Sandy Lyle		Tom Watson/Ben Crenshaw (5&4)	1
Nick Faldo/Bernhard Langer (4&2)	1	Lanny Wadkins/Craig Stadler	
José Maria Cañizares/Sam Torrance (4&3)	1	Raymond Floyd/Bob Gilder	
Seve Ballesteros/Paul Way		Tom Kite/Calvin Peete (2&1)	1
Afternoon fourballs			
Brian Waites/Ken Brown (2&1)	1	Gil Morgan/Fuzzy Zoeller	
Nick Faldo/Bernhard Langer		Tom Watson/Jay Haas (2&1)	1
Seve Ballesteros/Paul Way (1 hole)	1	Raymond Floyd/Curtis Strange	½
Sam Torrance/Ian Woosnam (halved)	½	Ben Crenshaw/Calvin Peete (halved)	
Morning fourballs			
Brian Waites/Ken Brown		Lanny Wadkins/Craig Stadler (1 hole)	1
Nick Faldo/Bernhard Langer (4&2)	1	Ben Crenshaw/Calvin Peete	
Seve Ballesteros/Paul Way (halved)		Gil Morgan/Jay Haas (halved)	½
Sam Torrance/Ian Woosnam	½	Tom Watson/Bob Gilder (5&4)	1
Afternoon foursomes			
Nick Faldo/Bernhard Langer (3&2)	1	Tom Kite/Raymond Floyd	
Sam Torrance/José Maria Cañizares		Gil Morgan/Lanny Wadkins (7&5)	1
Seve Ballesteros/Paul Way (2&1)	1	Tom Watson/Bob Gilder	
Brian Waites/Ken Brown		Jay Haas/Curtis Strange (3&2)	1
Singles			
Seve Ballesteros (halved)	½	Fuzzy Zoeller (halved)	½
Nick Faldo (2&1)	1	Jay Haas	
Bernhard Langer (2 holes)	1	Gil Morgan	
Gordon J. Brand Senior		Bob Gilder (2 holes)	1
Sandy Lyle		Ben Crenshaw (3&1)	1
Brian Waites		Calvin Peete (1 hole)	1
Paul Way (2&1)	1	Curtis Strange	
Sam Torrance (halved)	½	Tom Kite (halved)	½
Ian Woosnam		Craig Stadler (3&2)	1
José Maria Cañizares (halved)	½	Lanny Wadkins (halved)	½
Ken Brown (4&3)	1	Raymond Floyd	
Bernard Gallacher		Tom Watson (2&1)	1
Europe	**13½**	**US**	**14½**

SAM'S ANALYSIS: 1983

Europe

Seve Ballesteros	Three points towards Europe's cause and the greatest shot ever seen in a Ryder Cup on the pulsating last day. A brilliant senior partner for Paul Way.
Nick Faldo	With Langer contributed 3 points out of a possible 4 on the first two days and then won another point in the singles. Immense.
Bernhard Langer	Formed a superb partnership with Faldo – Europe's best in this Ryder Cup – and, like his fourball and foursomes partner, also captured a vital singles point.
Gordon J. Brand Senior	Unfortunate to be the only player Tony Jacklin ever left out of the team matches in his four Ryder Cups as captain. A steady if unspectacular player, he was perhaps unlucky not to get a half out of his singles match with Bob Gilder.
Sandy Lyle	Such a natural talent, but this was not his best Ryder Cup, by some distance. Dropped after defeat in the opening foursomes and slid to singles defeat too.
Brian Waites	A real steady Eddie of a player, and a gutsy one. Partnered Ken Brown in three of the four fourballs and foursomes but won only their first outing. Fought hard in a narrow singles defeat and performed highly creditably.
Paul Way	Remarkable debut for a 20 year old. Was in awe of Ballesteros but not overawed and more than did his bit in a successful if unpredicted partnership. Confident character, and his singles win over Curtis Strange took his personal contribution to 3½ points.
Sam Torrance	I played my best sustained burst of golf during my fourballs victory alongside Ian Woosnam on the first afternoon. Felt in good form throughout but only came away with 2 points from a possible 5. A fighting singles half.
Ian Woosnam	Only half a point in the end from his Ryder Cup debut but dealt brilliantly with the shock of seeing me drive out-of-bounds before he hit his own first Cup stroke. One of the best team men I've ever seen.

José Maria Cañizares	My partner in the two foursomes matches, he played his part in our opening-day win, but we then lost heavily in our second game in that format. Could easily have won a huge point over Lanny Wadkins in the singles, but then saw his opponent play one of the shots of the match to capture a half.
Ken Brown	Beat Morgan and Zoeller in the opening fourballs, in the company of Brian Waites, but then suffered two defeats with the same partner before producing his astonishing 4&3 singles win against Ray Floyd.
Bernard Gallacher	A bitterly disappointing eighth and final Ryder Cup as a player for the man who was to become Tony Jacklin's able deputy and then an excellent captain himself. Lost both his two matches, first with Lyle and then the anchor singles against Tom Watson.
Tony Jacklin (captain)	Inspirational, and the man who transformed both the European Ryder Cup team and the job of Ryder Cup captaincy itself. Attention to detail was total, and his on-course strategy was as strong as his off-course man-management. Deeply frustrated by defeat but knew it was also a victory in so many other ways and used the experience to plot and plan the famous wins to come at The Belfry and Muirfield Village. I am not convinced that Europe would definitely have won if Jacklin had been given two or three captain's picks – he was to be granted three picks in each of his remaining three matches as captain – but he was insistent after Palm Beach that he should be given the added flexibility of picks after inheriting a situation where none at all were granted for Florida.

United States

Fuzzy Zoeller	A delightful man with an effortless and rhythmic swing. Was given only one outing on the first two days, suffering a fourballs defeat, but then fought back to claim a half against the great Seve Ballesteros in the opening singles.

Jay Haas	Won 2½ points out of 3 in the fourballs and foursomes, with three different partners, but then ran up against Faldo in the singles and was beaten. Has latterly been a real star of Seniors golf.
Gil Morgan	A win, a loss and a half from his three team matches, but this highly talented golfer was then defeated by Langer in the singles. He was one of those sportsmen who just don't know at the time how good they are.
Bob Gilder	What exactly did happen way to the right of the final fairway in the singles victory over Gordon Brand, Bob? Two wins and two defeats from his four matches.
Ben Crenshaw	A win, a loss and a half over the first two days, but he ended up very much in credit with a crucial singles success against Sandy Lyle.
Calvin Peete	Another American to get 1½ points from his three games on the first two days – with a win, a half and a defeat – and then edged out Waites in the singles. Had a diamond in one of his teeth.
Curtis Strange	Not the best of Cups for my good friend Curtis, as he gained just 1 point – in the foursomes company of Jay Haas – out of three matches.
Tom Kite	One win and one loss coming into our singles battle, which was to be halved on the final green. Oh, that look he gave me!
Craig Stadler	'The Walrus' found the humidity and heat tough going but played only once on each of the first two days – losing one and winning one – before digging deep to overcome Ian Woosnam in the singles: another vital point for America on the last afternoon.
Lanny Wadkins	Took 2 out of 3 points on the first two days and then that memorable pitch at the 18th to give his captain, Nicklaus, the half that clinched the Cup.
Ray Floyd	Also played three times out of four on days one and two. He was beaten on each occasion and then, remarkably, ended the match still without even a half when Ken Brown, the man we all called 'Muscles', beat him up in the singles.

Tom Watson	The only American to play in all five matches, and he responded to Nicklaus's urgings to be his strong man on the course by winning 4 points.
Jack Nicklaus (captain)	We gave him a real fright, but he was still an impressive captain who mixed around his players on the first two days, in the traditional American manner, and then kept just enough power up his sleeve for the final five singles matches – Kite, Stadler, Wadkins, Floyd and Watson – to earn the 3 points from those games that he needed to retain the Cup by a margin of one. Was out-thought a little by Jacklin in the singles order – not expecting Ballesteros, Faldo and Langer all to be sent out at the top of the European list – but his overall strength, and wins in the middle order from Gilder, Crenshaw and Peete, played a big part in getting him across the line.

CHAPTER THREE

1985 THE BELFRY

Everyone still likes to remember my winning putt at the 18th on the final day – myself included – but, although that was the greatest moment of my life as a player, I also love to recall the build-up to the 1985 Ryder Cup. I cannot believe it is a quarter of a century ago now, because everything about how we all felt going into the match is still so fresh in the mind. Tony Jacklin, captain again, felt that it was merely a continuation of the 1983 Cup, and that's how I felt too. I think it is how all the players felt – well, especially the nine of us who remained to form the bulk of the side once more. How can I best sum up our emotions and our determination going into that 1985 match? Well, let's just say that we were all, metaphorically speaking, rubbing our hands together gleefully and saying to each other, 'Come on, we're going to f****** have them this time!'

Jacklin, the European captain, had been consumed during the previous 18 months by the planning and the final arrangements at The Belfry, which he felt were vital if he was to prepare his team properly for what was to become the biggest week that European golf had ever experienced.

He had also won a battle to have three captain's picks – in addition to the top nine automatic selections from the European Tour's Order of Merit – and he was determined to build on the giant strides the team had made in Florida. In particular, no detail in the way he set up the team's accommodation and both the on-course and off-course facilities at The Belfry was too small. Jacklin wanted to generate a real family atmosphere around the team, and he believed that creating an intimate and private team-room area, where the players and their partners and caddies could all relax and mix, was vital if the team were to forge a genuine and unbreakable togetherness.

Tony was brilliant that week, and I'm sure he felt the pressure of trying to win the Cup and doing everything he could to make it happen. But, as players, we simply believed – we absolutely believed – that our time had come. We had the current Open champion in Sandy Lyle, we had the current Masters champion in Bernhard Langer, we had Seve, we had Faldo, we had Woosnam. Tony's three picks were all very strong matchplay performers: Howard Clark, whom I was very pleased to see in the team and whom I was to partner in the team matches; the feisty Manuel Piñero, whom Tony would have picked for Florida if he had been given the chance; and José Rivero, who had won the World Cup for Spain the previous year in the company of José Maria Cañizares. Gordon Brand, Brian Waites and Bernard Gallacher were the only players, out of the 12 who formed Europe's team in Florida, who missed out this time. We felt we had a strong team, and, of course, we had such desire.

The match did not start well, however, for Jacklin and Europe. After the initial morning foursomes, the air of optimism and expectation surrounding the hordes of spectators thronging the course had been somewhat punctured. Comfortable wins for Tom Kite and Calvin Peete, Lanny Wadkins and Ray Floyd, and Craig Stadler and Hal Sutton had put the US into a 3–1 lead. Only Ballesteros and Piñero – paired up late on the final practice day by Jacklin after he felt that his original pairing of Seve and Rivero was not working – managed to gain a point for the European cause by beating Curtis Strange and Mark O'Meara 2&1.

Europe's three losing foursomes pairings were Faldo and Langer, Lyle and Ken Brown, and Torrance and Clark. Jacklin acted decisively. He kept Torrance and Clark together, sending them out again in the afternoon fourballs, but he ditched the Faldo–Langer partnership that had proved so strong in Florida and he also rested a slightly out-of-sorts Lyle from the day's second round of matches. Langer he put with Cañizares, and in came the small but long-hitting pairing of Woosnam and Paul Way. With Ballesteros and Piñero, he simply told them to go out and do it again.

It is interesting to look at the decisions that Tony made during that Ryder Cup, and a lot of them were hard decisions too. For a start, he decided to break up the successful Ballesteros–Way partnership from 1983. Many people might have expected him to continue with that, but he saw that he needed to freshen things up and also to harness Seve with one of the other three Spaniards in the team. That, initially, was Rivero, but Tony was not afraid to move away from his original thinking and bring in Piñero as Seve's partner very late in the day. It was an inspired move, as they won three of their four matches together. And he also had the proven Rivero–Cañizares partnership from the World Cup up his sleeve.

He also fancied the idea of pairing Way with Woosie in the fourballs, as they were both capable of shooting a lot of birdies and had similarly aggressive games. Way was a very confident young man, and it was a shame his game fell away so abruptly after such a remarkable start to his career, both individually and in Ryder Cup terms, in his early 20s.

But what is most significant about Tony's decision-making during that first day is that he had no hesitation in whipping both Faldo and Lyle out of the afternoon line-ups. They were, on paper, two of Europe's heaviest hitters, but Nick was struggling a lot with his game at the time and Sandy also seemed to need a bit of nursing through the first two days. He was also not too fond of playing foursomes, as many aren't.

Lyle was brought back on day two for the fourballs, partnering Langer, but Faldo was sidelined for the whole of the second day, too, and that is truly remarkable. But it is also pure Jacklin. He had, after all, picked Faldo as one of his three selections, alongside Rivero and Ken Brown, but he still allowed Nick to go away to work on his game, kept him in reserve in case things didn't go well, but then had the nerve to keep him out of things until the singles because the match began to go Europe's way. If it ain't broke, don't fix it, but it is still Nick Faldo you are talking about, and this was a very tough, and very brave, decision by Tony. It's a bit like dropping Wayne Rooney out of your England team during a major tournament because he's not playing very well. It's a very big call, but, of course, Jacklin got it totally right. It is the team that matters in a Ryder Cup, above and beyond any individual – even an all-time great like Faldo.

Way and Woosnam, leading off the European counter-attack after lunch, edged out Fuzzy Zoeller and that year's US PGA champion, Hubert Green, by one hole. Ballesteros and Piñero, in the next match, beat Andy North and Peter Jacobsen 2&1, and, suddenly, Europe were back on level terms. Then Cañizares and Langer claimed a half against Stadler and Sutton, and the only blot on Europe's afternoon was the one-hole defeat for Torrance and Clark by the combative Wadkins and Floyd partnership.

Torrance drew wild cheers by driving the green at the iconic par-four 10th, but Wadkins, who chose to lay up short of the water with his tee shot, still managed to halve the hole with a birdie three of his own. A twenty-five-foot putt from Wadkins edged the Americans ahead at the 16th, and two halved holes finally brought a titanic tussle to a conclusion.

It was a very tough and fiercely fought match, as you would expect against two blokes like Wadkins and Floyd. But Howard and I enjoyed playing together and it was a good match to be in. We were obviously disappointed when we came off the 18th green that evening. It had been a long and hard day, and we had not managed to get even half a point from our two matches. We could have been very disheartened. But, again, that's where Tony's captaincy shone through. He could see that we had played well and were both happy with our games and with being a partnership. He told us we would be out again the following morning in the second round of fourballs. It was exactly what we wanted to hear, and it boosted us just at the right time.

There is nothing better in the Ryder Cup than your captain coming up to you during the first two days of competition and telling you that you are playing. And, conversely, there is nothing worse than him telling you that you are not in his plans. But he could see that Howard and I were very comfortable with each other and very determined to come back out on the Saturday morning and get a point. So he went with us again, and it was a brilliant piece of captaincy because we rewarded him fully for his trust and faith.

Indeed, Torrance and Clark led Europe off in the fourballs and, with some inspired golf, overcame Kite and North by a 2&1 margin. Clark had five birdies, and Torrance finished things off with a birdie four at the long 17th, which matched Kite's four and prevented the Americans from fashioning an improbable escape with a half.

And, with Way and Woosnam brushing Green and Zoeller aside 4&3, the Europeans had seized the lead. Wadkins and O'Meara, however, then downed Ballesteros and Piñero 3&2, and the cut and thrust of the modern-day Ryder Cup was now at its sharpest. Craig Stadler, 'the Walrus', was just about to feel the pain of a cruel fate.

Stadler's short missed putt on the 18th green, which gave Langer and Lyle a remarkable half in their match against Craig and Curtis Strange, was a terrible moment for him but also a moment that gave us an incredible shot of extra belief and confidence going into the afternoon foursomes. It meant the whole match was tied up at 6–6, instead of the Americans being a point ahead, and so it was a really significant shift in the ever-changing momentum of the match.

The American pair of Stadler and Strange had, in fact, gone two up with two to play after Strange had put his six-iron approach at the 16th just a foot from the flag. Stadler birdied the par-five 17th, but Lyle then holed a twenty-two-foot eagle putt – after two huge blows to get on the green in two – to take the match down the 18th.

Both Langer and Lyle had birdie putts at the last to make sure of the half, but neither could hole from some distance. Stadler, fifty-five feet away from the hole in two, lagged up superbly to just under two feet, but the Europeans simply could not concede the par putt. Too much rested on it, and it was as if the realisation of that fact was too much for poor Stadler. He stabbed his putt nervously left of the hole and was left holding his head in horror at what he had done.

Now Jacklin had some more big decisions to make. Should he find room in the afternoon foursomes for Faldo? Ballesteros and Piñero had just lost, so should he split up that partnership? Had it any more mileage left in it? And, now Lyle had got that against-all-odds half alongside Langer, should he ignore Lyle's shaky form and dislike of foursomes and just send the German and the Scot out again?

Tony, again, got everything right that afternoon. He could easily have kept myself and Howard going, too, as we were on such a high after our victory against Kite and North. And there must have been a temptation to try to rehabilitate Faldo ahead of the singles. But he told Howard and me that he was standing us down, after playing in all three of the matches up until then, to give us just a little bit of time to get ourselves fully ready for the singles. He kept Seve and Piñero going, however, and also decided to give his successful – and so far unbeaten – Way and Woosnam pairing an initially unplanned outing in foursomes.

Both those decisions would have been him backing his gut feeling at the time, and he was to win one and lose one of those hunches, which is not a bad return. But Tony's biggest reward on that second afternoon came from his decisions to rest us in order to give José Rivero his first match, alongside Cañizares, and to withdraw Lyle from the firing line and give Bernhard Langer his fourth different partner of the match in Ken Brown. Those two decisions brought Europe 2 full points and thus a potentially decisive 9–7 lead going into the singles.

He wanted Rivero, in his debut Ryder Cup, to experience the unique atmosphere of the match before the singles, and he knew Cañizares – or 'Can O'Lager' as I called him – would be a comforting presence even in the difficult foursomes format, as they had played it so well together at the 1984 World Cup. As for Langer, it was also right for him to have a new partner for the foursomes, and, with Bernhard's magnificent temperament, it would not have bothered him a bit that Ken was his fourth partner in as many matches. And it showed how highly Tony regarded Bernhard, as he clearly felt he could pair him with anyone and get a result.

Cañizares and Rivero, in the first match out, came off spectacularly to trounce Kite and Peete 7&5, while the other irrepressible Spaniards, Ballesteros and Piñero, bounced back from their morning disappointment to beat Sutton and a shaken Stadler 5&4.

Jacklin's hunch with Way and Woosnam did not work, as they were defeated 4&2 by Strange and Jacobsen, but, in the now all-important anchor match, a triumphant Langer and Brown took out the big, previously unbeaten American pairing of Wadkins and Floyd. An edgy, close and tense affair was finally settled when Langer sank an eighteen-foot birdie putt on the par-five 15th and Brown fired an eight-iron approach to the next hole to a mere five inches. Two telling blows had pulled the European pairing to a 3&2 victory.

We knew that the point that Bernhard and Ken won right at the end of day two gave us the breathing space that we wanted going into the singles. If Wadkins and Floyd had won that match, it would have been 8–8. But a 9–7 lead was a very different situation. Tony's singles order might have been slightly different had it been 8–8, but with a 2-point lead he was able to hedge his bets slightly by putting most of his major strength in the number four, five and six slots.

Sandy Lyle, because he was left out of the afternoon foursomes on Saturday, worked hard on his game instead and came into the singles really feeling confident again, and he was able to do justice to his stature as the then Open champion. But what I remember most about the team meeting we had before Tony put in his singles order was Manuel Piñero's absolute determination that his captain should put him up against Lanny Wadkins. It was something I never saw at any other time, but Piñero – this little scrawny waif of a Spaniard – just stood up at the team meeting and said, 'I want Wadkins!' He stood up in front of all of us – and don't forget there were some pretty serious golfers of superstar status in that room, like Ballesteros and Langer and Faldo – and announced with huge passion that he knew that the Americans would put Wadkins out first in the singles order and that he, Manuel Piñero, wanted to be put up against him.

He virtually demanded it, and, as far as I was concerned, he could have him. Wadkins was the toughest American player, highly determined and skilful and quite cocky, in the best sense. No one wanted Wadkins! But Piñero did, and Tony – who had simply asked us all in a general sense if there was anywhere any of us didn't want to go in the order – immediately said to Piñero that he could go first.

In all the Ryder Cups I played in, the singles order was always decided by the captain because players were always happy to go wherever they were put, except on this occasion! And it was an extraordinary moment because Piñero was not one of our big players – in golfing terms, and not just in physical stature – and it must have taken real balls to stand up and demand Wadkins in such a way. Piñero was a real fighter in matchplay, however, and he had enjoyed a brilliant Ryder Cup in company with Seve, so I suppose he was on a high. And fair play to Piñero, too, because he went out first and beat Wadkins 3&1. Viva España!

Jacklin's singles order was Piñero (by personal demand), Woosnam, Way, Ballesteros, Lyle, Langer, Torrance, Clark, Faldo, Rivero, Cañizares, Brown. It was a clever line-up, with Ballesteros and Langer in the controlling positions of four and six, and the potentially explosive Lyle in between them at five. Woosnam and Way had also had an excellent Ryder Cup, and temperamentally they both relished the responsibility of being sent out behind the fired-up Piñero with orders to get early points on the board for Europe.

Then, at seven, eight and nine came the experienced and tough British trio of Torrance, Clark and Faldo. They were likely to be in the area of the draw from where the winning point might need to come, but that was not going to faze them. Faldo, despite his lack of form, was in his fifth Ryder Cup and had a proud playing record. He could be relied upon to give his very best.

At the back of the field were Rivero and Cañizares at numbers ten and eleven, fresh from their foursomes triumph the afternoon before and kept together again in the running order. Jacklin clearly hoped they would draw inspiration from each other, if necessary. As his anchor man, Jacklin had the experienced Brown – another unflappable character.

Ken was ideally suited to going out last. He had gone out second from last in the 1983 match, and he was to go out last again in the singles at Muirfield Village in 1987. Why? He was the slowest of our players, so no one really wanted to be behind him! But he was also a highly dependable player and quite a difficult customer in matchplay – as Ray Floyd discovered at Palm Beach and Lanny Wadkins was to find out in 1987.

Tony's order in 1985 played to the strengths of our team, with people in the positions their character and their abilities suited, and, again, it is a fine example of the thought and the subtlety he put into his captaincy. And Piñero gave us the start we wanted by taking out Wadkins in a match that turned on his chip-in for a birdie from off the green at the 10th. That established the momentum, and we knew we had such power in the middle order that the task of getting to the magic 14½ was within our grasp.

Although Woosnam found Stadler just too strong for him – with the roly-poly American winning himself a highly creditable point that went some way towards mending the hurt of his missed putt the previous day – another huge European point was won by Way, who produced a fine victory against Floyd, by two holes, after holding on gamely when his opponent fought back grimly from being four down with eight to play.

Ballesteros, three down with just five holes to play against Kite, clawed his way back into the match with three magnificent birdies at the 14th, 15th and 17th. On the par-three 14th he holed a forty-five-foot putt, at the 15th it was a fifteen-footer that dropped and then, on the 17th, the great Spaniard hit such a massive drive and three wood that he was through the green at the par five in two. A chip back then fell twelve feet short, but Ballesteros holed that one too and the roars from the crowd were deafening.

Kite out-drove Ballesteros at the last, however, and looked favourite to make a winning birdie when his approach shot came up just 15 feet from the flag. But neither he nor Seve could make a three, and the memorable match was halved – much to the delight of the Europeans more than the Americans.

Now, more than at any time on that tense last day, Jacklin's singles order brought its golden dividends. Playing immediately behind Ballesteros were Lyle and Langer, and both were never behind in their games with Jacobsen and Sutton respectively. Wins by 3&2 for Lyle and an even more emphatic 5&4 by Langer meant that Europe now led 13½ points to 8½. Just one more point was needed for European victory, but where was it to come from?

I played the worst golf of my life over the first nine holes. The atmosphere when I walked down to the first tee to begin my match against Andy North, at number seven in Jacklin's order, was simply amazing. There was so much expectation and excitement in the air. But, strangely and frustratingly, it didn't seem to inspire me. I was lucky when I double bogeyed the 6th that he did too, but Andy then birdied both the 4th and 5th to go two up, and, although I did manage to pull one back at the 7th when he bogeyed, I made a real mess of both the 9th and 10th to go three down with eight to play.

On the 9th tee I actually topped my tee shot – that's how badly I was playing – and it hopped over the burn running across the fairway. But I then had to hit three wood for my second shot to reach the green, as I was so far back, and it went into the water to the front and right. I remember telling myself that I had to stay calm and pull myself together. I saw a chink of light when Andy bogeyed the 12th, after missing the green with his approach, chipping to eight feet but then missing the putt.

With the tension surrounding the match tightening, and with no other match out on the course looking a sure-fire European bet, Torrance knew that he had to hang in and try to get something – anything – out of his own game.

Holes 12, 13 and 14 were all halved in par, and so the players went to the 15th tee with North still two holes up. From Europe's perspective, perhaps that final, Cup-deciding point might be needed from elsewhere.

I got a real break when North missed a very short putt for par at the 15th, a long par five, and when we halved the 16th in par fours I knew that I had to win at least one of the last two holes if I was going to get even a half out of the game. Tony had joined my match by now, and so I knew the importance of it all. But in those situations you are just totally focused on what you have to do. And, on the 17th tee, I knew I had to nail my drive and try to get on the green in two in order to crank the pressure right up on Andy. I hit a decent drive, and he ended up in the rough wide of the fairway, from where he could only hack it out about 15 yards.

Now, I thought, all I needed to do was get my second shot over the burn that runs across the fairway about 160 yards short of the green. I was just trying to get it up there so that I would have as short a third shot as possible into the green. What did I do? I hooked the approach, and the ball ended up in tall grass to the left of the fairway but, thankfully, well over the burn. Then, as I was thinking about what I had done, Andy hit an absolutely incredible one iron – his third shot – which ended with the ball almost hitting the flag as it ran across the green and on to just off the back edge. He was no more than 20 feet away from the hole. When I got to my ball, Jacklin was already there and everybody seemed to be there. But I not only got it out; the ball came to rest about six or seven feet away, and it was one of the shots of my career. Andy chipped up stone dead, for his five, and with a putt to win the hole I found that everything was shaking! But, thankfully, I managed to hole it for the four that brought the match back to all-square.

During one of his first visits to The Belfry, in the 1978 Hennessy Cup, Torrance had been so keyed up in his match against Seve Ballesteros that he had marched straight off the 17th green, after chipping in for a half in four, and – head down in concentration and with few spectators about – had mistakenly found himself standing on the 9th tee before realising his error.

There was no chance of that happening this time. Thousands of wild-eyed spectators thronged around every green and fairway, and the players had to walk through massed groups of them – held back only by ropes gripped by stewards – to get from each green to the next tee.

As I walked through to the 18th tee, with the roars echoing in my ears after my birdie putt and win at 17, I saw Tony Jacklin waiting by the side of the tee. I made to give him my driver, as if to say to him, 'What about if you hit this next shot?' But Tony merely grinned back and said, 'Go on, you can do it, son,' and I had to hit the most important drive of my life myself. Actually, I pulled it slightly, and I could feel it off the club even though I knew I had got a perfect contact. In fact, the ball flew well over three hundred yards – which shows just how pumped up I was – and left me with just a nine iron for my second shot on a hole that measured four hundred and seventy-four yards. But, from the tee, you cannot see the ball hit the fairway, and, with the water between you and the fairway getting wider for every yard further left you hit it, I did have my heart in my mouth until I heard the absolutely enormous roar from the galleries on the far side of the fairway, which greeted the sight of my ball landing on solid earth and bounding on up in the general direction of the hole. Thank God! I knew I had nailed it, but it did go much further left than I had intended!

Now it was North's turn to drive, and the pressure on him had suddenly been turned up to almost unbearable levels by the brilliance of Torrance's drive. The US Open champion, but Ryder Cup rookie, would never have experienced anything quite like this before, and it was too much for him.

Andy skied his drive, and as soon as he hit the ball I knew what was going to happen. There was no way he had hit it well enough to make the initial carry over water, and, sure enough, the reaction of the crowd told us the reality of it. And, as soon as I knew the ball was in the water, I knew we were going to win the Ryder Cup, and I could not stop the tears. I was crying as I left the tee for the long walk around the water to my ball, and the only thing that got me together again for a while was the fact that most of the American wives were waiting for us to walk past around the lake. I didn't want them to see me in that state, so I took a deep breath and pulled myself together before I went past them. I also had to wait while Andy took a drop, on the other side of the water, and then hit what was his third shot across it. And his ball was still not up with mine!

When he then hit a poor fourth, ending up about 20 feet left of the pin, I knew that all I had to do was get my second shot across the water and the Cup would be won. I didn't even have to hit the green. As I stood over the ball, after trying to compose myself, all I said to myself was that there was no way that I was going to hit it fat. I didn't care if I bladed it and it shot 50 yards over the green. As it happened, the connection was perfect with my nine iron, and the feeling when I looked up and saw the ball gently arcing its way towards the target was pure joy. After I hit the shot, I raised my arms wide in a salute to the crowd and my club actually hit Ian Woosnam, who had run up beside me, on the side of his head. He said he didn't feel a thing!

Jacklin, other members of the team who had already finished their singles matches and thousands upon thousands of European golf fans – both ringing the 18th green and watching transfixed on their television screens – were all in a state of ecstasy. Torrance was on the green in two, about twenty feet from the hole, and North was about to putt up and take six.

I know I had three putts to win the Ryder Cup, but I still wanted to hit a good putt and I am eternally grateful to Andy North for his wonderful sportsmanship and sense of theatre, because, of course, he could have picked up my marker and conceded the hole. But Andy, I think, wanted the crowd and myself to have that moment, and when my putt actually went in – wow! It was an unbelievable feeling. So, thank you Andy North for allowing me that moment, my moment. Even now, of course, 25 years on, so many people want to talk to me about that putt and that moment. It is wonderful, and it again tells you about how much the Ryder Cup means to people and how much it has caught the public's imagination during the last three decades.

What no one knew at the time, with the television cameras and every other media outlet concentrating on affairs in the Torrance–North match, was that Howard Clark actually had a putt to win the Ryder Cup himself but missed a four-foot putt for birdie on the 17th just before Torrance completed his memorable and historic three in front of a delirious crowd around the 18th.

Clark had always been in front in his match against O'Meara, but the American had fought back fiercely from being three down after five holes, and, after birdieing the 12th, O'Meara had got it back to just one down. The last six holes were all halved in par, however, and although that gave Clark a sweet victory by one hole, he missed his chance on the 17th green to claim his own moment of glory.

I would never wish a missed putt on Howard – or anyone, to be fair – but the BBC told me afterwards that they would have still stayed with my match on 18 even if Howard had holed out for that winning birdie and a 2&1 win on the 17th, which would, technically, have won the Ryder Cup before I had putted up ahead. They were never going to show his putt live. I think it was the sheer theatre and drama of what had happened in my match and because so many people were at the 18th. Plus the fact, of course, that the 18th at The Belfry is such an incredible setting. That's where the BBC wanted the match to be won!

Clark's win against O'Meara, and a further point gained when Cañizares overcame Zoeller by two holes – also finishing in front of the ecstatic hordes ringing the 18th green – meant that Europe had triumphed by 16½ points to 11½. It did not matter that Faldo, Rivero and Brown lost in three of the last four matches out on the course, to Green, Peete and Strange respectively. Europe, and Jacklin, had done it.

My own reaction on the 18th said it all as far as I was concerned. At moments like that, you never really know what you are going to do. Something happens deep inside you, and you just do things without thinking. It is always spontaneous. My tears all the way up that 18th hole, and then again when that final putt went in, were unstoppable and were of sheer joy. We had worked so hard, and played so passionately, and suddenly the prize was ours. The pledge we had made in Florida had been fulfilled. It was a deserved triumph for us and especially for Tony Jacklin. We were all so delighted for him. It was time to celebrate, and, my, how we celebrated!

After the initial jubilation with Seve and others spraying champagne from the roof of The Belfry hotel and Jacklin on my shoulders and Concorde doing a fly-past, and all the cheers of the crowd, there was a slight pause in the celebrations because we then had to attend the victory dinner. That must have been the worst concept in the history of the Ryder Cup – and now thankfully discarded – because neither team, in truth, wanted to be there. The winners just wanted to get on with the celebrations and didn't feel they could be too outrageous in the company of the vanquished, and the losers simply didn't want to be there at all. But that at least didn't last for long, and having sat through the dinner as modestly as we could, because you really don't want to embarrass either yourself or your opponents, we all really let our hair down when we got back to our team room. Later, too, we all ended up in the spa area of the hotel and everyone – Seve, Faldo, everyone – threw themselves into the pool. Well, the only bloke around who didn't was Bill Elliot, a golf journalist who did a runner because he didn't want his suit to get soaked. I never forgave Bill for that!

The following morning my old mate John O'Leary and I enjoyed a champagne breakfast, and, when I finally left The Belfry late on that Monday afternoon, it was merely to drive south to a friend's house near Woburn where another big celebration party soon started. Then, on the Tuesday, it was down to London to fly out with a lot of other players for that week's Spanish Open, and for me that was also one of the best parts of the 1985 Ryder Cup win. Meeting up again with so many other European Tour players, and being able to celebrate our victory with them – on the flight out and when we got to Spain – really brought it home to you what the win meant to the rest of Europe's golfing community. You get a real sense of how much you are representing the rest of the European Tour's players, and it was magnificent to get the chance to celebrate again with them.

I don't think the partying really stopped for me until about 4 a.m. on the Wednesday night, after the pro-am on the day before the tournament started. But, by then, I knew I had really made the very most of enjoying the moment! And, what is more, I made the cut in that tournament on the Friday evening, which must go down as one of the best performances of my career! Yes, the parties after the 1985 Ryder Cup were the biggest celebrations of all time, but winning the Cup back after a gap of 28 years made it the perfectly natural thing to do. Now, though, we knew we were capable of living with the Americans, and beating them, and the knowledge that we were now faced with perhaps the even bigger task of winning on US soil for the very first time in history, at Muirfield Village in 1987, was the perfect incentive for us to take the 1985 win and make it just the start of further glories. As for me, I knew that I was going to do all that it took to be a part of the 1987 team. I just had to be there.

1985 Ryder Cup Results: 13–15 September, The Belfry *Captains: Tony Jacklin (Europe), Lee Trevino (US)*			
Europe		**US**	
Morning foursomes			
Seve Ballesteros/Manuel Piñero (2&1)	1	Curtis Strange/Mark O'Meara	
Bernhard Langer/Nick Faldo		Calvin Peete/Tom Kite (3&2)	1
Sandy Lyle/Ken Brown		Lanny Wadkins/Raymond Floyd (4&3)	1
Howard Clark/Sam Torrance		Craig Stadler/Hal Sutton (3&2)	1
Afternoon fourballs			
Paul Way/Ian Woosnam (1 hole)	1	Fuzzy Zoeller/Hubert Green	
Seve Ballesteros/Manuel Piñero (2&1)	1	Andy North/Peter Jacobsen	
Bernhard Langer/José Maria Cañizares (halved)	½	Craig Stadler/Hal Sutton (halved)	½
Sam Torrance/Howard Clark		Raymond Floyd/Lanny Wadkins (1 hole)	1
Morning fourballs			
Sam Torrance/Howard Clark (2&1)	1	Tom Kite/Andy North	
Paul Way/Ian Woosnam (4&3)	1	Hubert Green/Fuzzy Zoeller	
Seve Ballesteros/Manuel Piñero		Mark O'Meara/Lanny Wadkins (3&2)	1
Bernhard Langer/Sandy Lyle (halved)	½	Craig Stadler/Curtis Strange	½
Afternoon foursomes			
José Maria Cañizares/José Rivero (7&5)	1	Tom Kite/Calvin Peete	
Seve Ballesteros/Manuel Piñero (5&4)	1	Craig Stadler/Hal Sutton	
Paul Way/Ian Woosnam		Curtis Strange/Peter Jacobsen (4&2)	1
Bernhard Langer/Ken Brown (3&2)	1	Raymond Floyd/Lanny Wadkins	
Singles			
Manuel Piñero (3&1)	1	Lanny Wadkins	
Ian Woosnam		Craig Stadler (2&1)	1
Paul Way (2 holes)	1	Raymond Floyd	
Seve Ballesteros (halved)	½	Tom Kite (halved)	½
Sandy Lyle (3&2)	1	Peter Jacobsen	
Bernhard Langer (5&4)	1	Hal Sutton	
Sam Torrance (1 hole)	1	Andy North	
Howard Clark (1 hole)	1	Mark O'Meara	
Nick Faldo		Hubert Green (3&1)	1
José Rivero		Calvin Peete (1 hole)	1
José Maria Cañizares (2 holes)	1	Fuzzy Zoeller	
Ken Brown	1	Curtis Strange (4&2)	1
Europe	**16½**	**US**	**11½**

SAM'S ANALYSIS: 1985

Europe

Manuel Piñero	Fierce matchplay competitor who teamed up with Seve and won 4 points from 5. 'I want Wadkins!'
Ian Woosnam	Formed impressive new partnership with Paul Way but lost his singles match and did not hit his very best form.
Paul Way	Who would have thought this was going to be his last Ryder Cup? Beat Ray Floyd in singles and won 3 points out of 4.
Seve Ballesteros	So strong, and Europe's established leader on the course. Took 3 points out of 4 alongside Piñero and a vital half in his singles against Kite.
Sandy Lyle	Not his best Ryder Cup but won a crucial singles point in Europe's Sunday charge to victory.
Bernhard Langer	Only lost one match from the five he played, including a thumping singles win. Four different partners over the first two days? No problem.
Sam Torrance	Perhaps my golf was not at its best during the three days, but the honour of sinking the winning putt will live with me for ever.
Howard Clark	A great partner for me during the first two days, and he also picked up a singles point against Mark O'Meara.
Nick Faldo	That Europe still won by 5 clear points without Nick contributing anything is one of the more remarkable statistics of 1985. But he only played twice and was in a rut of poor form.
José Rivero	The only rookie in the team had to wait until Saturday afternoon before being given an outing. But what an outing: a 7&5 win in the second round of foursomes alongside Cañizares.
José Maria Cañizares	Unbeaten in three matches, he underlined his reputation as a dependable and highly competitive matchplay performer. The 38-year-old veteran was Europe's only unbeaten player.
Ken Brown	Won a vital point in the final foursomes match with Langer but got nothing from his other foursomes outing and his anchor singles.

| Tony Jacklin (captain) | He will say it was his players who did it, but this was truly a triumph for Jacklin's leadership and captaincy skills. The man who transformed the European Ryder Cup side showed all his management flair and intimate knowledge of who to play and who to leave out. Who would think that Faldo and Lyle would only play in three of the fourball and foursomes matches between them? And what about the late hunch in putting Ballesteros and Piñero together, a partnership that then produced three out of four points? He also failed to panic when we went 3–1 down after the opening round of matches. In his preparation, his deployment and management of his troops, and his singles order, Jacklin was flawless. |

United States

Lanny Wadkins	Three wins from his first three matches, but then America's strong man lost in the pivotal final foursomes and also his singles against Piñero.
Craig Stadler	Poor Craig will never forget that short missed putt on the 18th on Saturday lunchtime, but he won 3 points overall.
Ray Floyd	Like fellow tough guy Wadkins, he began brilliantly with 2 points from his first two outings but then lost his remaining two matches – and both were vital moments for Europe.
Tom Kite	Only 1½ points from a possible 4 for him, but he was one of the toughest Americans.
Peter Jacobsen	Popular and personable, he enjoyed a good foursomes win on the second day but found Lyle too strong in the singles.
Hal Sutton	Another American who started strongly but then fell away. Trounced by Langer in their singles: a portent for 2004?
Andy North	Although the US Open champion, he lacked the stature of other Americans and ended up without a point from his three matches.

Mark O'Meara	Fine fourballs victory on day two was to be his only point from three matches. Another American on the fringes of the team.
Hubert Green	The recent US PGA champion but curiously only used twice on the first two days. Lost both games but bounced back against an out-of-form Faldo in the singles. Had the deepest-set eyes I've ever seen.
Calvin Peete	Took 1 from 2 in the foursomes, alongside Kite, and a steady if unspectacular player. But won his singles against Rivero to emerge in credit overall.
Fuzzy Zoeller	Poor old Fuzzy did not enjoy the match much: played three, lost three and even when he hit the heights with his golf – as in his first day fourball – he found that the Europeans played even better.
Curtis Strange	Won his anchor singles to finish with 2½ points from a possible 4. One of the better American performers.
Lee Trevino (captain)	Surprisingly, he was never really his ebullient self in public either at press conferences or in the formal speeches that captains have to make before and after the match. He was obviously a highly experienced player in Ryder Cups, and he seemed to organise his team in the traditional American way of giving every member a decent run-out in the team element of the match. Curtis Strange, one of his stronger players, was also wasted down at number 12 in the singles order, but, overall, I just think that the Americans were outplayed by Europe.

CHAPTER FOUR

1987 MUIRFIELD VILLAGE

If 1985 was special, then 1987 topped it. Thirteen previous British, British and Irish, and European teams had travelled to the United States to try to win the Ryder Cup on American soil, and all had failed to do so.

Tony Jacklin's first team, of course, had come closest; indeed, the narrow defeat at Palm Beach, Florida, in 1983 had acted as a spur for the triumph to come two years later at The Belfry. Seven of the players who had appeared in 1983, furthermore, were able to form the heart and soul of the 1987 team. Nine players from the 1985 victory made it to Muirfield Village, in Columbus, Ohio.

The three wild cards, this time, were José María Olazábal, the exciting 21-year-old from Spain making his Cup debut, Sandy Lyle and Ken Brown. Lyle and Olazábal had not qualified by right only because they had played so much on the PGA Tour in America, and Brown too had split his time between Europe and the States and so had not given himself the best chance of making the team through the European Tour's Order of Merit.

For Tony Jacklin, and for all the players, our 1987 win must go down as the greatest ever Ryder Cup performance by a European side. But, when I look again at the names in our team that year, and reflect on what they were doing in their individual careers at the time, it is very clear to me that the 1987 team was also the best Europe have ever fielded. Perhaps not quite up there with the 1981 US line-up, but not a million miles short either. Remember, Seve was in his absolute pomp, Nick Faldo had just won the Open that summer, the first of his six major titles, and Bernhard Langer, Sandy Lyle and Ian Woosnam were, at the end of 1987, ranked third, fourth and sixth in the world. Sandy was to win the Masters six months or so later, and Ballesteros the 1988 Open. Indeed, between them, Faldo, Lyle, Woosnam, Langer and Olazábal were about to win eight of the next twelve US Masters green jackets, and Faldo two more Opens. Nick, Seve, Bernhard and Sandy were all major winners by the time the 1987 match was played, with Woosie and Olazábal already established as major talents. It was a tough team to get into!

Manuel Piñero, José Maria Cañizares and Paul Way were the three players from 1985 to miss out, but Olazábal, the feisty Bristol-based Scot Gordon Brand Junior, and the veteran Irishman Eamonn Darcy – who had made three previous Cup appearances – were more than capable additions to the nine who had contributed so much to the 1985 breakthrough.

The year 1986 had been one of my worst, both on and off the golf course, with the break-up of my first marriage, but by the time the 1987 Ryder Cup came along I had met Suzanne, and I proposed to her during the flight out to America on Concorde. It is by now a very well-known quote, but there was indeed more than a grain of truth in Tony Jacklin's line to me on the Thursday evening before the start of the 1987 match: 'Sam, I'm resting you tomorrow morning – you're playing!' Before the Cup's opening ceremony, Suzanne and I had been like a couple of kids when, having walked once around the 18th green in front of the clubhouse to the stage with the rest of the teams and their partners, we dashed fully 500 yards around the back of the clubhouse and did the walk through the crowds again! It had been such an indescribable feeling of pride and excitement, and we just wanted to do it all again! We got a tremendous reaction from the spectators, and, at that Ryder Cup, the European support in particular was incredible. But I suppose, when the match began, they soon had a lot to shout about.

Torrance and Howard Clark were paired up again by Jacklin and sent out first in the opening foursomes matches, but nothing went right. Soon, they had lost three of the first five holes, against Tom Kite and

Curtis Strange, and could not recover. In the end, they were beaten 4&2, and neither played again until the singles. After a couple of hours' play, moreover, Europe were down in all four matches and, as in 1985, it looked as if the Americans would be the ones to make a fast start.

In the second foursomes match, Langer and Brown lost four of holes two to eleven, after winning the first, and eventually went down to a 2&1 defeat to Hal Sutton and Dan Pohl. At 2–0 behind, Europe needed a boost, and it was provided by the remaining two foursomes pairings, Faldo and Woosnam and Ballesteros and Olazábal.

It was just one of those things that Howard and I could not get into our match, and it cost us the opportunity of playing again before the singles. But that's the way it sometimes goes in the Ryder Cup. It wasn't as if either of us was playing badly. In fact, at that match, I would say that all 12 of us were playing great. It's just that only eight can play in each fourball and foursomes series, and Tony quite rightly went with his big guns. Both the Faldo–Woosnam and Ballesteros–Olazábal partnerships won twice on that opening day, having come through grittily in the opening foursomes to win on the 18th green and peg America back to 2–2, and by the end of the day Tony also had the Langer–Lyle pairing doing the business. For the second day, therefore, it was just a case of putting those fantastic three partnerships back out there again twice more and sitting back to watch. Unbelievably, those three pairings won 9½ points out of a possible 11 in fourballs and foursomes. They might have been a bit tired by the time we got to the singles, but they'd almost won the Ryder Cup for us again by then.

By the end of day one, after an incredible afternoon whitewash of the Americans in the fourballs – the first time the US had gone down 4–0 in a team session – it was 6–2 to Europe.

Brand Junior and Rivero had joined the big three in the afternoon fourballs, winning their match 3&2 against Ben Crenshaw and Scott Simpson and playing so well that they were on course for a better-ball 66 or 67 when they finished on the 16th green.

Lyle and Langer won on the 18th against Andy Bean and Mark Calcavecchia, who messed up at both the 17th and 18th holes to throw away a one-hole lead, while Faldo and Woosnam were six under par when they took out Sutton and Pohl 2&1 and Ballesteros and Olazábal seven under when they defeated Strange and Kite, America's other morning winners, by the same margin.

The next morning saw Strange and Kite attempt some kind of US fightback by beating Brand and Rivero 3&1 in the top foursomes game, while Faldo and Woosnam managed a scruffy half against Sutton and Larry Mize. But, once again, Europe's bottom two pairings were inspirational. Lyle and Langer were heading for a score of sixty-five or sixty-six – remarkable in foursomes – when they beat Lanny Wadkins and Larry Nelson on the 17th green, and Ballesteros and Olazábal dug deep in typical fashion to hold on to a one-hole advantage against Crenshaw and Payne Stewart in the anchor match.

Jacklin then gave Faldo and Woosnam the added incentive of leading off the afternoon fourballs against America's most productive partnership of Strange and Kite, and the tall Englishman and little Welshman – not natural partners off the course but deadly together on it – responded by waltzing to a brilliant 5&4 win.

They birdied the first five holes and went to the turn in a barely believable twenty-nine strokes. Three more birdies followed, and Faldo and Woosnam were ten under par for their better-ball score when the match ended on the 14th. It was golf of the highest standard, and the Americans could not live with the pace that Europe were setting.

That win took the European points tally to 9½, from just thirteen completed matches, and only a first defeat for Ballesteros and Olazábal later in the afternoon – following a perhaps more predictable loss for Brand Junior and his new partner Darcy – slowed Europe's rampaging bandwagon a little.

Bean and Stewart, in fact, also went out in twenty-nine before beating Brand and Darcy, who were themselves five under par at that stage, 3&2. And it was to prove, over the years, to be a rare beating indeed for 'Seve and Ollie' as Sutton and Mize ran out 2&1 winners.

For the fourth time out of four, however, the anchor match brought a European point. Lyle and Langer were three up with three to play against Wadkins and Nelson but had to go to the 18th to make sure of the win. And it was clinched with one of the shots of the entire match, which in itself is saying something, with members of both teams joining the huge crowd surrounding the final green.

Wadkins, ever the fighter, had put his approach shot to within a couple of feet of the hole, guaranteeing the birdie three that might have snatched an unlikely half. But Langer's second shot, in fading light, then managed to deposit his ball inside that of Wadkins. Hole halved in three, and the European pair had won by one hole.

At the end of day two, therefore, Europe led by 10½ to America's 5½. Only 3½ more points were required to retain the Ryder Cup, with 4 points needed for outright and historic victory.

Our 1987 team was also the first from this side of the Atlantic to win or tie each series of fourball and foursomes matches, and on the Saturday night we were more than confident that we could go on to win the Cup outright. We weren't taking anything for granted, because America were always favourites to take the singles due to their greater strength in depth – over the entire 12-man team – and because their players knew the Muirfield Village course so intimately from often playing on it on their regular tour. It was literally the course that Jack built, and America's captain, Nicklaus, did not take kindly to the European dominance of the first two days.

We knew the Americans would make a huge effort on the final day and that we would have to fight extremely hard for every point or half-point. But we were still very confident, because our lead of 5 points was a massive one to take into the singles. In effect, the Cup was ours to lose, even though that adds to the intensity of the final day in that you know that you should win from that position.

I know that Tony received some criticism at the time for depending so much on his big players to form partnerships and to play them in every series of foursomes and fourballs. Langer, Faldo, Woosnam, Ballesteros and Olazábal played in all four rounds on the first two days, while only Strange, Kite and Sutton did that for the US. Those critics say that Europe's big six, including Lyle, who played in three of the team matches, then only won 1½ points between them in the singles. They say that this showed how fatigued they were. But I believe that Jacklin got this exactly right.

In those days, we simply had to make the most of our best players during the fourballs and foursomes. Our strength in depth was not as good as America's, even in a team like the 1987 one. That was our biggest weakness. Indeed, in 1987, it was not stretching things too much to say that our top six were the best six players in the world game – so why not play them as much as possible? Tony was absolutely correct to go for it on the first two days, and I think it is a great mark of his captaincy skills that he not only got his reward with the numbers up on the scoreboard on that Saturday evening but he also made sure that every member of our twelve-man team got at least one piece of the foursomes or fourball action before the singles.

From numbers eight to twelve in our team, we always struggled against the Americans in that era, and especially on their courses, and so for Jacklin to blood everyone over those first two days was brave – even knowing he had much of the work being done by his three power pairs. To me, and even compared with his opposite number, Nicklaus, in this match, Jacklin was way ahead of his time in the skills and decision-making he brought to the job of Ryder Cup captain.

There was still much drama to come on the final day, though, as Europe struggled to make it over the line against a ferocious American counter-attack. It never looked as if Europe would fail to get the 3½ points needed as a minimum requirement, but it was still uncomfortably close.

Torrance, too, found himself in the thick of the action after being put out at number three in the singles 'batting order' by Jacklin. The legacy of his tense but vital half with Larry Mize was to stay with Torrance for years, as was also the case for Darcy after his heart-stopping encounter with Crenshaw that finished in glorious victory for the Irishman.

We were all playing so well that we went into the singles with supreme confidence. But I suppose, after all the disappointments that we had suffered in America, it was also an unreal situation in a way. How could we be an amazing 5 points ahead? Was it really true? The Ryder Cup, especially on American soil, had always been something of a massacre for us, but now, suddenly, we were the dominant force. I remember that we had a wonderful sense of unity, and desire to get the job done, when we went out there on that Sunday. But it didn't make the task any easier, even though in many ways it is a more straightforward golfing challenge when you are playing singles. In the team matches, you have a very deep sense that your partner is relying on you and that you do not want to let him down. But, in singles, it is just you and your own ball, and that is more of a natural comfort zone for a professional golfer. So, even in as tense and pressurised a situation as the singles of a Ryder Cup in which we could win it for the very first time in America, you tee off with a bit of relief inside you that it is now just down to you.

Woosnam, sent out by Jacklin at the head of the field, could not get the better of his opponent, Andy Bean, as hard as he tried. Finally, one down with two to play, Woosnam's fate was sealed when Bean managed to halve the 17th even though his drive ended up in heavy rough and Woosnam found the heart of the fairway. When the 18th was also halved in par, the Americans had the first singles point on the board.

In the next match, Clark was also involved in an equally dour struggle with Pohl, but this time the 18th, as so often that week, saw a swing in fortunes to Europe. Pohl made a mess of it, leaving Clark to win the hole and the match with a par four.

Now it was Torrance. His battle against Mize was yet another closely fought affair, with never more than one hole in it in favour of either man. But, when they came to the last hole, Mize was one up.

He pulled his drive into a water hazard that ran up the left side of the 18th hole, and after a long delay in which the rules officials were called, he took the option of a free drop because of a TV tower, which gave him line-of-sight relief. But he still had to drop in the hazard and could then only advance the ball back onto the fairway. It may not have been quite that long, but it felt like I was waiting about 20 minutes before I could play my second shot. He was still well short of the green, and, standing over my ball, after a perfect drive, I knew I had a glorious chance of winning the hole and grabbing a priceless half for the team.

I hit the five iron of my life to about fifteen feet below the hole, which, on that green, with its slope from back to front, was exactly where you wanted to be. But Mize, after playing into the front bunker and chipping out about fifty feet past the hole, then holed the putt for a five! It was an incredible five by Larry, but having been expecting to have three putts for the hole I now knew that I could only afford two. And, settling over the putt, I felt my hands shaking uncontrollably – or so I felt. Looking at the video of that putt now, nothing seems to be moving at all, but I can categorically state that I did not know, when I eventually hit it, if the ball would come up six feet short or twenty feet past.

Somehow, though, and to this day I don't know how, the ball was knocked stone dead. What I remember most about that moment, as I then just tapped the ball into the cup for a four, and a halved match, was an American woman in the crowd who started whooping because, having seen Larry hole from just off the green and me miss my birdie putt, she assumed that we had halved it in four and that Mize had won the game by one up. I was in such a state of relief, after my shakes over the ball, that I was hardly celebrating, and my one big emotion was that I wanted to pick my ball out of the hole and hurl it at that woman! I'm very glad that I didn't. But that is where my putting twitch began, and the subsequent struggles that I had with the putter were only fixed when I adopted the broomhandle putter during the winter of 1988–9. I suppose that is what a Ryder Cup can do to you!

Faldo and Olazábal, Jacklin's main strengths in the middle of his singles line-up, and playing directly behind Torrance at four and five in the order, could not win even a half-point between them, however. Faldo seemed to run out of steam as he twice bogeyed on the inward nine and saw Mark Calcavecchia turn around the Open champion's narrow lead and secure his match for America on the 18th.

And Europe still needed 2 more points to retain the Cup and 2½ to win it outright when Olazábal – never ahead against Payne Stewart – bogeyed both the 16th and 18th to lose by two holes. Rivero, too, seventh out, was in the process of going down 2&1 to Scott Simpson, that year's US Open champion, and everywhere you looked on the course the Americans were fighting for their lives.

Langer, eighth out, was involved in a tremendous scrap with Larry Nelson, who had been three up early in their match, but both Ballesteros, three up with six to play against Strange, and Brand Junior, four up at the turn in match number eleven against Sutton, were beginning to fritter away holes. Lyle, too, playing at nine in between Langer and Ballesteros, was down in his match with Kite and was to lose that one by a 3&2 margin. In the anchor game, meanwhile, there was little hope of Ken Brown turning things around against Wadkins.

There was still hope with Brand, Langer and especially Ballesteros, of course, but in an increasingly fraught atmosphere it was clear that much could depend on the outcome of Darcy's extraordinary game against Crenshaw, in match number six.

Darcy, the ninth and final qualifier by right in Jacklin's twelve, had also endured a largely unhappy previous Ryder Cup career. Indeed, when he stood on the first tee on that Sunday lunchtime at Muirfield Village, Darcy knew he was, in all probability, facing his last chance to win a full Ryder Cup point in what was his eleventh individual match. In three previous appearances – in 1975, 1977 and 1981 – Darcy had gained only two half-points, from a foursomes and a fourball outing, and he had also been beaten, alongside Brand, in the previous afternoon's fourballs. Was this to be a ninth defeat or a first win?

He also had a bad start, losing the second hole, but then three birdies in four holes from the fourth saw Darcy win all four and spring into a decisive lead. Moreover, Crenshaw, after three-putting the 6th hole, had banged his putter into the ground in sheer frustration – and broken it. Unable to replace it, Crenshaw was now forced to putt with either his one iron, for long putts, or the leading edge of his sand wedge, for short ones. But if this was to Darcy's advantage, it was not apparent, as Crenshaw – renowned as one of the best putters in the game – began to hole putts from all angles.

Three up to Darcy soon became one down with just two to play, and the poor Irishman was looking as if he would be unlucky yet again. Crenshaw, however, then gave his beleaguered opponent a welcome boost by making a mess of the 17th. All square. And then, remarkably,

Crenshaw also drove into the water hazard to the left of the 18th that Mize had found against Torrance.

After dropping under penalty, Crenshaw could only find a greenside bunker with his third shot. Darcy, from the fairway, put his second shot into the same sand trap. Crenshaw came out to ten feet below the hole, and Darcy to five feet above it.

Any golfer would have wanted Crenshaw's putt rather than Darcy's, even though it was twice the length. On the slope on that green, if Darcy had missed then his ball would have had nothing to stop it. It would have rolled at least eight feet past. Of course, Eamonn would have been praying that Ben did not hole his ten-footer – especially as he had a one iron in his hand! But Crenshaw did, with a magnificent effort under the circumstances, and now Darcy had to hole out for the four if he was to get his full point, his first Ryder Cup win and – as it was looking at that time – the extra half-point that would make all the difference to the European cause. No pressure then!

It was difficult to look as Darcy bent over his putt, and poor Eamonn really got the shakes with his putting after that moment. I know it was only five feet, but it was one of the toughest putts to make in that sort of situation and Darcy never really got over the stress of it – even though, to his everlasting credit, he coaxed it in with the faintest brush of the ball. But I wonder if Eamonn would, or could, have holed that putt if Jacklin had not made sure that he put him out in the fourballs the previous afternoon to get a taste of the course and the electric atmosphere out there?

I think Tony's captaincy decision-making was again rewarded to the full with Darcy's putt. Those greens at Muirfield Village were so incredibly quick that week that the so-called lesser Europeans, who in those days had little chance outside of Ryder Cups to play in America, were at an enormous disadvantage because conditions were so alien to them. Perhaps 60 per cent of our team had previously had little, or no, experience of greens like that. In fact, I also think that Nicklaus and the Americans got it badly wrong by deliberately, as a tactic, making the greens so quick. That was an error, because they were so fast that even the American players had never really seen anything like them before!

With Langer finishing with a tough half, and Ballesteros by now also assured of at least a half in his match, Darcy's full point meant that the Cup was still Europe's. And, fittingly, when Ballesteros finished off Strange on the 17th, to win 2&1, victory itself was clinched with the 14½-point mark reached.

Brown, in the last match, lost 3&2 to Wadkins, but Brand claimed a half against Sutton and the final score read US 13, Europe 15. History had been made, and Jacklin's brilliant team had done it.

The European support throughout the match had been tremendous, and, after the closing ceremony, myself and Woosie and Faldo went into the buggy storage room beneath the Muirfield Village clubhouse, where, all week, Europe's fans had gathered to meet and have a few drinks. Well, the atmosphere in there after we had won was simply amazing, and the half-hour or so we spent in there mingling with the supporters and drinking and singing remains, for me, one of the most special of all the Ryder Cup memories. It was almost a crying shame when we were dragged out to go to the official victory dinner. But the feelings of warmth we got from our own fans, and the chance to celebrate our achievement with them for a while, was an incredible privilege. And it started something, as a post-match mingle with the supporters, that we then did at every Ryder Cup afterwards. I hope it is also a tradition that will always remain.

Even before the team and its supporters left Ohio, there were big questions on everyone's lips: would Jacklin now step down as captain on the grounds that he could not achieve anything more in the job? And what peak was there left for Europe's team to conquer, now that the ultimate victory had been won on American soil? These were questions for which Ian Woosnam, for one, knew relevant answers. Standing up in front of the rest of the players in the team room, he said that Jacklin had to continue on as captain for 1989 so that Europe could have the best chance of winning the Cup for a third time in a row.

I don't think any of us wanted this rollercoaster ride to stop. We were having the time of our lives, and for all of us the lure of the Ryder Cup was now so strong. We enjoyed the camaraderie that Tony, in particular, had helped to create, and we had so many top-class players who had found that Ryder Cup competition had enabled them to hone and celebrate their talents in a supportive team environment too. Some of the golf that had been played in that 1987 match was just extraordinary. It was breathtaking, and even Jacklin said he had never seen golf of that sustained quality before. At Muirfield Village we had twelve golfers, and six world-class ones in particular, playing to the very best of their ability and showing that they could perform in the biggest cauldron – the biggest amphitheatre, really – that the game could produce. It should be harder than usual to perform to that sort of level under those conditions, but everyone had seemed to rise to the occasion, and the result was an achievement beyond our wildest dreams, to be honest.

We knew we were in with a great chance of winning when we landed in America. But it was the manner of our domination, despite the Americans' courageous showing on the final day, that made it heady stuff for us, and for our fans. I've always maintained, too, that the advantage of setting up your home course for the benefit of your own players is worth – over the course of a Ryder Cup match – at least 2 points to the host team. That's why our eventual 2-point winning margin, though so hard-fought in the end, was worth double that in terms of what was really the gap between the two teams in that match at Muirfield Village. That's also why I still rate it the best Ryder Cup performance, the best team and the best achievement of my time. It was the best everything.

1987 RYDER CUP RESULTS: 25–27 SEPTEMBER, MUIRFIELD VILLAGE
Captains: Tony Jacklin (Europe), Jack Nicklaus (US)

Europe		US	
Morning foursomes			
Sam Torrance/Howard Clark		Curtis Strange/Tom Kite (4&2)	1
Ken Brown/Bernhard Langer		Hal Sutton/Dan Pohl (2&1)	1
Nick Faldo/Ian Woosnam (2 holes)	1	Lanny Wadkins/Larry Mize	
Seve Ballesteros/José María Olazábal (1 hole)	1	Larry Nelson/Payne Stewart	
Afternoon fourballs			
Gordon Brand Jr/José Rivero (3&2)	1	Ben Crenshaw/Scott Simpson	
Sandy Lyle/Bernhard Langer (1 hole)	1	Andy Bean/Mark Calcavecchia	
Nick Faldo/Ian Woosnam (2&1)	1	Hal Sutton/Dan Pohl	
Seve Ballesteros/José María Olazábal (2&1)	1	Curtis Strange/Tom Kite	
Morning foursomes			
José Rivero/Gordon Brand Jr	½	Curtis Strange/Tom Kite (3&1)	1
Nick Faldo/Ian Woosnam (halved)		Hal Sutton/Larry Mize (halved)	½
Sandy Lyle/ Bernhard Langer (2&1)	1	Lanny Wadkins/Larry Nelson	
Seve Ballesteros/José María Olazábal (1 hole)	1	Ben Crenshaw/Payne Stewart	
Afternoon fourballs			
Nick Faldo/Ian Woosnam (5&4)	1	Curtis Strange/Tom Kite	
Eamonn Darcy/Gordon Brand Jr		Andy Bean/Payne Stewart (3&2)	1
Seve Ballesteros/José María Olazábal		Hal Sutton/Larry Mize (2&1)	1
Sandy Lyle/Bernhard Langer (1 hole)	1	Lanny Wadkins/Larry Nelson	
Singles			
Ian Woosnam		Andy Bean (1 hole)	1
Howard Clark (1 hole)	1	Dan Pohl	
Sam Torrance (halved)	½	Larry Mize (halved)	½
Nick Faldo		Mark Calcavecchia (1 hole)	1
José María Olazábal		Payne Stewart (2 holes)	1
Eamonn Darcy (1 hole)	1	Ben Crenshaw	
José Rivero		Scott Simpson (2&1)	1
Bernhard Langer (halved)	½	Larry Nelson (halved)	½
Sandy Lyle		Tom Kite (3&2)	1
Seve Ballesteros (2&1)	1	Curtis Strange	
Gordon Brand Jr (halved)	½	Hal Sutton (halved)	½
Ken Brown		Lanny Wadkins (3&2)	1
Europe	**15**	**US**	**13**

SAM'S ANALYSIS: 1987

Europe

Ian Woosnam	Majestic ball-striking and unbeatable in the company of Faldo for two days. But still waiting for that first singles victory . . .
Howard Clark	A doughty singles point in the furnace of the final day, in his only outing after being beaten with me in the opening foursomes.
Sam Torrance	I might have only played twice, but I got a precious half-point in the singles and this was one of the happiest times of my life, especially with Suzanne there for her first experience of the Ryder Cup.
Nick Faldo	One of four of the big six who lost in the singles, but with Woosnam he was a cornerstone of our victory with his golf over the first two days.
José María Olazábal	Took 3 points out of 5 on his debut and the beginning of his wonderful partnership with Seve. His little victory dance on the 18th green at the end said it all about how he took to Ryder Cup battle.
Eamonn Darcy	Heroic final putt on the 18th green to beat Crenshaw and give Europe perhaps its most important point of the last day. A fighter, and it was a worthy end to his own Ryder Cup career.
José Rivero	Won one of his two team matches, a fourballs outing with Gordon Brand, in fine style but could not follow that up with a singles point. Like many of us, forced to adopt merely a supporting role because of the brilliance around us.
Bernhard Langer	Beaten only once in five matches, his 3½ points were again central to the cause and his partnership with Lyle inspirational.
Sandy Lyle	Left out of the opening foursomes but then formed a superb partnership with Langer before being beaten in the singles by Tom Kite.
Seve Ballesteros	Won 4 points out of 5 and formed with Olazábal the beginning of the Ryder Cup's greatest partnership. Totally focused on the job he had to do out on the course – which was leading us all by his brilliant example.

Gordon Brand Junior	A very worthy debut for a tenacious player, with an opening fourballs win and then a singles half to take out of his four outings.
Ken Brown	One of three players to appear in the opening foursomes and then not play again until the singles. Not Ken's most memorable Ryder Cup from an individual standpoint, but he more than played his part in the best team I've known.
Tony Jacklin (captain)	Victory at Muirfield Village was, in many ways, the culmination of his ambition as a Ryder Cup captain. Why has he never been knighted for his services to golf on this side of the Atlantic? Involved all twelve of his players on the first two days, despite rightly depending on the world-class talents of his big six to garner as many points as they possibly could in the foursomes and fourball matches. As in 1985, his preparation and man-management were exemplary, and his singles order – with his top six players spread out in the order at numbers one, four, five, eight, nine and ten – was designed to withstand the shocks of an American fightback. It was a clever strategy, rewarded when 3 of the points needed on that tense last day came from elsewhere.

United States

Andy Bean	Tall and powerful striker who should have been pleased with his debut performance: a win and a loss in the fourballs and then a singles victory over Woosnam.
Dan Pohl	This was to be his only Ryder Cup appearance, and after his opening foursomes win he then lost in the afternoon, sat out day two and lost his singles.
Larry Mize	The 1987 Masters champion finished with 2 points out of four matches, with a high point of beating Seve and Ollie, with Hal Sutton, in the Saturday fourballs.
Mark Calcavecchia	Took Nick Faldo's scalp in the singles, but otherwise it was a forgettable Cup for 'Calc', who lost in his only other match.
Payne Stewart	One of five US rookies, he lost his first two matches before showing his true class with a Saturday fourballs win and then victory over Olazábal in the singles.

Ben Crenshaw

Did his broken putter cost him that match against Darcy? We will never know, but it was a miserable three days for Ben, who lost all three of his matches.

Scott Simpson

The 1987 US Open winner did not look comfortable in his only Ryder Cup, losing his only team match but at least beating Rivero in his singles.

Larry Nelson

The 1987 US PGA champion had remarkably won all nine of his matches at the 1979 and 1981 Ryder Cups. Here, though, he lost three before managing a half against Langer in the singles.

Tom Kite

He and Strange played in all four of the team matches, winning two and losing two, but he then beat Lyle in the singles to emerge with great credit.

Curtis Strange

One of only three Americans, along with Kite and Sutton, to appear in all five matches, but he ended up with just 2 points as Ballesteros beat him in the singles.

Hal Sutton

His 3 points out of 5, with only one lost match, was an excellent effort for a tough matchplay competitor.

Lanny Wadkins

The resurrection of his previously unbeaten partnership with Nelson did not work, and the whole match was over before he won his only point from a possible four, against Brown in the anchor singles.

Jack Nicklaus (captain)

It was a difficult defeat for Jack to take, on his own course and in his own home city, but he was gracious as ever and privately was unhappy with the American selection system, which, he felt, militated against their being able to field their strongest team. Scott Simpson and Larry Nelson, for example, only qualified because they happened to win the US Open and US PGA titles, respectively, that year. He would have liked proven performers such as Ray Floyd or Tom Watson in his side. Nicklaus was also heard voicing his concern that, on the first afternoon, there seemed to be little vocal support for the Americans out on the course. But that was probably because all four of his fourball teams were in the process of getting beaten. In truth, the play of the Europeans was just too good – especially on the first two days. Nicklaus's policy of putting out his best four golfers at the end of his singles order could also be questioned, especially as they went into the final day with a 5-point deficit.

Chapter Five

1989 The Belfry

The return to The Belfry in 1989 was billed as 'the Match of the Century' by an increasingly frenzied media, and hype now surrounding the biennial contest was taking the Ryder Cup into uncharted territory.

No fewer than 50 of the 380 assembled press personnel were from the United States, too, illustrating in itself just how quickly the Ryder Cup had caught the imagination of the American public, as well as that of Europe. At 350,000 square feet, the tented village at The Belfry that year was then the largest ever at a British sporting event. There were almost 5,000 people working at the course that week, controlling or catering for the vast crowds.

Jacklin was also still Europe's captain. Pressed into serving his continent just one last time, he needed little persuasion. Then, when his first wife, Vivien, tragically died from a brain haemorrhage while driving her car near their Spanish home, scarcely six months after the triumph at Muirfield Village, Jacklin found that thinking about the 1989 contest, then eighteen months away, became more and more cathartic.

Sandy Lyle's form had dropped away too much for him to be considered as a wild card, even though he was still ranked just outside the world's top ten, but five of the big six of '87 were still very much at the peak of their careers. Jacklin chose Bernhard Langer as one of his three captain's picks alongside Christy O'Connor Junior, who had just missed out in 1985, and Howard Clark, for whom this was a fifth Ryder Cup.

Eamonn Darcy, Ken Brown and José Rivero were – along with Lyle – the players missing from the 1987 line-up, but two of the three who had qualified by right for the team were the highly experienced pair of Mark James and José Maria Cañizares. James, indeed, had finished in second place on that year's Order of Merit to Jacklin's other newcomer, Northern Ireland's highly talented Ronan Rafferty, who was thus only one of two rookies in the team, alongside O'Connor Junior.

There was a good amount of experience on that 1989 side, and Faldo had won the first of his three Masters titles at the start of that summer. But our leader on the course was still very much Seve, who had himself won the third of his Open Championship titles the previous summer at Royal Lytham. And Seve was always pumped up for the Ryder Cup – really pumped up. He didn't like Americans very much, and it all stemmed from what he believed was poor treatment of him by the US Tour authorities at the start of his great career. There was this television interviewer once who kept calling him 'Steve' when he was doing the interview. Seve never forgot that incident: 'Who is this f****** Steve?' he would say. 'My name is Seve . . . Sev-er-i-ano . . .' He was not happy! Even among all the great players he played with in many Ryder Cups – Faldo, Langer, Lyle, Woosnam, Olazábal – he was regarded as the greatest. Some of the shots he played were shots you did not think were possible. He was our inspiration.

In Raymond Floyd, the American captain, however, Jacklin had his most worthy opponent in four Ryder Cups. And in the team that gathered around Floyd, one of his country's toughest competitors, were 12 players who would give even Seve and his fellow European star names a run for their money.

Curtis Strange had won his second US Open in a row in 1989, Mark Calcavecchia had captured the Open at Troon and Payne Stewart also became a major winner with the US PGA title at Kemper Lakes. And Floyd also had Tom Watson back in his team, plus a couple of other proven Ryder Cup players in Lanny Wadkins and Tom Kite. In addition, there were some hugely talented rookies: Fred Couples, Chip Beck and Paul Azinger.

I think it is true to say that the 1989 American team was a little stronger than the one in 1987, but don't forget the match was still on foreign soil for them and at a venue that we liked and that was associated with European glory. And, of course, we had seven players in our team who had their own fresh and special memories of the 1985 win there to bolster us further. We were certainly confident of victory again, but getting the outright win we desired was not to be.

The European team's motivation, moreover, was even further heightened when Floyd, no doubt intentionally, introduced his own players at the Gala Ball – which was held a couple of nights before the match in Birmingham – as 'the 12 greatest players in the world'.

It only added to the general hype, though, and when the match began it was to a background of tremendous excitement and anticipation. And, as in Ohio two years previously and at The Belfry in 1985, it was the Americans who got off to the best start before being hauled back.

Only the two proven partnerships of Faldo and Woosnam, and Ballesteros and Olazábal managed to get anything out of the opening four foursomes matches – and only halves at that. Howard Clark and Mark James were edged out by Lanny Wadkins and Payne Stewart, while Mark Calcavecchia and Ken Green won 2&1 against Bernhard Langer and rookie Rafferty.

But 3–1 down at lunchtime became 5–3 up that evening as Europe repeated the clean sweep of fourballs matches that had also occurred on the opening day of the 1987 match at Muirfield Village. It was a stunning turnaround that whipped The Belfry's hordes of European supporters into a frenzy.

When Ballesteros and Olazábal both drove the ball onto the iconic par-four 10th green – with Olazábal then holing for an eagle two and with Seve's own eagle putt not required – the noise was simply incredible from the thousands packed not just around the green but down the whole of the fairway too. The 280-yard hole, guarded by water to the front and left and demanding a fade off the tee to avoid overhanging trees, was witnessing amphitheatre golf – and the two Spanish conquistadors marched off like true conquerors before their adoring crowds after winning that hole on their way to a 6&5 thrashing of Tom Watson and Mark O'Meara.

I didn't play in the morning foursomes, but Tony sent me out alongside Gordon Brand Junior in the first match of the afternoon fourballs. It was good to be given that responsibility, and at the head of the field you can play at your natural pace with no one to hold you up. Gordon was a good partner, and it was he who played a wonderful bunker shot at the 18th to make sure of our victory by one hole against the tough combination of Curtis Strange and Paul Azinger. I had hit a low one iron into the final green, but it had gone long, and, after chipping down onto the second tier, I then putted up stone dead, but for a bogey five. But Gordon's bunker play and par four saved me, and the team, and our full point got things going nicely for us for the rest of a sensational afternoon.

What I also remember from our match was that Seve, having finished his own match, came up alongside us as we played the 18th, and, when he saw where Gordon's second shot had finished up, he came up to me and told me to tell Gordon that he should not use a sand wedge for what was a long bunker shot but a pitching wedge. Now, you just don't do that sort of thing to a fellow professional. You can't tell someone how to play a particular shot – they will know their own best option. I felt like saying to Seve, 'I'm not telling him. You tell him if you want to,' but I just kept quiet and, of course, Gordon was more than equal to the shot facing him. But that's Seve for you: he just couldn't help himself, and we were to see that side of him when he was captain himself at Valderrama. He was so enthusiastic and wanted to win every point for Europe that he possibly could.

Clark and James, whom Jacklin kept faith with despite their earlier defeat, bounced back with a 3&2 win over Couples and Wadkins, and, in the third fourballs match out, Faldo and Woosnam were too strong for Calcavecchia and Mark McCumber. Then, of course, came Seve and Ollie, and the 4–0 afternoon scoreline was complete.

At the end of the first day we had turned things around and were now 5–3 up. We felt in control of our own destiny, and, to be honest, that is how things remained for virtually the rest of the 1989 match. We just didn't contemplate not winning it.

On the Saturday it was, however, a case of nip and tuck as the Americans fought fiercely to remain in touch. In the morning foursomes it took all the formidable skill and willpower of Ballesteros and Olazábal to close out the anchor match by one hole, against Kite and Strange, to give Europe a 2–2 share of that series.

Faldo and Woosnam had beaten Wadkins and Stewart 3&2 in the opening game, but Torrance and Brand Junior ran up against the in-form Beck and Azinger and lost the second match 4&3. O'Connor, given a debut run-out alongside Rafferty in game three, went down 3&2 to Calcavecchia and Green.

There was no place for Gordon and me in the afternoon line-up. We were a good team as well as good friends, and worked well together, but Tony wanted to get Howard Clark and Mark James – another pair of good friends, and winners in their fourball match the previous afternoon – back out there. He also wanted to give José Maria Cañizares his first taste of action before the singles and teamed him up with Bernhard Langer, who had only played in one match before that and also needed another run-out ahead of the singles. Langer was suffering from a bit of a neck complaint that week, and also the course was playing very long. With the Faldo–Woosnam and Ballesteros–Olazábal pairings primed to go out for a fourth time, that was the afternoon line-up taking care of itself.

Clark and James delivered another important point too, after Faldo and Woosnam, going out first, had lost their unbeaten record against Beck and Azinger, and then Langer and Cañizares had also been defeated 2&1 in match two by Kite and McCumber.

Stewart and Strange were edged out by one hole as Clark and James put Europe back in the lead at 8–7, and then it was left to the Spanish maestros to complete a wonderful two days by beating Calcavecchia and Green 4&2 in the anchor match. Ballesteros and Olazábal had won 3½ points out of a possible 4 and had once again been instrumental in giving the Europeans a significant advantage going into the singles.

At 9–7 we felt totally in control. Yes, the Americans had given it their all on that second day, but a two-point lead with the singles to come was a good place to be in, and, as I keep saying, the feeling in the European team room throughout that entire week was that we had the measure of the opposition. The Seve–Ollie combination was magnificent again, and although the Faldo–Woosnam partnership was not quite as good as in 1987 – they had lost a little bit of edge compared with how they played in America two years earlier – they were still a brilliant pairing to have, as their 2½ points out of 4 shows.

In his singles line-up, Jacklin once again stuck to his belief that, when a captain feels in control of a Ryder Cup, power should be put both at the top and at the bottom of the order.

He led off this time with Ballesteros, as the natural leader of the pack, and followed him with the dependable Langer and then his second unbeaten Spaniard, Olazábal. At the foot of the line-up was the experience and grit of Torrance, at ten, and the class of Faldo and Woosnam, at numbers eleven and twelve.

In places four to nine, Jacklin had stationed his lesser six players, although Rafferty, at four, was that year's leader of the European Order of Merit and Clark and James, at five and six, were both Ryder Cup veterans and in excellent form and spirits following the team matches.

At seven, eight and nine were O'Connor, the second rookie, along with Rafferty, and then the tough and experienced duo of Cañizares and Brand Junior. It was a line-up with balance, and it showed that Jacklin expected the winning of the Cup to be a hard-fought battle.

He had put some of his big players up front but had not simply gone out with all guns blazing in a bid for a quick kill. With Torrance, Faldo and Woosnam at the back of the field, indeed, he was giving himself some added insurance in case things should not go according to plan.

When I look at that 1989 singles order, I always see what I took from that day and translated into my own captaincy in 2002. At seven and eight were Europe's two supposedly lesser players – in terms of sheer talent and achievement, that is – in O'Connor and Cañizares. But look at where the Cup was eventually decided. It was those two players who, in the end, made the crucial difference, and it was a lesson I learned.

I decided, in 2002, to put my supposedly lesser players right at the end of the order, because I don't care who you are – Tiger Woods or Joe Bloggs – you will feel the pressure of playing in the final singles matches of a Ryder Cup, and, if the whole match itself then ends up coming down to those last singles, anything can happen. In the cauldron of a Ryder Cup anybody can produce unbelievable golf, and I never felt that my own lesser players in 2002 would not be able to handle that pressure. It shines out to me that, in 1989, it was his middle order and supposedly lesser players who delivered enough points for us to tie 14–14 and thus retain the Cup.

At an early stage of that last day, in fact, Europe were down in nine of the twelve singles, but early nerves at the defeats sustained by Ballesteros and Langer at the head of the order were steadied by the victories of Olazábal and Rafferty in the next two games. It was, however, a close-run affair.

Ballesteros was beaten by one hole by Azinger in a controversial, ill-tempered match that was to have ramifications too at Kiawah Island in 1991. Langer went down 3&1 to Beck, who thus completed a superb unbeaten Cup debut with 3½ points from a possible 4.

The finish to the opening singles match, between Seve and Azinger, was like you wouldn't believe. Azinger was one up going down the last, but he snap-hooked his tee shot and it finished up on the edge of the big water hazard. But he was given a drop, and it was so dubious where it was. If you go in the water then there should be no way of getting the ball up to the green, but from where he got the drop he was able to hit the ball up into a greenside bunker and over all the water in between. Seve was so angry at where Azinger got the drop, especially as he had hit a perfect drive. I think Seve lost focus, as he couldn't beat Azinger's bogey five, and the match was lost, by one hole.

There had already been some controversy earlier in the match when Seve wanted to change a marked ball, and all that bad feeling spilled over into 1991 and especially into the opening foursomes of that match, which featured Seve and Olazábal against Azinger and Beck. But in 1989 it was Azinger who came out on top, and his early point on the board – in conjunction with Beck's winning point against Langer – squared the match again at 9–9.

Drama at the 18th, however, was far from over. One of The Belfry's great matchplay holes was to see a remarkable seven more matches decided there before the day was out, including the next two.

In the third singles match, Payne Stewart was another one of four Americans to find water off the tee, costing him a one-hole defeat against Olazábal. And, soon after, Calcavecchia suffered a similar fate to gift Rafferty his one-hole victory: 11–9 to Europe. Or, rather, 11–10, because, in the fifth match, a shell-shocked Howard Clark had already been crushed 8&7 by Tom Kite, who was in simply imperious form. At that stage of the Cup's history, no one had ever won an 18-hole singles match by such a margin.

I felt very sorry for Howard, because, when they shook hands on the 11th green, he was himself one or two under par! If he had drawn one of the other Americans that day, instead of Kite, he might even have gone on to win his match. Against Tom that day, though, there was simply nothing he could do except congratulate his opponent on some quite stunning golf. That's matchplay, of course.

With seven matches still out on the course, Europe needed 3 more points to retain the Cup and 3½ to win it again outright. By now, however, Mark James was very much in control against Mark O'Meara in match six and soon was closing out his man for a 3&2 win. The scoreboard clicked round to 12–10.

Victory for Europe was tantalisingly close, but there was nothing more that could be guaranteed when Jacklin and his cohorts looked at the state of play in the other matches still to finish, and at that stage only Ian Woosnam, in the bottom game against Curtis Strange, had a potentially decisive lead.

Christy O'Connor Junior's two-iron shot on the 18th hole became, quite rightly, the story of that last day, although, technically, it was José Maria Cañizares, in the next match, who won the point that made sure the Cup would stay in Europe. Christy had been thrilled to make the team, after his near miss in 1985, but after he and his opponent, Fred Couples, had driven on the final hole – after standing on the tee all square – it looked for all the world as if the American had a decisive advantage. Christy was not a big hitter, and he was facing a 230-yard second shot over water into that multi-tiered green. Couples had launched a massive drawn drive and, a little like myself in 1985, was now looking at only a nine-iron in for his second shot. But Christy somehow managed to coax that remarkable two-iron stroke to within three and a half feet of the hole, and Freddie, completely flummoxed by this turn of events, then half-shanked his nine iron well to the right of the green, chipped up and missed the putt for a four. All Christy then had to do was bend down and pick up his marker as Freddie conceded his three, and Europe had won a vital point. But I know for a fact that, to this day, Christy is delighted that Couples did not get his four and that he therefore didn't even have to putt his ball! But what a shot Christy hit, and what a Ryder Cup moment it was.

With the galleries around the 18th in a state of high excitement, Ken Green became another American to find water off the tee, and Cañizares's victory in the next match to finish confirmed that Europe had reached the magic 14-point mark. Jacklin was besieged by interviewers around the packed final green, and the European supporters were celebrating as if the Cup had been won. It hadn't.

Steve Rider, working for BBC television, got his ear bitten off by Tom Kite, whom he spoke to by the side of the 18th green soon after the Cañizares win. When Steve said something to the effect that the Americans had lost again, Kite quickly rebuked him. Tom said that the match itself could still be tied, and that there were enough points still out there on the course for the United States to reach 14 themselves. And Tom was absolutely right, sadly for us.

There were four singles matches still to be resolved, and, although Europe now led 14–10, it was becoming increasingly uncertain whether the half-point required to win the Cup outright could be found from the games involving Brand Junior, Torrance, Faldo and Woosnam.

Brand's match against McCumber, like those of Faldo and Woosnam, came down the 18th, but this time there was no joy on that hole for Europe. McCumber completed a one-hole win, to raise American hopes of a tied match, and then Faldo hit it into water off the tee to lose his match against Lanny Wadkins by a similar one-hole margin. Faldo, later in his career, said it was one of the biggest disappointments of his golfing life.

Those of us still out there in the last few matches knew that, somehow, we just had to squeeze a half out of the Americans to give us the Cup by an outright margin. Of course, we knew by then that we had retained it, but there was absolutely no letting up or easing off. We desperately wanted to complete the job, and it is still heartbreaking to recall that we couldn't do that. Tony had put a significant amount of power in those lower matches, but even that didn't do the job. It is astonishing to look back and see that, between them, there was not even half a point in the singles from our big four of Ballesteros, Langer, Faldo and Woosnam.

In many ways, it is a measure of how well the rest of the team played that we came away with a 14–14 tie and retained the Cup, but I totally reject the notion that our big guns had run out of steam on that final day. To me, Seve, Nick and Woosie had not lost an edge, because they had also played in all four of the matches on the first two days. That is too simplistic. Yes, you are going to be a bit more tired on the Sunday night than you would be if you had not played in every match, but during the actual matches you have so much adrenalin coursing through your body that tiredness really doesn't come into it. I played in all five matches in 1983, and again in 1995, and that's my honest opinion.

Torrance himself, in match ten, was having a fierce struggle against Tom Watson. Three down at the 11th, he was then in a bunker at the 12th, and, although coming out to two feet, he was irked when Watson opted not to concede the putt and also said, 'I should probably give you that, but I think I will test you.' Watson, however, then sank his own birdie putt, and so the hole was lost anyway and Torrance was now four down with just six to play.

It was just one of those days when I could not buy a putt. It was very frustrating, especially as Watson seemed to be able to hole it from anywhere. From tee to green there was hardly anything in it, but he just kept on popping them in – often from further from the hole than I was – and I didn't. But, because of what happened on the 12th green, there was steam coming out of my ears when we walked onto the 13th tee, and I almost drove the green with a tee shot approaching 350 yards, chipped up to three feet and won the hole with a birdie three. I birdied the 14th as well to win that, and suddenly I was back to just two down. But, from there on in, I couldn't make any more putts, and we eventually shook hands on the 17th green. In the scorebooks, by the way, it says that I lost that match 3&1, but in fact it should be recorded as 2&1. He had two putts for the half, which would clinch him the match, but was fully 20 feet or so away. I conceded them, and so in the scorebooks it goes down that he won the hole. I know it's only a technicality, but it annoys me when I see it!

When Torrance's match with Watson ended, it was still possible for Europe to gain the half-point that would give them the Cup outright. But then came Faldo's agony at the 18th and, in the anchor match, an incredible fightback by Strange.

Woosie was actually offered a halved match by Curtis when they reached the 15th green, when the news filtered through that the Cup was still in European hands. But that was not allowed in the rules, and they had to play on. It was a bit cheeky by Curtis, because he was one down at the time and Woosie had been in charge of the match throughout. But then Curtis birdied every one of the last four holes, including that 15th, and his brilliant birdie three at the last ensured that Woosie could not get us our missing half. One down, standing on the 18th tee, he would have had to win that hole to achieve it, but Curtis ended up winning by two holes and so the overall match was squared 14–14.

To lose all those last four games meant that we felt gutted, despite holding on to the Cup. There had been no complacency. You are only as good as your last game, aren't you? We wanted to nail them, to show that we could back up 1987 and 1985. And we had them, and we let them off the hook. It was a bittersweet feeling for us players. The crowd at The Belfry were celebrating, because, to them, a tied match meant we had won the Cup again. But, to us, and to me personally, because I was one of the last four who had failed to bring home that one little half-point, it was hard to take. We felt all week that we had the beating of the Americans, and I think they felt they were going to be beaten too, and so when you are in that ascendancy for so long in a Ryder Cup it truly is a deflating experience not to finish it all off at the end.

Of course, if you can look at it dispassionately, it makes it even clearer after a 14–14 tie how much the Ryder Cup, in modern times, has become such a closely fought contest. The evidence is right there, in that scoreline, and so many of the Ryder Cups of the 1980s and 1990s came down to little swings one way or the other. So many of them could have gone either way, in truth, but in 1989 we did feel devastated not to have won outright, because we felt we were the better team.

In terms of the growth of the Ryder Cup as a modern sporting phenomenon, however, the 1989 tie – only the second in the event's history – succeeded merely in cranking up the excitement and its profile to even higher levels. And, for Europe, it was time to find a successor to Tony Jacklin as captain.

We all knew that 1989 was going to be Tony's last time, and I think he only agreed to do a fourth captaincy stint because of the unanimous opinion that, after 1987, he deserved one more go at home – and back at The Belfry – as a sort of thank you for all that he had done in making the European team so competitive. And what a record he had built: a narrow defeat in Florida in 1983, the historic wins at home in 1985 and away in 1987, and then a tie! It should have been a third win out of four, of course, but at least Tony was able to hold the Ryder Cup aloft again at The Belfry at the end of the 1989 match. It was a fitting end to his captaincy reign.

He had also deserved the honour of saying when he wanted to stand down. All the players were still 100 per cent behind him, and his tactical decision-making and his leadership of the team was as good in 1989 as it had ever been. He had changed everything for us, and if Seve Ballesteros has been the single biggest influence for good on the European Tour in my lifetime then Tony Jacklin is not far behind, and – in terms of the Ryder Cup alone from a European perspective – he has been the biggest influence of all.

1989 RYDER CUP RESULTS: 22–24 SEPTEMBER, THE BELFRY
Captains: Tony Jacklin (Europe), Raymond Floyd (US)

Europe		US	
Morning foursomes			
Nick Faldo/Ian Woosnam (halved)	½	Tom Kite/Curtis Strange (halved)	½
Howard Clark/Mark James		Lanny Wadkins/Payne Stewart (1 hole)	1
Seve Ballesteros/José María Olazábal (halved)	½	Tom Watson/Chip Beck (halved)	½
Bernhard Langer/Ronan Rafferty		Mark Calcavecchia/Ken Green (2&1)	1
Afternoon fourballs			
Sam Torrance/Gordon Brand Jr (1 hole)	1	Curtis Strange/Paul Azinger	
Howard Clark/Mark James (3&2)	1	Fred Couples/Lanny Wadkins	
Nick Faldo/Ian Woosnam (2 holes)	1	Mark Calcavecchia/Mark McCumber	
Seve Ballesteros/José María Olazábal (6&5)	1	Tom Watson/Mark O'Meara	
Morning foursomes			
Ian Woosnam/Nick Faldo (3&2)	1	Lanny Wadkins/Payne Stewart	
Gordon Brand Jr/Sam Torrance		Chip Beck/Paul Azinger (4&3)	1
Christy O'Connor Jr/Ronan Rafferty		Mark Calcavecchia/Ken Green (3&2)	1
Seve Ballesteros/José María Olazábal (1 hole)	1	Tom Kite/Curtis Strange	
Afternoon fourballs			
Nick Faldo/Ian Woosnam		Chip Beck/Paul Azinger (2&1)	1
Bernhard Langer/José Maria Cañizares		Tom Kite/Mark McCumber (2&1)	1
Howard Clark/Mark James (1 hole)	1	Payne Stewart/Curtis Strange	
Seve Ballesteros/José María Olazábal (4&2)	1	Mark Calcavecchia/Ken Green	
Singles			
Seve Ballesteros		Paul Azinger (1 hole)	1
Bernhard Langer	1	Chip Beck (3&1)	1
José María Olazábal (1 hole)	1	Payne Stewart	
Ronan Rafferty (1 hole)	1	Mark Calcavecchia	
Howard Clark		Tom Kite (8&7)	1
Mark James (3&2)	1	Mark O'Meara	
Christy O'Connor Jr (1 hole)	1	Fred Couples	
José Maria Cañizares (1 hole)	1	Ken Green	
Gordon Brand Jr		Mark McCumber (1 hole)	1
Sam Torrance		Tom Watson (3&1)	1
Nick Faldo		Lanny Wadkins (1 hole)	1
Ian Woosnam		Curtis Strange (2 holes)	1
Europe	**14**	**US**	**14**

SAM'S ANALYSIS: 1989

Europe

Seve Ballesteros	Beaten in the singles, after that rancorous struggle against Azinger, but unbeaten on the first two days, when he and Olazábal gained 3½ points from a possible 4. Once again, Europe's rock.
Bernhard Langer	Not at his best in this Ryder Cup, and as a result was only selected for one foursomes and one fourballs outing before the singles. Unusually for Bernhard, he didn't win a point.
José María Olazábal	Peerless once more in the foursomes and fourballs, alongside Seve, and also won a vital singles point against Payne Stewart. Europe's biggest contributor to the cause, with 4½ points.
Ronan Rafferty	A tough Ryder Cup baptism and lost his two foursomes matches before bouncing back with a crucial singles victory against Mark Calcavecchia.
Howard Clark	Excelled in the team element, winning 2 points from 3 in the company of his great friend Mark James, but then ran up against a raging storm called Tom Kite in the singles.
Mark James	An outstanding performance, and at the top of his game at the time of this match. Won 2 points from 3 alongside Clark in the foursomes and fourballs and then beat Mark O'Meara convincingly in the singles.
Christy O'Connor Junior	If it was me in 1985 who got all the attention on the last day then this time it was Christy. What a shot into the 18th! There's a plaque on the spot from where he hit his two iron on that fairway, and nothing more needs to be said. Such moments are only supposed to happen in your dreams.
José Maria Cañizares	Only used once on the first two days and suffered fourballs defeat alongside Langer, but his experience and fine temperament came in more than handy in the singles. Beat Ken Green with a great putt on the 18th to win the point that kept the Cup in Europe.

Gordon Brand Junior	Played well with me when we won our Friday fourballs match against Strange and Azinger but had no luck after that and was another European player who could have expected at least a half out of his singles match.
Sam Torrance	Like Gordon, I started well but could not get going again in my two remaining matches. Just could not buy a putt for much of my singles match against Tom Watson.
Nick Faldo	The 1989 Masters champion continued his successful partnership with Ian Woosnam, established in 1987, over the first two days but then lost his singles to Lanny Wadkins to take much of the gloss off his excellent performance.
Ian Woosnam	Like the rest of us involved in those final singles matches, Woosie took his own defeat hard – especially as he had been in control against Curtis Strange for much of it. But, in the team element, he was again masterful alongside Faldo.
Tony Jacklin (captain)	This match marked the end of the Jacklin era. He had been the best Ryder Cup captain of my time, and what a legacy he left behind for European golf. We now knew we could take on the Americans as equals, and the Ryder Cup itself had been transformed by Jacklin's leadership, passion and attention to detail. He had some wonderful players at his disposal, but he still had to deploy them and enthuse them. Jacklin believed in us and believed that the Americans could be beaten in the Ryder Cup. Look at the situation, historically, when he took over, and then look at the situation when he left, just eight years later. What he achieved was incredible, and the European Tour – in terms of sponsorship support and the raising of standards at every level – has grown up so fast over the past three decades as much on the back of our Ryder Cup successes as the individual successes of a group of magnificent players led by Ballesteros and Faldo.

United States

Paul Azinger

Lost his debut Ryder Cup match on the first afternoon, courtesy of Gordon Brand and myself, but soon began to show what a natural matchplay scrapper he was. Two wins followed on day two, alongside Chip Beck, and then he topped it all off with victory over Seve in the singles, which showcased his toughness.

Chip Beck

Another rookie who performed wonders for his captain and his country. Indeed, Beck was unbeaten after gaining a highly creditable half against Ballesteros and Olazábal in the opening foursomes, alongside Tom Watson, and then winning both his matches with Azinger on day two and beating Langer in the singles.

Payne Stewart

Came into the European team room late on the Sunday night and joined in our party until the early hours of Monday. A wonderful man and a tragic loss to the game when he died in a plane crash in 1999. Only 1 point from 4 here, though.

Mark Calcavecchia

The 1989 Open champion played in all five matches – one of only two Americans to do so – but ended up with just 2 points, both in foursomes with Ken Green. His drive into the water on the 18th in the singles cost America dear, as did the similar fate of three of his colleagues.

Tom Kite

Hit a remarkable vein of form to win his singles by a record 8&7 margin and also earned a further hard-fought point and a half from his three foursomes and fourballs outings. One of America's best players in this match.

Mark O'Meara

An unhappy match, being beaten 6&5 by Ballesteros and Olazábal when playing alongside Watson in the Friday fourballs and then not appearing again until being beaten 3&2 by Mark James in the singles.

Fred Couples	His Ryder Cup debut ended with his implosion on the 18th against Christy O'Connor, and he also lost his only other match when he and Wadkins were beaten 3&2 by Clark and James in the Friday fourballs.
Ken Green	I cannot think about poor Ken these days without my mind turning to the terrible car accident last year in which a number of his family members were killed and he lost a leg. His dog, which he had saved many years previously by wrestling it from a crocodile that had snatched it from his back garden in Florida – I kid you not – was also killed in that accident. This was Ken's only Ryder Cup, but he distinguished himself with two foursomes wins alongside Calcavecchia.
Mark McCumber	Like Green, this was to be the steady if unspectacular McCumber's one Ryder Cup appearance, but he won two out of his three matches, after starting with a loss against Faldo and Woosnam, and his narrow singles victory against Gordon Brand Junior helped the Americans to fight back to tie the overall match. He was a funny kind of player, with a slicing style, and he's a very nice man. I've always called him 'Cucumber'.
Tom Watson	In his final Ryder Cup as a player, Watson gained just half a point from his two outings on the opening day before being left out altogether on day two. But he putted like a dream to beat me in the singles and end up with 1½ points from a possible 3.
Lanny Wadkins	There were 2 points out of 4 from America's long-serving Ryder Cup strong man. Mixed fortunes in the team matches, but his singles win against Nick Faldo was a big moment for him and the United States team.
Curtis Strange	Earlier that summer he had won his second successive US Open title, and he was the only American, bar Calcavecchia, to be sent out in all five matches by his captain. But, before recovering remarkably to beat Ian Woosnam in the anchor singles, he had gained only a solitary half-point from his four outings in the team matches.

Ray Floyd (captain)   Led the Americans as he had played in the Ryder Cup: with an uncompromising attitude and no little skill. Probably the best captain that Jacklin faced in his four matches, and he was well served by his rookies, Azinger, Beck, McCumber and Green. He would, however, have expected better returns from his three major champions of 1989, with Strange, Calcavecchia and Stewart only picking up 4½ points between them out of a possible 13. Watson, too, disappointed, and only Kite from his more experienced men really performed to the expected level.

He juggled his pairings well on the Saturday to limit the damage of Europe's 4–0 whitewash in the Friday fourballs, and it is to Floyd's credit that his team did not throw in the towel when the Cup was retained by the Europeans on another tumultuous Sunday at The Belfry. His singles order also showed imagination, with his aggressive decision to send out his in-form rookies, Azinger and Beck, at the top of the list being royally rewarded with the big scalps of Ballesteros and Langer. In the end, indeed, it was only the mess that Stewart, Calcavecchia and Couples all made of the 18th hole that prevented Floyd from raising the Ryder Cup himself in triumph.

CHAPTER SIX

1991 KIAWAH ISLAND

This was the Ryder Cup that was called 'the War on the Shore', but, although it did have its controversies, it was nothing like that at all. Corey Pavin was criticised by some for wearing a US-marine combat-style cap and for fist-pumping celebrations that got the crowd overexcited. Rubbish. He might have gone a bit crazy after holing brilliantly from a bunker, but he meant nothing by wearing that cap and why shouldn't he react to a great shot like that? It is the Ryder Cup, after all. No, it was not a war on the shore. But it definitely was a totally fantastic Ryder Cup, on a brilliant course for the event, and it was a magnificently contested match.

In fact, the dramatic Kiawah Island course, in the sand dunes of South Carolina, had not been the original choice of venue for the 1991 Ryder Cup. A course in Palm Springs had been earmarked, but a couple of months before the event it was realised that TV schedules of the prime East Coast channels would be compromised by the two sets of matches – foursomes and fourballs – that had to be played on each of the first two days.

That meant that Landmark, the company who had acquired the staging rights for that year's match, simply switched it to their number-one East Coast location, Kiawah Island. The Ocean Course, however, was not fully finished in its construction, and, lashed by Atlantic winds and tides, its facilities were far from what would be considered acceptable for one of golf's major tournaments, for example.

Access for the public was also difficult and viewing almost impossible in certain parts of the course, with the fairways and greens raised up to protect them from high tides. As a place to guarantee excitement in a Ryder Cup, however, it was spectacular.

Both teams were given large Portakabins in which to change and to hold team meetings, because the actual clubhouse was, in essence, merely a locker room and a bar raised up on stilts. Facilities were fairly rudimentary, but I loved the course and thought that it would be impossible to find a more exciting venue. It also had some great matchplay holes, as was soon to become apparent when the match began. But the weirdest thing about the course was the distance between the 9th green and the 10th tee. It was officially measured at some 900 yards, but I'd swear it was almost a mile! Obviously, us players and caddies were whisked from the 9th to the 10th on buggies, but for the spectators it was a totally different matter. And what we soon found was that when you reached the 10th it was like meeting up with a brand-new crowd. They used to wait there for the players to come through, and so they hadn't a clue about what had been happening in the holes before we got there. The spectators who had been following us during the front nine would then start turning up again at about the 12th, or the 13th. It was bizarre, and quite tough on the spectators. Kiawah's inaccessibility, meanwhile, meant that there were not as many European supporters there as had travelled to Muirfield Village in 1987. That made the American support sound more vocal too.

Europe's team was now under the command of Bernard Gallacher. He had been assistant to Tony Jacklin in each of the 1985, 1987 and 1989 Ryder Cups, after playing under Jacklin in 1983 in what was the last of his own eight appearances as a player. Indeed, since 1969 he had been at the heart of the Great Britain and Ireland and then European teams.

Gallacher was never the official vice captain, simply because that job title never existed at that stage. He was a helper and sometimes did not even attend official team meetings. But he had been one of Jacklin's most trusted aides and advisers, and it was only natural that he should succeed him as captain.

I don't think there was any other credible candidate for the Ryder Cup captaincy. Bernard, a dear friend, had the complete respect of every member of the team and of the entire European Tour. He had been a tenacious matchplay opponent in his own Ryder Cup playing career, and he knew the event inside out. He was different in character from Tony, but he had all the attributes needed for the job and we all totally trusted him to make the right decisions for the team.

Sensibly, Gallacher aimed simply to continue on as Jacklin had done. He made it his business to make sure everything was done for the team that could be done, and he also knew that the bedrock of what had been such a successful team in the 1980s was still there. Sandy Lyle, sadly, had not recovered the form that had seen him reach the peak of his profession in the mid '80s, but the team Gallacher led in 1991 was an intriguing and powerful mix of old and new blood.

First, there was the core of experienced and battle-hardened players who were unafraid of the Americans and – in the case of those around at the time – had not lost to them since 1983: Seve Ballesteros, Nick Faldo, Ian Woosnam, Bernhard Langer, Sam Torrance, Mark James and José María Olazábal.

Then there were the five rookies: Colin Montgomerie, David Feherty, Steven Richardson, Paul Broadhurst and David Gilford. Indeed, due to this influx of new players, Gallacher had gone solely for experience when he named his three wild card picks, which were Faldo, Olazábal and James.

America's captain, Dave Stockton, had also gathered around him a strong team, headed by the experience of Lanny Wadkins, Hale Irwin, Ray Floyd, Payne Stewart and Mark Calcavecchia. Paul Azinger, Chip Beck, Mark O'Meara and Fred Couples also had previous Ryder Cups to draw on, while Stockton's three rookies were Corey Pavin, Wayne Levi and Steve Pate.

Of the European newcomers, though, Montgomerie had qualified in second place on the tour's Order of Merit, behind only Ballesteros, and Richardson had also finished third to underline his rich current form. The final three players to qualify, in a tight finish to the season, had been Broadhurst, Feherty and Gilford, who had just edged out the gallant veteran Eamonn Darcy for ninth place on the money list.

I was absolutely delighted when Feherty made the team, because he was my very best friend in the game. We went everywhere together on tour, we were inseparable and it was no surprise when Bernard decided to pair us up during the match itself. Before we got to America, David was keen to hear from me what he could expect. 'What was the Ryder Cup actually like to play in?' he kept asking. All I could do was to tell him it was like being someone who has children, as he has, and the fact that people who have children find it very difficult to put into words what having kids is like if they try to describe being a parent to those who don't have them. You just can't explain it, because you can't explain the strength and nature of that bond you feel with your own kids. And, I told him, that is exactly what the Ryder Cup is like, because it's just so different from anything else you experience in golf. It is unique; it is so very special.

The match, meanwhile, could not have started more explosively. The opening foursomes, between Azinger and Beck and Europe's finest, Ballesteros and Olazábal, was always likely to be combustible, given the acrimony that still existed between Ballesteros and Azinger following their singles clash at The Belfry two years before.

It was the Americans who made the fastest start, and at the turn they were three up. The Spaniards, however, were not just unhappy at the scoreline. They had spotted that Azinger and Beck were changing their ball illegally during holes, and Seve in particular was livid.

I was out walking with this match, as I was only due to play in the afternoon fourballs and I wanted to soak up a bit of the atmosphere. On the 7th hole a clearly agitated Seve came over to me and told me he wanted Bernard Gallacher to get himself over to that match. Could I get Bernard on the radio, he asked. But, on the radio, I couldn't raise him, so I ran off from the match to try to find him. Bernard, in fact, was sitting at the back of the 9th green, where the opening match would soon come through, and he had been having a bit of trouble with the radio, because – it is alleged – Stockton had found out which wavelength we were using and was listening in to what Gallacher was saying. So Bernard had turned it off, although it was a situation that was soon sorted out and he was able to use it again for the rest of the match.

Anyway, my message to Bernard soon grabbed his attention, because I said there was a major incident and that Seve wanted him there immediately. At the root of the incident was the fact that, in the rules at that time, two players in foursomes cannot switch the ball they use during any one hole. In other words, if I am using Dunlop and you are using Titleist, we can either use the same ball all the way around or I can tee off on my holes using my ball but not the other player's ball. And you can tee off with your ball on your numbered holes, but the same ball must then be used for the rest of that hole. What you can't do is switch balls around, which is what Azinger and Beck were doing. To the uninitiated, this may not sound too much of a big deal, but at that level it certainly is. For example, some balls spin more than others, so you would want to use a spinning ball more if you are playing downwind but a ball that spins less if you are playing into the wind.

Everything came to a head on the 9th green when Bernard and Seve challenged the Americans and called for the referee. And so, as the players all moved across to the 10th tee, there was a hold-up of about 15 to 20 minutes while all this was sorted out. In the end it was ruled that the Americans should lose the 9th hole. And, nothing tells you more about Severiano Ballesteros than the fact that he and Olazábal then turned that match around. From three down, they ended up winning what, of course, had by now become a real grudge match 2&1. Seve was so angry, but he controlled his anger and put it all into his golf. His passion was blazing, and with Olazábal at his side he dug out an extraordinary victory. But that is what the man can do. It was amazing.

It was also a good job that Ballesteros and Olazábal came in with their point, because it was all Europe were to get in those opening foursomes matches. The three other games all went America's way, and, as in 1985 and 1989, Europe were 3–1 down.

Langer and James were beaten 2&1 by Floyd and Couples, Gilford and Montgomerie went down 4&2 to Wadkins and Irwin, while the most damaging defeat from a European perspective was the one-hole loss for Faldo and Woosnam against Stewart and Calcavecchia.

Gallacher, however, stuck to his afternoon plans and led off the first round of fourballs with Torrance and Feherty, while asking both the Spanish pair and that of Faldo and Woosnam to go out again. In between them, in the third match, he teamed up James and the big-hitting Richardson.

At the time of the 1991 match, Ian Woosnam was ranked at number one in the world, and Nick Faldo was at number two. Their record as a Ryder Cup partnership was magnificent, and in both the 1987 and 1989 Cups they were at the heart of the European effort. Their 3½ points out of 4 in 1987 and then another 2½ out of 4 in 1989 had made them one of the greatest pairings in the event's history. But in 1991 the dynamic between the two had changed, and the magic had gone. Perhaps their personalities had come through fully by then! But also, as the two best players in the world, they had become used to being big rivals throughout the rest of the year, and with Ian supplanting Nick at the top of the rankings and having won the Masters earlier that year, the whole nature of the relationship between them had changed. I don't blame Bernard for going into the match with them still as a pairing: you would have expected them to deliver more points for the team, as they had done before. But perhaps they should have told him that they did not want to play together, if indeed that was the case. Whatever, they lost for the second time on the first day in the afternoon fourballs, going down in flames by 5&3 against Floyd and Couples, and that was the end of their partnership. After that, Bernard knew they were a pairing that had run its course.

Fortunately for Gallacher and Europe, however, the other three fourballs pairings all brought something home. Ballesteros and Olazábal continued to build the legend of their partnership with another superb 2&1 victory over Azinger and Beck. There was no way Seve was going to lose to that pair following the morning's epic confrontation.

And, in match three, the unsung English pairing of James and Richardson triumphed 5&4 over Pavin and Calcavecchia. With Torrance and Feherty fighting back from three down to grab a half with Wadkins and O'Meara, it meant that the scoreboard at the end of a fierce first day was US 4½ points, Europe 3½.

Feherty was white with nerves when we started the match. We had both played well in practice, and we were confident as a partnership. In practice, we had even challenged Seve and Ollie to a game, which cost us money, of course, but showed that we fancied our chances against anyone. But David admitted to me later that walking to the first tee, and hitting his first shots, was easily the most terrifying thing he had ever done in his professional golf career. I took it upon myself to have a word. We were soon three down, and I told him that if he didn't pull himself together that I was going to join Wadkins and O'Meara and he could take on the three of us. I told him to enjoy it, because very few golfers ever get the chance to experience the unique thrill of playing in a Ryder Cup. To his eternal credit, Feherty did buck up, and he played some wonderful golf as we battled back to take the match down the 18th, all square.

On the 17th, in fact, which is probably the hardest par three I have ever played, I hit a four iron to about eighteen inches with what was one of the best shots of my whole career. I thought we were going to win it to go one up, but Wadkins then responded by hitting his own four iron to three feet and holing it for a half in birdie two. Up the 18th, Feherty was in a bit of trouble and I hit a terrible second shot, which ended up in a greenside bunker. They made sure of their better ball par, but I missed my par putt after coming out of the sand and so it was left to Feherty to make a ten-footer straight up the green for his par four and a halved match. It was left edge, and he stroked it in like a man. It was a magnificent effort, especially at the end of his debut match and particularly when you remember how he looked and felt at the start of those 18 holes. That putt was a true test of David's resolve, as well as his golfing ability, and he passed it with flying colours.

The next morning, Torrance and Feherty were sent out again by Gallacher, this time at the head of the second round of foursomes, but they could not prevent their opponents, Wadkins and Irwin, from completing a highly competent 4&2 victory.

Indeed, as 24 hours previously, only Ballesteros and Olazábal held up an end for Europe, beating Couples and Floyd 3&2 in the anchor match and preventing an American clean sweep.

James and Richardson, despite going into their match in confident mood after their fourballs win, lost on the 18th to Calcavecchia and

Stewart, and – most damagingly for European morale – there was a real hammering for Faldo and Gilford in their match against Azinger and O'Meara.

Bernard had by now decided to split up his Faldo–Woosnam pairing, and, because it was foursomes, he decided to keep Nick going and give him a new partner. Gilford had been playing superbly in practice, and he had a steady game ideally suited to the foursomes format. He hit a lot of fairways and was a very consistent player. You could see what Bernard was thinking when he put them together, but it went horribly wrong. I think Faldo let himself down. He did not seem to help Gilford or try to take him under his wing, in the manner Seve did with David so brilliantly at Oak Hill in 1995. But that was the difference between Faldo and Ballesteros. In 1995 Seve charmed Gilford, put his arm around him, joked with him and got him to play some incredible golf. And, to me, that's what you want from your elite players. You want them to give a little bit to their partners and help them through. But Nick seemed to be sadly lacking on that morning, and it ended up being a terrible defeat and a horrible experience for Gilford in particular. So, after a bad morning, in which only yet more heroics from Seve and Ollie kept us afloat, we were down by 7½ points to 4½. We were in deep trouble.

Europe's team, however, reacted marvellously to the crisis and produced golf on a level with what had been seen at Muirfield Village four years earlier to claw back the deficit in the afternoon fourballs.

Woosnam, now paired with Paul Broadhurst, in his first Ryder Cup outing, led the counter-attack, and some great shot-making saw them beat Azinger and Irwin 2&1. Next out were Langer and Montgomerie, forging a new partnership that would become one of Europe's best and beginning their liaison with a 2&1 win over Pate and Pavin.

Stockton, also opting to give Wayne Levi his debut match alongside Wadkins, saw his third fourballs pair beaten 3&1 by a rejuvenated James and Richardson. Only a fighting half by Couples and Stewart, against Ballesteros and Olazábal, prevented a 4–0 clean sweep. It was some comeback, and it left the match thrillingly poised at 8–8.

Even a small lead going into the singles is a huge advantage, and what an afternoon's golf it was from the European team. On that Saturday night we were jubilant, because we had played our way right back into the match. It could have been so different if those fourballs matches had not swung our way like that. But, once again, we had rattled the Americans, and so much of our position, going into the singles, was down to the sheer brilliance of Ballesteros and Olazábal. Their 3½ points from a possible 4 was a tremendous effort: in three successive Ryder Cups they had now won an astonishing 10 points out of 12 in foursomes and fourballs matches. And they still had 1993 to come to improve that record still further. Unbelievable.

It was now that the second great controversy of the 1991 Ryder Cup reared its ugly head. To Gallacher's astonishment, he learned at breakfast on the Sunday morning that Stockton had withdrawn Pate from the singles draw.

At the gala dinner before the event began, there had been a minor shunt involving some of the cars carrying the players to the function venue. Pate, who attended the dinner, was later said to be suffering from a bad back as a result of the accident. But, when he finally appeared on the course, in the Saturday afternoon fourballs, he had played apparently without discomfort.

To this day I have to wonder about how hurt Pate actually was. I was in one of the cars that bashed into each other, and it wasn't much of a concertina effect at all. Pate seemed absolutely fine that evening, and when he played in the second round of fourballs he hit a driver and five iron to get up in two on the par-five 11th. I couldn't get near it in two! So his back must have deteriorated incredibly quickly on the Saturday evening, after playing those 17 holes against Monty and Langer, and it was a real shock when he was withdrawn overnight.

But, to add to our feelings of doubt about the whole thing, it soon emerged that Pate had been drawn to play against Seve in the original singles draw. And, that week, and despite Pate being a fair golfer, there is no doubt that Seve was in the mood to beat any American drawn against him. As it was, because of Pate being withdrawn, the names on the draw list were shifted

down and Seve then found himself playing Wayne Levi, who was undoubtedly
America's weakest player. That was not a good result for us, because it was a
real waste of Seve's point. Also, I reckon anyone in our team could have beaten
Levi. Actually, I'm not sure who I was drawn against in the original singles
line-up, but I could have done without facing Freddie Couples, who ended up
beating me 3&2. Perhaps I would have got O'Meara, who Paul Broadhurst
beat 3&1 in the match above me – who knows, but I would much rather have
played O'Meara than Couples!

As a result of Pate's withdrawal, too, Gallacher had to hand in the
brown envelope in which – before the singles draw had been made
on the Saturday night – he had been required by the rules to write the
name of a player to be taken out of the draw should there be an illness
or injury on the other side.

With a heavy heart, and simply because he had lost his only two
matches and was one of his rookies, Gallacher had written Gilford's
name. At the time, however, he was fully expecting Pate to play in the
singles, as he had just completed 17 holes out on the course in the
second series of fourballs.

By the time Stockton's withdrawal of Pate was known, Gilford had
departed from the team hotel to the course to prepare for his singles
match. When Gallacher's message reached him, informing him of the
sorry turn of events, it completed a miserable Ryder Cup debut for the
Englishman.

We all felt so sorry for David Gilford, and, although he and Pate were both
given a half-point, it all left a sour taste in the mouth. We felt that it was the
Americans who had gained a half-point out of the affair. But, at the time,
we just had to get on with things because the match was still wide open,
and the singles draw was intriguing. Bernard had slightly wrong-footed the
Americans, too, by putting out Faldo at the head of our field. That was the
last place they expected to see him. They might have expected Woosie or Seve
but not Nick. But Bernard knew that Faldo was fretting about his own game,
following the break-up of his partnership with Woosie, and then the disaster of
pairing him with Gilford in foursomes, and by asking him to go out first it was

a clever way of clearing Nick's mind and giving him the huge responsibility of leading our line. And it worked, too, because he beat Ray Floyd by two holes and that game featured some of the best golf of the match.

Both captains had opted to spread their main strength across the singles order, and the tussle it produced on that final day will live long in the annals of Ryder Cup history. It always promised to go right down to the wire, and it did.

But, thanks to Faldo and to David Feherty, in the second match, and then to a truly extraordinary finish to the third game involving Montgomerie and Calcavecchia, it was Europe who came out of the blocks faster in the singles battle that would decide the destiny of the Cup.

Feherty, clearly inspired by what would be his only Ryder Cup appearance, produced a brave 2&1 victory against Stewart, that year's US Open champion, and soon Europe reached the eleven-point mark – with Gilford's half – when Montgomerie somehow managed to come back from being five down with six to play, and then four down with four to play, to gain a miraculous half with Calcavecchia.

Colin did incredibly to get that half, which of course kicked off a long Ryder Cup singles career in which he was to remain unbeaten, but it was also a case of Calcavecchia imploding horribly. Take the 17th: I know that at that stage Monty had come back to two down with two to play, and so the nerves must have been really rattling around, and I also know that the 17th at Kiawah is a par-three hole I would rate as the most difficult I have ever seen, but when Monty put his tee shot into the water to the front and right of the green, the match was over. All Calcavecchia had to do was to hit his ball anywhere left – it didn't matter how far left. Monty was then taking three off the tee anyway, so Calc would have won the match right there if he had kept his own tee shot dry.

But, unbelievably, Calcavecchia shanked his tee shot straight into the water too! Then, when Monty put his ball on the green with his second tee shot, Calcavecchia put it into the water again! I've never seen anything like it, even in a Ryder Cup. Finally, when they went up the 18th, Calcavecchia hit two great shots to get his ball to about thirty-five feet from the hole in two, but, with Monty getting his four, he then three-putted to lose that hole as well. It was perhaps the greatest collapse ever seen in a Ryder Cup, and allegedly Calcavecchia could not be found for about an hour after he shook hands on the half with Monty. Apparently, he went down to sit on the beach, and people say he was hyperventilating because of the stress of it all.

Behind Montgomerie, however, things were not looking so rosy for Europe. Olazábal and Richardson were beaten after struggles with Azinger and Pavin respectively, and although Ballesteros saw off Levi, as expected, with a 3&2 win, the rest of the scoreboard did not make for pleasant reading from a European standpoint.

In match seven, Woosnam could not get the better of Beck and lost 3&1, and although Broadhurst fought tigerishly to mark his own debut with a 3&1 win over O'Meara – making it two wins from two outings for the Midlander – the final three matches all seemed to be going America's way.

When Broady won his singles it put us up to 13 points, but I was always down to Freddie Couples in match nine, and, behind me, the same was the case with Mark James against Lanny Wadkins. I was three down at the turn, we halved the 10th and then at the 11th I was addressing the ball and the ball moved. There was nothing I could do but take the penalty stroke, and so I lost that hole to go four down. I tried to come back, but Couples made sure at the 15th, where he holed from off the green after I had hit a great shot in and thought I might get a win. But I then missed my birdie putt, and that was that. Freddie is a great friend, but I would have dearly liked to have beaten him on that day. And, even though it was Freddie, who is one of the most laid-back guys in the game, I don't think we had much of a conversation, and certainly no jokes, throughout that round. In the last round of a major championship, maybe, but not in a Ryder Cup! It is different, totally different.

With Torrance and James both losing by a 3&2 margin, all eyes turned to Bernhard Langer, who by now was two down with four holes to play in the anchor match against Hale Irwin.

America now led 14–13, but if Langer could pull his match around then Europe would still retain the Cup with a second successive 14–14 tie. And, this time, if the German could get a full point, it would not feel like the anticlimax of 1989. This time, and especially after the Pate controversy, it would feel like victory itself.

Both Langer and Irwin are naturally slow players, and, at the back of the field, they had fallen a bit behind the other matches in front, which, of course, had also by now finished on the 16th green. All attention was suddenly focused on their match, and huge crowds descended upon it. One of the most remarkable hours of golf in the game's history was about to unfold.

Bernhard won the 15th with a six-foot putt to get back to just one down, and then the up and downs he made from sand at both the 16th and 17th were incredible. The first one was for a half in four, and then he won the 17th with a great putt – and, suddenly, the match was all square, and Langer and Irwin found that they were, in effect, playing off for the entire Ryder Cup as they stood on the 18th tee. Irwin needed only a half at the final hole to make sure America regained the Cup, but Langer knew that the 18th at Kiawah is a tough closing par four and that he had a good chance of winning the hole if he could get his par.

Irwin is not a long hitter, and his drive went left. It was not as wide a drive as some commentators have said, simply because the crowds were so vast as they tried to watch the drama of this final hole that many of them were spilling out virtually onto the fairways on either side. There are even rumours that Irwin's drive was 'improved' by American supporters in the crowd and that it was much wider than where the ball ended up, but to me that is rubbish. I reckon Irwin's ball landed just off the fairway to the left, even though it did go into the spectators, but it was still quite short and he could not get up in two.

At this stage, I was sitting at the back of the green next to José María Olazábal, and Ollie's eyes were blazing with intensity. He said to me, 'Come on, Sam, come on. Watch the ball as it comes into the green – if we will it, we can make it move!' And he was utterly serious, 100 per cent serious. I think, in that one little moment, I saw the kind of intensity and willpower that the

Americans must have come up against whenever they played against Seve and Ollie in a Ryder Cup!

Langer did get on in two, meanwhile, with or without our combined willpower, but was about fifty or sixty feet away, and his approach putt – a putt to win the match itself, remember – finished up about six feet past the hole. Irwin, meanwhile, got to about three or three and a half feet in four, and Langer gave it to him! I would not have done – and we all looked at each other because I don't think any of us would have given it. It was not like the Nicklaus–Jacklin concession, to me, because Irwin would have had to hole it to win the match. America had already retained the Cup when Jack conceded to Tony in 1969.

For myself, I don't think Hale Irwin would have holed that putt in a million years, as short as it was. In that situation, and with all that pressure, he was looking so shaky – and had been looking shaky all down the stretch. You could see it in his demeanour. Great man that Irwin is, and golfing legend that he is, he was gone. But Langer, being Langer, wanted to clear his mind of everything other than the fact that he now had a putt to win his match, and the Ryder Cup itself. And so he gave Irwin his five, because now all he had to do was make his four.

The putt was inside left, but there was a spike mark directly on the line that Bernhard wanted. Now, Langer is very precise, and so he decided that he could still hole the putt by hitting it just a little bit harder and by missing the spike mark he would hit the right side of the hole. I think I would simply have taken my chances with the spike mark, and hit it exactly on the right line. Sometimes spike marks can throw the ball off course, and sometimes they don't. But, again, Bernhard has not got to where he has in golf by not knowing his capabilities, and he was totally sure that he could make the putt while also taking out of the equation the uncertainty of what would happen if the ball hit the spike mark. Langer is happy he hit the putt he wanted, but it hit the right edge of the hole and stayed out. We had lost. It was devastating, and even now I think it was just fate: only three matches had played that 18th hole before Langer and Irwin, so what were the chances of that spike mark being exactly on the line of Bernhard's putt? For me, odds so great that it must have been fate.

The epic, exhilarating Langer–Irwin half meant a final result of US 14½, Europe 13½. America had regained the Cup, and the American celebrations were unrestrained. Dave Stockton, the captain, was just one of those thrown into the Atlantic waves when the celebrations reached the beach.

In the end, of course, it made the Europeans feel even more angry and frustrated that it was the Steve Pate half that had made the difference.

The scenes afterwards back in the Portakabin that passed for our team room and changing area were indescribable. Seve, Ollie and Langer were all crying their eyes out, amongst others. To see these great men weeping was heartbreaking, but I could not say anything to them. What was there to say? I wasn't man enough to tell them not to cry and to think about the next match in 1993. In those circumstances, and after what we had just witnessed, I just couldn't say it. Langer said he'd made the stroke he wanted but that the ball had broken too much to the right. But he had achieved marvels just to get himself into the situation to win the match in the first place.

The Pate incident, in particular, also meant there were some grievances on our part, but when you lose – even by half a point – you have to be graceful to your opponents, and that is what we tried to be. But, for a while in that team room, there was desolation. No wonder Monty has felt like he's felt about the Ryder Cup over the past two decades. He'd seen what it had done to Calcavecchia in his singles, up close and personal. And then he saw how much it all meant to some of the greatest players Europe had ever produced. What an introduction he had to it all at Kiawah Island!

1991 Ryder Cup Results: 27–29 September, Kiawah Island
Captains: Bernard Gallacher (Europe), Dave Stockton (US)

Europe		US	
Morning foursomes			
Seve Ballesteros/José María Olazábal (2&1)	1	Paul Azinger/Chip Beck	
Bernhard Langer/Mark James		Raymond Floyd/Fred Couples (2&1)	1
David Gilford/Colin Montgomerie		Lanny Wadkins/Hale Irwin (4&2)	1
Nick Faldo/Ian Woosnam		Payne Stewart/Mark Calcavecchia (1 hole)	1
Afternoon fourballs			
Sam Torrance/David Feherty (halved)	½	Lanny Wadkins/Mark O'Meara (halved)	½
Seve Ballesteros/José María Olazábal (2&1)	1	Paul Azinger/Chip Beck	
Steven Richardson/Mark James (5&4)	1	Corey Pavin/Mark Calcavecchia	
Nick Faldo/Ian Woosnam		Raymond Floyd/Fred Couples (5&3)	1
Morning foursomes			
Sam Torrance/David Feherty		Hale Irwin/Lanny Wadkins (4&2)	1
Mark James/Steven Richardson		Mark Calcavecchia/Payne Stewart (1 hole)	1
Nick Faldo/David Gilford		Paul Azinger/Mark O'Meara (7&6)	1
Seve Ballesteros/José María Olazábal (3&2)	1	Fred Couples/Raymond Floyd	
Afternoon fourballs			
Ian Woosnam/Paul Broadhurst (2&1)	1	Paul Azinger/Hale Irwin	
Bernhard Langer/Colin Montgomerie (2&1)	1	Steve Pate/Corey Pavin	
Mark James/Steven Richardson (3&1)	1	Lanny Wadkins/Wayne Levi	
Seve Ballesteros/José María Olazábal (halved)	½	Fred Couples/Payne Stewart (halved)	½
Singles			
Nick Faldo (2 holes)	1	Raymond Floyd	
David Feherty (2&1)	1	Payne Stewart	
Colin Montgomerie (halved)	½	Mark Calcavecchia (halved)	½
José María Olazábal		Paul Azinger (2 holes)	1
Steven Richardson		Corey Pavin (2&1)	1
Seve Ballesteros (3&2)	1	Wayne Levi	
Ian Woosnam		Chip Beck (3&2)	1
Paul Broadhurst (3&1)	1	Mark O'Meara	
Sam Torrance		Fred Couples (3&2)	1
Mark James		Lanny Wadkins (3&2)	1
Bernhard Langer (halved)	½	Hale Irwin (halved)	½
David Gilford (halved)*	½	Steve Pate (halved)	½
Europe	**13½**	**US**	**14½**

*Steve Pate withdrawn because of injury

SAM'S ANALYSIS: 1991

Europe

Nick Faldo

Three defeats from three as his great partnership with Ian Woosnam came to an end, and then a new one with David Gilford failed to find any spark. But then a superb singles win on Sunday against Ray Floyd to set up what was so nearly another glorious last day for Europe.

David Feherty

The Northern Irishman stood up manfully to the test on his Ryder Cup debut, finishing with a brilliant singles win against Payne Stewart that looked as if it might be pushing Europe closer to retaining the Cup.

Colin Montgomerie

Began his own epic Ryder Cup career with a foursomes defeat alongside fellow rookie David Gilford but then won a vital fourballs point with Bernhard Langer – so starting that productive partnership – and will never forget his miraculous half in the singles. Nor will Mark Calcavecchia!

José María Olazábal

He and Ballesteros were unbeaten for the second successive Ryder Cup in foursomes and fourballs – a truly remarkable record. But Ollie could not get the better of Paul Azinger on his own in the singles, which was a great disappointment to him.

Steven Richardson

Like Feherty and Broadhurst, playing in his only Ryder Cup. But, like them, he performed excellently, with two points in the fourballs alongside Mark James being the highlight. Tried to change his swing soon after this match, and it was a fatal mistake, as he was never the same player again. A great character and great team member.

Seve Ballesteros

As in 1989, another 3½ points out of 4 in the company of Olazábal, and his singles point against Wayne Levi was inevitable. What would have happened in the overall match, however, if Ballesteros had played Steve Pate, as originally intended, and Levi had played another of the Europeans?

Mark James drives from Walton Heath's 17th tee during practice before the 1981 Ryder Cup. Watching (from left to right) are fellow players Howard Clark, Sam Torrance, Sandy Lyle and European team captain John Jacobs (in dark sweater). (© Press Association)

Lee Trevino, in characteristic pose during the 1981 Ryder Cup at Walton Heath. (© Press Association)

Members of Europe's 1983 Ryder Cup team are pictured in front of Concorde at a rainy Heathrow before the flight to Florida. From left to right: Ken Brown, Sandy Lyle, Gordon J. Brand Senior, Tony Jacklin (captain), Bernard Gallacher, José Maria Cañizares, Ian Woosnam, Nick Faldo, Brian Waites. (© Press Association)

Severiano Ballesteros played the shot of the 1983 Ryder Cup with a three-wood from a fairway bunker. (© Getty Images)

Europe's great victory in 1985 was even briefly celebrated from the roof of The Belfry Hotel. From left to right: Ian Woosnam, Howard Clark, Seve Ballesteros, captain Tony Jacklin on Sam Torrance's shoulders, Paul Way, Bernhard Langer. (© Getty Images)

Europe's 1987 Ryder Cup team celebrate their historic victory at Muirfield Village. (© Getty Images)

Ireland's Christy O'Connor acknowledges a higher power after his unforgettable two-iron approach to the final green at The Belfry to clinch 1989 singles victory against Fred Couples. (© Press Association)

Bernhard Langer's agony on the 18th green at Kiawah Island in 1991. (© Getty Images)

An emotional Seve Ballesteros hugs Nick Faldo after the Englishman's crucial singles-winning putt on the final green at Oak Hill. European triumph in 1995 was soon to be confirmed on the same green by Ireland's Philip Walton. (© Getty Images)

Justin Leonard has just holed his monster putt across the 17th green at Brookline in his singles match against José María Olazábal, and the 1999 Ryder Cup is about to become the most controversial in the event's long history. (© Getty Images)

Cares of a Ryder Cup captain:
Sam Torrance is deep in thought at the 2002 match. (© Getty Images)

THE 34th RYDER CU   ATCHES

Sam with his father, Bob Torrance, in the moments after 2002
Ryder Cup victory was clinched. (© Getty Images)

A kiss for Mrs Torrance: Sam and
Suzanne share an intimate moment as
Europe begin to celebrate victory
in 2002. (© Getty Images)

We did it! Captain Sam with
Lee Westwood. (© Getty Images)

Sam, flanked by wife Suzanne and son Daniel, walks to the closing ceremony in 2002 with Curtis Strange, the US captain, and his wife, Sarah. (© Getty Images)

A proud Sam Torrance gets his hands on the Ryder Cup trophy, with master of ceremonies Renton Laidlaw in the background. (© Getty Images)

Sam with his vice captain, Ian Woosnam, and the Ryder Cup trophy. (© Getty Images)

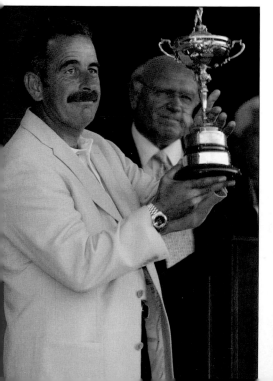

The 2002 Ryder Cup team celebrate victory as
darkness falls outside The Belfry. (© Getty Images)

Lifting the holy grail of golf: Sam
Torrance holds the Ryder Cup on the
small bridge leading to the 10th green at
The Belfry on the morning after Europe's
2002 triumph. (© Getty Images)

Sam and Daniel Torrance.
(© Getty Images)

Ian Woosnam	Woosie's search for a singles win goes on, this time beaten by Chip Beck. Teamed up to good effect with Paul Broadhurst in the Saturday fourballs, after his partnership with Faldo hit the skids, but overall Europe would have expected more from the then world number one.
Paul Broadhurst	Won 2 points out of two matches, and Broadhurst was never again to play in a Ryder Cup. But he can be proud of his efforts in both his fourballs win, with Woosnam, and his singles victory against Mark O'Meara that so nearly helped Europe over the finishing line. A real fighter and a great man to have on your side.
Sam Torrance	Mixed fortunes in the fourballs and foursomes with Feherty and disappointment in the singles, where Fred Couples was too strong on the day and won 3&2.
Mark James	Played in every match, after winning one of Bernard Gallacher's wild-card spots, and repaid his captain with a typically gutsy performance. Formed a good partnership with Richardson, after initial disappointment with Langer, but could not pull a singles half out of the bag when it was badly needed.
Bernhard Langer	His heroic half with Hale Irwin provided one of the Ryder Cup's most iconic moments. How I wish that putt on the final hole, in the final match, had dropped! But Bernhard, as ever, gave it everything for the cause, and only he could have gone out the following week and won a tournament. What mental strength.
David Gilford	Poor David, after foursomes defeats alongside first Montgomerie and then Faldo, then ended up with an unwanted half-point after being chosen by Gallacher to sit out the singles following Pate's withdrawal. But at least he got his revenge in 1995!

Bernard Gallacher (captain)

He would have been excused for thinking the Fates were against him following his debut as Ryder Cup captain, especially with regard to the Steve Pate incident. Gallacher had every right to think that this probably cost his team a half-point on the final day, but, even then, if Langer's putt had dropped, he would have been celebrating a famous win. He was handicapped, too, by the Faldo–Woosnam partnership not working as it had in 1987 and 1989, and then by the failure of the Faldo–Gilford experiment. Gallacher otherwise handled his team skilfully in terms of pairings and his singles order – before it was undermined somewhat by the late withdrawal of Pate.

United States

Ray Floyd

America's captain in 1989 made his seventh appearance as a player at the age of forty-nine and responded initially with 2 points from two outings on the opening day, partnering Fred Couples. But he played only once on day two, tasting defeat against Ballesteros and Olazábal, and was then also beaten in the singles by Faldo.

Payne Stewart

US Open champion in 1991, he won 2 foursomes points alongside Calcavecchia and then helped Couples to take a half-point from Ballesteros and Olazábal in the Saturday afternoon fourballs. But losing his singles to Feherty was a big disappointment.

Mark Calcavecchia

Two foursomes victories and a fourballs defeat left him in credit, but then came the astonishing halved singles match with Montgomerie, which felt like the most crushing of defeats. In the end, though, perhaps Calcavecchia could console himself with the thought that his half made the difference!

Paul Azinger

Followed up his fine debut at The Belfry in 1989 with another decent performance. Only won 2 points from his five matches, but his singles point against Olazábal was crucial.

Corey Pavin	He had nothing to show for his two fourballs outings but came through on the Sunday with a vital singles point against Steve Richardson. A debut to remember, and it was clear that he had the temperament and the fighting qualities for matchplay golf. He will be a formidable captain in 2010.
Wayne Levi	Only given one outing before the singles, in the final fourballs matches alongside Lanny Wadkins, but Levi was clearly the weakest of the American players and it was no surprise that he finished with no points in his only Ryder Cup. Should have stuck to making jeans!
Chip Beck	His partnership with Azinger, so successful in 1989, failed to function here, and he was stood down throughout the second day. But he then produced a telling singles victory against Ian Woosnam that was central to the American last-day effort. He was such a good player.
Mark O'Meara	Alongside Azinger, he was the beneficiary of the failure of Europe's Faldo–Gilford experiment in the second-day foursomes, and he also gained a fourballs half-point on the first afternoon. Lost his singles, however, and was not regarded as one of America's strongest players.
Fred Couples	There were 3½ points out of 5 for Freddie, and he was one of only three Americans to play in every match, together with Azinger and Wadkins. Played near to his best in this match, which was very good indeed.
Lanny Wadkins	Another 3½ points from five matches, adding to Wadkins's stature as one of the best Ryder Cuppers produced by America. He had three different partners, too, over the first two days, before presenting his captain with a vital singles point in the penultimate match.
Hale Irwin	Won 2 points out of three matches in the team stage, forming a strong pairing with Wadkins, but will always be associated with the epic singles struggle with Langer at the death. Should he have been made to putt out for the win?

Steve Pate	His name will for ever be linked with the 1991 Ryder Cup, and not for the reasons he would have wanted. How bad was his back, hurt in that minor car crash before the gala dinner? He played in 17 holes on the Saturday afternoon, losing his fourballs match with Pavin against Langer and Montgomerie, but was then withdrawn from the singles.
Dave Stockton (captain)	He was a tough captain with a no-nonsense attitude and a real regard for the Ryder Cup and its unique demands. He was unafraid to use every trick in the book, and that was definitely something I learned from him before my own captaincy in 2002! A good guy, and he did a good job with a decent team. He was also a big influence on Paul Azinger, and it was no surprise that Azinger turned to Stockton to be one of his assistants when he was captain at the 2008 Ryder Cup.

With a 3-point lead going into the Saturday afternoon fourballs, however, I would have been tempted to leave out both Wayne Levi and Steve Pate from his four-team line-up. To me, winning the Cup is all that matters – even if some of your players don't get a game before the Sunday. And the Americans ended up winning only half a point that afternoon, bringing the overall score back to 8–8. He left Floyd, Calcavecchia, Beck and O'Meara on the sidelines for that session, and it could have come back to bite him. Then again, if Pate had not played then he would have presumably played in the singles the following day . . . and that might have cost America even more dearly.

CHAPTER SEVEN

1993 THE BELFRY

Although losing the 1991 Ryder Cup by such a hair's breadth was a devastating experience, the year ended on a very positive note for Torrance and four of his teammates from Kiawah Island. In terms of the rest of his senior golfing career, too, it brought him something extremely significant: his first taste of captaincy. It was to be a successful and fulfilling experience, moreover, and it shocked Torrance how much he enjoyed it.

Out of the blue, I got a call from the European Tour asking if I would captain a six-man side in the Asahi Glass Four Tours World Championship, which was being held that November in Australia at the Royal Adelaide club. My team was Paul Broadhurst, David Feherty, Colin Montgomerie, Ronan Rafferty, Steve Richardson and myself, and it was a complete shock to be asked to lead it. But I realised it was also a great honour, and I found myself really getting into it.

The Ryder Cup it was not, of course, but it was still a different feeling to be the captain, and it surprised me how much I enjoyed it. My message to the team was a simple one, because it was an end-of-year competition and I just wanted everyone to relax and enjoy themselves – almost as if we were on a bit of a golfing holiday. But we were still highly competitive about the golf, and I remember Paul Broadhurst in particular played some magnificent stuff as we ended up beating the US PGA Tour team to get to the final, in which we then beat the Australia/New Zealand Tour team to win the event. Of course, back in 1991, and even though I had just played in my sixth Ryder Cup, I had no thoughts at all about one day being a captain of my continent. I thoroughly enjoyed being the skipper at that Asahi Glass event, but if you had told me there that one day I would be a Ryder Cup captain I would have laughed at you.

The lead-up to the 1993 Ryder Cup, and the match itself, was highly traumatic for Torrance and undoubtedly the low point – from a personal perspective – of his whole association with the event.

For the European team as a unit, however, confidence and expectation were high both before and for long periods of the match itself. After the agonising near-miss of 1991, Europe's best golfers were determined to win the Cup back again on home soil, and they had reflected in the two years that had passed since Kiawah that there was absolutely no reason why they should not make sure of coming out on top on the return to The Belfry.

We were very much up for it, and we felt we had a strong team. We also badly wanted to win it for Bernard Gallacher, our captain for the second time and who had also been devastated by the nature of our defeat at Kiawah. Our world-class players were still at or near the peak of their games, Colin Montgomerie was beginning to come through as one of Europe's new elite and then there were players like myself and Mark James who had tons of experience to help to balance the fact that we also had four rookies in the line-up: Barry Lane, Peter Baker, Joakim Haeggman and Costantino Rocca.

But my own troubles began a month or so before the event when, staying at The Belfry, I suffered one of my occasional sleepwalking episodes and threw myself at a four-foot-high plant that was in a pot standing decoratively in my bedroom. In the middle of the night, and in the shadowy darkness, I had obviously mistaken the plant for some sort of intruder, and I threw myself at it. The result – apart from waking me up – was a painful bruise on my chest and what was later diagnosed as a cracked sternum bone. You can imagine how embarrassing the incident was, and how many terrible jokes I had to endure afterwards, but it was also a genuine fear for a time that I would be forced to pull out of the 1993 match. Fortunately, the injury healed up very quickly, and by the time late September – and the American team – arrived, I was able to practise fully with the rest of the European team when we all assembled at The Belfry. I had not played competitively for a month, but practice went well and I was hitting the ball well. Surely nothing more could go wrong for me now?

The Fates, though, seemed to be conspiring against Torrance making any sort of contribution to the European mission to regain the Ryder Cup. On the second practice day, the Wednesday, he began to become aware of an irritating pain in his left foot.

More precisely, when he removed his golf shoe and his socks, he saw that a tiny blister had formed between the nail of his left little toe and the tip of the toe. It was becoming very sore, but, seeing the small size of it, Torrance felt it was something that would soon go away. It didn't.

By the time we played in Thursday's practice it was very sore indeed, and I found I was in agony on some shots. Being right on the end of the left little toe, it was also not helping that when I completed my swing a lot of my weight was transferred in the turn of my body into that area of my left foot. It was becoming a real concern. But we are all big boys, and I felt it was still not the kind of pain that I couldn't handle. I told Bernard Gallacher on the Thursday night that the toe was getting very sore, but I also said that I felt that I would be fine to play in the morning – when Mark James and I were drawn to lead off the opening foursomes match against Lanny Wadkins and Corey Pavin.

Of course, I was absolutely desperate to play. This was the Ryder Cup, for goodness' sake, and the adrenalin was already kicking in and my mentality was that nothing was going to stop me from taking on the Americans again. If there was pain, I was just going to ignore it, take some painkillers and get on with it. The Ryder Cup was that important. What I didn't realise until about halfway through the foursomes match, though, was that the pain – which I could handle mentally – was also having an influence on my swing. Jesse [James] had driven superbly down the middle of the 8th fairway, but when I came into the ball with my five-iron second shot I felt this sudden stab of searing pain and my instinctive flinch made the club twitch just as I impacted with the ball, and it shot off thirty or forty yards right of the target. I had completely blocked the ball right, and that was a shot I never hit in my entire career.

From then on, I couldn't hit a decent shot, and we lost the next five holes – four of them to pars. It was horrendous, and I felt so sorry for Jesse and for Bernard and the rest of the team when we were finally beaten 4&3. I felt as if I had let the whole team down and had let everyone rooting for Europe down. It was the worst feeling on the planet, and I also instinctively knew that my Ryder Cup was over. That night, I had an operation in a hospital in Birmingham to remove the nail. When I took my shoe off at the end of our foursomes defeat there was pus everywhere, and it was horrible knowing that I probably should not have played. It was even worse knowing that I was virtually certain not to be able to play again in the match – although officially it was initially hoped that I might be able to take part in the singles on the Sunday – and it meant that Europe now had to battle on with just eleven men over the next three rounds of fourballs and foursomes.

Torrance's injury, and the news that he was probably out of action for the rest of the match, was not the only shock for Gallacher and the Europeans to absorb on that first morning of competition.

Playing in the third foursomes match, Seve Ballesteros and José María Olazábal were beaten 2&1 by Tom Kite and Davis Love III in what was only their second defeat in 13 Ryder Cup matches together. They were Europe's talismans; was Gallacher's team literally falling apart right from the start of the contest?

Seve had needed a captain's pick from Bernard to get into that 1993 team. His form had begun to fall away, and we were seeing the start of his sad decline, although he did pick things up again in 1994, when he won twice and finished third in the Order of Merit. He also won his last European Tour victory in 1995 and, of course, played in that year's Ryder Cup too, but in 1993 he failed to win a tournament in Europe for the first time since 1976, and he ended up finishing in 42nd position in the Order of Merit. It was absolutely, totally correct to pick him – his partnership with Olazábal was too valuable and his sheer presence was also vital – but he ended up not feeling that he was playing well enough that week to appear in all four of the team matches and asked to sit out the final fourballs. Seve also lost a singles match that he would have been a certainty to win in his prime, and so his

contribution in terms of points won on the course was not quite what he would
have expected from himself.

Gallacher, besides fretting over Seve's form and Torrance's injury
absence, also had a worry with Bernhard Langer. The German had led
the qualifying table for the 1993 match, beating Faldo and Montgomerie
into second and third place respectively, but arrived at The Belfry having
not played for six weeks because of a neck injury.

Langer was lacking in match practice as well as match fitness, and
Gallacher was therefore resigned to the fact that he could use potentially
his very best player – in terms of both huge experience and current
form – in a maximum of only four of the five matches. If Langer's neck
condition worsened during the week, indeed, it might only be three
matches. Gallacher had Langer inked in for both foursomes, in addition
to the singles, but he knew that to give him even one fourballs outing
would be a bonus, given the heavy workload of the first two days.

Gallacher had selected Haeggman and Olazábal, who had finished
10th and 12th respectively in the points list, alongside Ballesteros as
his three captain's wild cards, and in Langer he had the 1993 Masters
champion – the German's second green jacket – while Faldo had
finished as runner-up to Greg Norman in that summer's Open at Royal
St George's after taking his third Open title in 1992.

Also, Europe's captain was highly optimistic that he had the makings
of another big-hitting foursomes and fourballs partnership – to set
alongside that of Ballesteros and Olazábal – in the shape of Faldo and
Montgomerie.

Colin's golfing hero as he was growing up was Nick Faldo, and so to play
alongside him in a Ryder Cup was the stuff of dreams for him. Nick was not
the easiest of partners in that he liked to be the dominant decision-maker,
but Colin was happy to go along with that at that stage of his career. It was
a pairing that was flagged up before we got to The Belfry and was eagerly
awaited, and it certainly proved to be as potent a combination as we had
hoped. But a pointer as to how much Colin was the junior partner at that
time came right at the start of their first foursomes together. All week, in

practice and in discussion, they had gone with Colin hitting off on the odd-numbered holes and Nick on the even-numbered ones. Of course, Colin had thus mentally prepared himself not just to hit off first at the opening hole, but also at the third, the fifth and so on. But then, when they got onto the first tee on that Friday morning, Faldo went over to Colin and whispered into his ear, 'I'm drawing the ball well – I'm going first.' And that was it; he did!

On the opening morning, especially with Ballesteros and Olazábal suffering that rare reverse and Torrance's injury scuppering the chances of his tried-and-tested partnership with James, Gallacher and Europe were more than happy to see the immediate impact made by the other two pairings, Woosnam and Langer and the Faldo–Montgomerie alliance.

Paul Azinger, the 1993 US PGA champion, and Payne Stewart, who had finished as runner-up to Lee Janzen in that summer's US Open, were crushed 7&5 by some brilliant golf from Woosnam and Langer, the latter of whom was thankfully showing few ill effects from his neck complaint. Faldo and Montgomerie, meanwhile, playing in the anchor foursomes, took out another high-profile and highly experienced American partnership of Fred Couples and Ray Floyd by a 4&3 margin, dovetailing efficiently in exactly the manner Gallacher had foreseen.

At 2–2 following the opening series of matches, the performance of the Woosnam–Langer and Faldo–Montgomerie pairings had more than compensated for the problems thrown up elsewhere, and at least Torrance knew – as he nursed his injury and his deep personal disappointment – that Europe's overall chances still looked good.

It is the team that matters in a Ryder Cup, over and above any personal feelings, and if we had gone on to win that 1993 match then everything would have been fine. As it was, my frustration was not helped by the eventual outcome, and it was a forgettable Ryder Cup all round for me. The incident with Tom Watson, the American team captain, at the gala dinner before the match began, did not help my mood either. I had walked over to Tom during the dinner and asked him if he could sign my menu, and had been completely taken aback when he declined to do so. His point was that, as a team, the Americans had decided not to sign autographs during that evening and so if he had done it for me it would have gone against that policy decision. I felt embarrassed and flabbergasted, and the incident caused quite a bit of fuss in the media in the lead-up to the match. I was very angry but was happy to go to the press tent the following day in an effort to play it down for the sake of diplomacy. But it remains, for me, another aspect of that match that I do not remember with any fondness.

Europe's fortunes on the course, however, continued to flourish in the first day's afternoon fourballs. Gallacher decided to split Woosnam and Langer, who was fit enough for another outing, and to give them two of the rookies to look after. Other than that, he merely asked the Ballesteros–Olazábal and Faldo–Montgomerie partnerships to go out again.

Both Peter Baker, paired with Woosnam, and Barry Lane, who joined Langer, were ideally suited to the fourball format, being streaky players well capable of a string of birdies. As it turned out, the Woosnam–Baker pairing was an inspired choice.

By the end of that first day, we were up in the match and Seve and Ollie had re-established their authority with a 4&3 win against Davis Love and Tom Kite in the anchor fourballs. With Woosie and Baker winning on the 18th, and Faldo and Montgomerie halving with Azinger and Couples, Europe led by 4½ points to 3½, and as a team we had managed to come through a day that could easily have been a traumatic one.

Only Langer and Lane had lost in the afternoon, beaten 4&2 by the ultra-competitive Wadkins and Pavin combination, but the real bonus for Gallacher was the way Woosnam and Baker gelled, with the younger man seemingly inspired by the unique atmosphere of the Ryder Cup while also being relaxed and reassured by the company of Woosnam. It was like Ballesteros and Way in 1983 all over again, with the added piquancy here that Baker, from Wolverhampton, was something of a local hero to many of the European supporters in the galleries.

It was on the second morning, however, that Europe looked as if they might run away with the entire match. The second set of foursomes proved to be a showcase for the talents of the three leading European pairings. Once again, it seemed as if the six best players in the Europe line-up were capable of inflicting decisive damage on an American team with the greater strength in depth.

Given the responsibility of leading the charge, Faldo and Montgomerie reacted by shooting down the previously unbeaten Wadkins–Pavin partnership by a 3&2 margin in the first match out. Then came Langer and Woosnam, with a 2&1 win over Azinger and Couples.

Baker and Lane, put together on something of a hunch by Gallacher, following their blooding in the fourballs on Friday afternoon, were defeated 3&2 by Floyd and Stewart, but surely it was certain that Ballesteros and Olazábal, in the anchor match, would avenge their loss to Love and Kite of 24 hours earlier.

Seve and Ollie came through 2&1 against Love and Kite, but, sadly, it was to prove to be their final Ryder Cup match together, as Seve was still struggling with his game. Bernard was called out to the 14th fairway during that foursomes match, with the Spaniards two up and in control, and Seve told him that, because the afternoon pairings had to be put in 15 minutes later, at 12 noon, he didn't want to be considered for the fourballs. Bernard tried to persuade him to reconsider, saying that his partnership with Olazábal was central to the European cause and that it could always get points, as was being proved again at that moment. But Seve was adamant that too much pressure was beginning to build on Olazábal, as a result of his own poor play, and that he would be better served by working on his game on the range that afternoon in preparation for the singles.

Then, minutes later, Bernard also got word from Langer, up ahead, that his neck was starting to hurt again and that, as a precaution, he too should sit out the afternoon matches. Suddenly, and despite the situation in which we were about to go ahead by 7½ points to 4½, Bernard was faced with having to rethink his intended fourballs pairings. It just shows that, as a Ryder Cup captain, you have to be prepared to deal with anything. In that intense heat of competition, and especially with thirty-six holes having to be played on each of the first two days, the physical and mental strain on players is so great. But Bernard immediately rejigged two of his pairings, bringing in Haeggman to partner Olazábal and also deciding that Costantino Rocca would become the fourth and final rookie to be given a run-out ahead of the singles, alongside Mark James.

There is no doubt, however, that the European momentum was stalled by the news that both Ballesteros and Langer were standing down from the Saturday afternoon fourballs.

It was a crucial stage of the match, and the Americans, 3 points down, were desperate to regain some sort of ground before Sunday, the day of reckoning, dawned. If the 3-point deficit had remained, going into the singles, and with Torrance also assured of a half because of the same 'brown envelope' rule invoked when Steve Pate was injured during the 1991 match, then America would have been right up against it.

And so, with a frustrated Gallacher condemned now merely to watch and muse on what might have been, the whole match turned as the United States fought back tenaciously to win the second session of fourballs by a convincing 3–1 margin.

James and Rocca were swept away 5&4 by Pavin and Jim Gallagher Junior, and Olazábal and Haeggman could not get the better of Floyd and Stewart in the anchor match, going down 2&1 in the end.

Europe's only bright spark was the blazing, red-hot golf played by Woosnam and Baker as their brilliant partnership overwhelmed Couples and Azinger 6&5. Yet the biggest disappointment of all was the failure of Faldo and Montgomerie to overcome the pairing of John Cook and Chip Beck. They could easily have grabbed at least a half-point, too, when coming up the 18th one down. Faldo's second-shot approach to the multi-tiered green was by far the best of all, leaving his ball only some ten feet from the flag.

Montgomerie was furthest away, and clearly out of the hole, but both Americans were around fifty feet from the pin and looking at difficult putts even to make sure of their par fours. Faldo could have instructed Monty to go first, to try to ensure the European par, before sitting back to see if either of the Americans could make their pars or even a remarkable birdie three.

Instead, Faldo, as is permissible in fourball matches, chose to opt – with his partner technically the next to play – to putt his ball first. His reasoning was obvious: if he made the birdie three then the two Americans would be faced with making either of their long-range efforts simply to halve the hole and protect their one-hole advantage. But Faldo missed, and, when an American ball was rolled up alongside the cup, the match was conceded.

It is difficult to criticise. Nick and Colin had been previously unbeaten, winning 2½ points out of 3, and it is undoubtedly a physical as well as mental challenge to play in every match over the first two days. On paper, though, you looked at their top match against Cook and Beck – one a rookie playing in his debut match and the other not in his best form and making his first appearance of this Cup – and you wrote down a guaranteed European point. That Cook-and-Beck point represented the biggest swing towards America in the whole match. If Faldo and Monty had won it, rather than losing by the official margin of two holes in what was a game that could easily have gone their way, we would have gone into the singles with a 2-point lead, plus my half for being withdrawn. As it was, the Americans were right back in it at, in effect, only 9–8 down following the fourballs matches and the half-point both myself and Lanny Wadkins were awarded following the handing-in of the two brown envelopes.

Sensing the momentum shift, Gallacher now opted to hedge his bets somewhat in his singles order. He wanted a fast start, to build on the slender one-point lead if possible, and so he sent out Woosnam first with Montgomerie placed at three and Baker, who was on a high after his birdie blitz in the fourballs, at four.

Then, in an effort to safeguard himself against any sort of concerted American effort, he placed four of his top six players in the final four places in the order: Ballesteros at eight, Olazábal at nine, Langer at ten and Faldo in the anchor position at eleven.

Lanny Wadkins, because he had played in so many Ryder Cups, had volunteered his name to go into the American envelope and therefore be drawn against me in the singles. That was a terrific gesture by him and one that I am sure Watson was grateful to get, because no captain likes to put any player's name into it. I know how bad Bernard felt about picking out David Gilford for that treatment at Kiawah Island.

On the Saturday evening, before the singles draw was made, Watson was invited into the European team room so that he could see for himself that I was in no fit state to play a singles match the following day. I had even tried to hit a few balls on the range, to see how the foot felt now that the nail on my left little toe had been removed, but it was hopeless. Anyway, I'd only got the bandage covering the side of my foot partly off when Tom could see all the gunge that was still oozing out of the wound. 'Stop, stop! I don't want to see any more!' he told me.

I also remember, on the first afternoon of the match, when he didn't know about my injury, that Peter Withe – the former Aston Villa centre-forward, a lovely guy and someone I knew quite well – jumped onto my back when I was standing at the putting green in front of The Belfry hotel. He said something like, 'Hi Sam, we're going to whip these Americans, aren't we?' or words to that effect, but I was so choked up that I couldn't even answer. I just had to walk away, with tears beginning to run down my cheeks. I'm sorry, Peter.

At first, the singles matches seemed to be going well for Europe. Woosnam, in what was, remarkably, to be the first of three successive Ryder Cup singles tussles with Couples, ended with a half, and – in matches three, four and five – there were brave and narrow victories for Montgomerie, Baker and Haeggman against Janzen, Pavin and Cook respectively.

Moreover, in match two it seemed as if Lane was assured of at least something against Beck. With five holes to play, Lane was three up. But the Englishman blew up as Beck fought back, and, on the 18th, the match finally went the American's way. Europe, with 3½ points gained from the first five matches, even with Lane's collapse, now needed just 2½ more points from the remaining six matches to regain Samuel Ryder's trophy.

In the end, the whole match slipped away from us when poor Costantino Rocca lost his game against Davis Love. After reaching the 17th green in two, and with his opponent one down and still some way short on that par-five hole after two shots of his own, Rocca failed to make his birdie four. His approach putt went six feet past the hole, after Love had pitched in to about three or four feet with a wonderful stroke under pressure. Then Costantino missed his return putt, and Love holed for his birdie to win the hole and get back to all square. When Love then won the 18th, too, it was a distraught Rocca who came back into the team room.

Even if we had got just one point, with two halves, from the Lane and Rocca matches, we could have still won that Ryder Cup. At one stage, indeed, it looked as if we would get a full point from both those games, and that would have been the Cup right there, but in the end we got nothing at all from them. It just shows on how much of a knife-edge so many Ryder Cups in the past three decades have been played. Sadly, too, the next three matches involving Seve, Ollie and Langer were also slipping away from us by then, and Nick Faldo's hole-in-one against Azinger at the 14th hole, in the anchor singles, was ultimately to no avail.

Mark James, playing ahead of Rocca, had also lost 3&2 to Payne Stewart before the Italian lost his way at the 17th, and Ballesteros was a shadow of his usual Ryder Cup self as he stumbled to a 3&2 defeat against Gallagher.

There was hope for a while from Olazábal, but then he succumbed to the canny Floyd by two holes, while Langer's bad neck played up again as he was beaten 5&3 by Tom Kite.

Faldo, who had been involved in a tremendous battle with Azinger at the bottom of the field, the highlight of which was undoubtedly his ace at the par-three 14th when the overall match was still technically alive, shook hands on a half with his American opponent when news filtered through that the United States had come through to retain the Cup.

Losing 15–13 was a bitter disappointment for us, and I also felt doubly bad for Bernard Gallacher. As captain, he had done little wrong, but had been undermined in his planning by injury to Langer and myself and by the drop-

off in form suffered by Seve. To lose so many potential points, or half-points, on the 18th green was also very hard to take for a team that still had so many good memories of the stirring deeds done on that final hole both in 1989 and, especially, in 1985. Seven of the first nine singles matches went to the last hole, but this time we only got 3½ points from those games. The 1991 defeat at Kiawah had been heartbreaking, but at least there we had played well as a team on their course and we could leave with our heads held high. In 1993, for a combination of reasons, we had underperformed as a team, and that made the defeat even harder to take.

For my part, and for Bernard Gallacher's sake as much as anything else, I left The Belfry in that late September of 1993 incredibly determined – even though I had just turned 40 – to try to put it all right again in 1995. That is why I was so delighted when the European Tour decided to give Bernard one last go as captain in 1995, with Seve also lined up too for one last effort as a player in that match before he could turn his attention to captaining Europe in his native Spain in 1997. But, whatever happened, I did not want my own Ryder Cup career to come to an end with those frustrating events of 1993.

1993 RYDER CUP RESULTS: 24–26 SEPTEMBER, THE BELFRY
Captains: Bernard Gallacher (Europe), Tom Watson (US)

Europe		US	
Morning foursomes			
Sam Torrance/Mark James		Lanny Wadkins/Corey Pavin (4&3)	1
Ian Woosnam/Bernhard Langer (7&5)	1	Paul Azinger/Payne Stewart	
Seve Ballesteros/José María Olazábal		Tom Kite/Davis Love III (2&1)	1
Nick Faldo/Colin Montgomerie (4&3)	1	Raymond Floyd/Fred Couples	
Afternoon fourballs			
Ian Woosnam/Peter Baker (1 hole)	1	Jim Gallagher Jr/Lee Janzen	
Bernhard Langer/Barry Lane		Lanny Wadkins/Corey Pavin (4&2)	1
Nick Faldo/Colin Montgomerie (halved)	½	Paul Azinger/Fred Couples (halved)	½
Seve Ballesteros/José María Olazábal (4&3)	1	Davis Love III/Tom Kite	
Morning foursomes			
Nick Faldo/Colin Montgomerie (3&2)	.1	Lanny Wadkins/Corey Pavin	
Bernhard Langer/Ian Woosnam (2&1)	1	Fred Couples/Paul Azinger	
Peter Baker/Barry Lane		Raymond Floyd/Payne Stewart (3&2)	1
Seve Ballesteros/José María Olazábal (2&1)	1	Davis Love III/Tom Kite	
Afternoon fourballs			
Nick Faldo/Colin Montgomerie		John Cook/Chip Beck (2 holes)	1
Mark James/Costantino Rocca		Corey Pavin/Jim Gallagher Jr (5&4)	1
Ian Woosnam/Peter Baker (6&5)	1	Fred Couples/Paul Azinger	
José María Olazábal/Joakim Haeggman		Raymond Floyd/Payne Stewart (2&1)	1
Singles			
Ian Woosnam (halved)	½	Fred Couples (halved)	½
Barry Lane		Chip Beck (1 hole)	1
Colin Montgomerie (1 hole)	1	Lee Janzen	
Peter Baker (2 holes)	1	Corey Pavin	
Joakim Haeggman (1 hole)	1	John Cook	
Mark James		Payne Stewart (3&2)	1
Costantino Rocca		Davis Love III (1 hole)	1
Seve Ballesteros		Jim Gallagher Jr (3&2)	1
José María Olazábal		Raymond Floyd (2 holes)	1
Bernhard Langer		Tom Kite (5&3)	1
Nick Faldo (halved)	½	Paul Azinger (halved)	½
Sam Torrance (halved)*	½	Lanny Wadkins (halved)	½
Europe	**13**	**US**	**15**

*Sam Torrance withdrawn because of injury

SAM'S ANALYSIS: 1993

Europe

Ian Woosnam

The undoubted star of the European effort, and he remained unbeaten in all his five matches. Won 4 points out of 4 in the company of Bernhard Langer in the foursomes and Peter Baker in the fourballs, and then gained a half in his singles match against Fred Couples. A lionheart.

Barry Lane

His only Ryder Cup was an unhappy experience, with fourballs and foursomes defeats preceding his collapse in the singles against Chip Beck. At three up with five to play he would have been looking at a half as even the most pessimistic of outcomes, but he then lost four of those last five holes.

Colin Montgomerie

Teamed up with Nick Faldo to create another heavy-hitting European pair. Won both foursomes and halved the opening fourballs but then disappointed with a loss to Cook and Beck in the final fourballs. But also won a hard-fought singles battle against Lee Janzen to emerge very much in credit.

Peter Baker

Enjoyed a wonderful Ryder Cup debut by playing in four matches and winning 3 points for Europe. Formed a joyous fourballs partnership with Woosnam and also beat Pavin by two holes to record a famous singles win. Such a shame that he could not make another Ryder Cup team.

Joakim Haeggman

A captain's pick after just missing out on automatic qualification, and he put in a worthy effort. A popular member of the team who did well when pressed into last-minute service as Olazábal's Saturday-afternoon fourballs partner and then won a vital singles point with a one-hole victory against John Cook. I'll never forget his little gesture of celebration when he got to his ball way up in the bunker that flanks the far side of the 18th fairway, after a ridiculously long drive, and realised that it was lying so well in the sand that he could easily get a wedge to it and plop it over the water and onto the green.

Mark James	I felt I let Mark down very badly, with my toe injury affecting the overall quality of our foursomes play in the opening match of the Cup. He also suffered defeat in the final fourballs, alongside Rocca, and it became a match to forget for him when he was beaten by Payne Stewart in the singles.
Costantino Rocca	The tears flowed for poor Costantino after he lost his singles match against Davis Love after being one up and on the green in two at the 17th. But he then three-putted to let Love in, and his defeat at the 18th then confirmed that Europe would fall short. Also lost his one other match, and it was hard to bear for the Italian rookie.
Seve Ballesteros	His great partnership with Olazábal survived the match, with 2 points coming from their three outings, but Seve's own form was so worrying for him that he took the terrible decision to pull himself out of a scheduled fourth match alongside his Spanish compatriot. He then lost his singles, which illustrated just how far his game and his confidence had fallen, and, although he still had one more Ryder Cup appearance in him, Seve was never again to play a foursomes or fourballs match with Olazábal.
José María Olazábal	Two wins from three with Seve took their partnership record to an unbelievable P15 W11 H2 D2 over four consecutive Ryder Cups, but he could not find another point – or even half-point – from his remaining fourballs outing alongside Haeggman nor from his singles against Ray Floyd.
Bernhard Langer	Did not play for six weeks before the match because of a troubling neck injury, and it flared up again after he had played in the first three sessions. Won 2 superb foursomes points in the company of Woosnam, but by the time his singles match came along the German had run his race. Nevertheless, in the circumstances, another great Ryder Cup effort from Langer.

Nick Faldo	Only one defeat in five matches, which was, unfortunately, the key fourballs reverse on Saturday afternoon, but Faldo can look back with pride on another rock-like display in what was his ninth consecutive Ryder Cup appearance – a run he was to stretch to a record-breaking eleven.
Sam Torrance	There is little more I can say about my own non-contribution to the 1993 Ryder Cup. The bad toe infection came out of nowhere, and I was totally gutted.
Bernard Gallacher (captain)	Endured a difficult Ryder Cup because of my injury, Langer's bad neck and Seve's bad form. But, by midday on the Saturday, it seemed as if Gallacher was presiding over a runaway European victory. He had engineered a 3-point lead going into the final fourballs session, but then momentum was lost with the late withdrawals of Langer and Ballesteros from their matches, through injury and form respectively.

His new Faldo–Montgomerie power partnership came off well, as did the pairings of Woosnam and Langer, and Woosnam and Baker – in spectacular fashion. He was hoping, however, for more than 2 points – and only three matches – from the great Ballesteros–Olazábal partnership, and there was absolutely nothing from the supposedly lesser players in the team, other than Baker, until Haeggman, and Baker, came up with heroic singles points on the final day. Europe lost this Ryder Cup through the ill fortune of circumstance, not because of any decision that Gallacher made. Thankfully, though, his reward was still to come.

United States

Fred Couples

One of three Americans, with Pavin and Azinger, to be played in all five matches, but Freddie found it tough going as he emerged with only two half-points to show for all his efforts. But one of those halves was at least the vital one against Ian Woosnam in the important opening singles on Sunday.

Chip Beck

Out of sorts in this match after his strong showings in both 1989 and 1991, and only appeared for the first time in the final round of team matches. Yet he still came away with a 100 per cent record, to illustrate the essential unpredictability of the Ryder Cup, after winning with Cook in the match-turning Saturday-afternoon fourballs against Faldo and Montgomerie and then fighting back from three down with five to play to beat Lane in one of the ultimately decisive singles matches.

Lee Janzen

The 1993 US Open champion was a significant disappointment in his debut Ryder Cup, being played in only one fourballs match before the singles, in which he was beaten by Montgomerie to finish without even a half-point to his name. Another of the stronger US opponents.

Corey Pavin

Won 3 points from his four team matches but then lost his singles against Peter Baker for some of the shine to be taken off his performance. Overall, however, he showed again what an asset he was to the American team.

John Cook

Like Jim Gallagher Junior, this was to be his only Ryder Cup appearance, but, like his fellow rookie, he featured in one of the key matches of the whole contest. Cook lost his singles on the Sunday, but on the previous afternoon he and Chip Beck beat Faldo and Montgomerie in the final fourballs to turn the match back towards America.

Payne Stewart	Suffered a thrashing in the foursomes in the opening session and did not play that afternoon, but the rest of the match was a delight for Stewart. First he teamed up with Ray Floyd to record points in both the Saturday foursomes and fourballs, and then he beat Mark James convincingly in the singles.
Davis Love III	One of four rookies in the American line-up but was already considered a senior member of his team by Tom Watson and was played in three of the four team matches. Began his Ryder Cup career with a memorable foursomes win against Ballesteros and Olazábal, but he and Tom Kite then lost their next two matches. His singles win against Rocca was central to America's overall victory.
Jim Gallagher Junior	Blooded on the first afternoon, suffering fourballs defeat alongside Lee Janzen, but Gallagher then showed his shot-making ability when paired with Pavin in the Saturday fourballs and in his highly significant singles victory against an out-of-form Ballesteros. That win was a great moment for him.
Ray Floyd	At 51, the grand old man of this American team returned in triumph to the scene of his captaincy appearance in 1989, which had ended in a 14–14 tie but with Europe retaining the Cup. Lost his one match on the opening day but from then on was unbeaten, winning twice in the company of Payne Stewart and also in a vital singles clash against Olazábal.
Tom Kite	There were 2 points out of 4 for the steady Kite, with the highlight of his pairing with Love undoubtedly being the first morning foursomes victory against Ballesteros and Olazábal. Also won his singles against Langer by a hefty 5&3 margin as America edged ahead on the Sunday afternoon.
Paul Azinger	Had a very similar Ryder Cup to Couples, with whom he was paired three times. Played in all five matches but gained only a half-point from his four team-session outings and an agreed half with Nick Faldo in the singles when the overall result of the match was known.

Lanny Wadkins	His last act as one of the greatest American Ryder Cup players was the selfless one of volunteering to be sat out of the singles when my own injury prevented me from teeing off on the Sunday. But he had already more than played his part in the American victory with 2 points out of 3 alongside Pavin on the first day and a half. Played thirty-four matches in his eight Ryder Cups, winning 21 points.
Tom Watson (captain)	It was mission accomplished for one of America's greatest players, and he showed his tough side in his leadership of a team built around the experience of Wadkins, Floyd, Kite and Stewart and the fierce competitiveness of the likes of Pavin, Azinger and Beck. In truth, this was not a vintage United States line-up, but it performed to the best of its ability, and, with Europe's team suffering problems of injury and poor form, it was just enough in the end.

Unlike some American captains of the recent past, Watson clearly decided to identify what he considered to be his strong pairings – such as Wadkins and Pavin, Couples and Azinger, Kite and Love, and Floyd and Stewart – and to stick with them during the first two days. Like Gallacher, his singles order was an attempt to spread his strongest players right across the line-up. Ultimately, however, it was the late and unlikely fightbacks of Beck and Love that won it for him.

CHAPTER EIGHT

1995 OAK HILL

The 1995 Ryder Cup was all about redemption for me. I wanted to make up for my personal horror show at The Belfry two years earlier, and I so dearly wanted to help the European team to win again after two agonising and narrow defeats. All 12 of us in the team wanted to win it for Bernard Gallacher, who was captain for the third and – we all knew – the last time. Looking back on all my Ryder Cup experiences now, I am still enormously proud of the way I played in 1995 at Oak Hill, and, for me personally, the whole experience out there that week in New York State comes very close to my winning captaincy in 2002 and my winning putt and our historic win of 1985. It's tough to have to rank 1995 as low as joint third on my list, alongside the thrill of our 1987 win in America but that just goes to show how memorable the other two experiences were in my life.

Gallacher only had two captain's picks available for the trip to the Oak Hill Country Club in Rochester, with ten of Europe's team now qualifying automatically through the Ryder Cup points list.

Torrance qualified in third place, behind Colin Montgomerie and Bernhard Langer, and was in such a rich vein of form as he went past his 42nd birthday in the August that he ended up just being pipped by Montgomerie for the Order of Merit title itself a few months later at the Volvo Masters, the final tournament of the year.

Also qualifying by right for Gallacher's team, from fourth place to tenth on the points list, were Costantino Rocca, Seve Ballesteros, David Gilford, Mark James, Howard Clark, Per-Ulrik Johansson and Philip Walton, who just edged out Miguel Ángel Jiménez.

Gallacher's original two picks had been Nick Faldo and José María Olazábal, both of whom were playing most of their tournament golf in the United States, but Olazábal was later forced to pull out because of the chronic foot injury that was, ultimately, to cost him two full years out of the game and a huge amount of heartache.

Ollie was given as much time as possible to shake off the injury, as, of course, he was a central part of any Ryder Cup team of that era. His great partnership with Ballesteros might have reached into a fifth successive match had he been fit, as Seve himself had qualified with ease, and he had also won the first of his two US Masters titles in 1994. It was devastating for Ollie when he had to admit that his injury was too bad for him to play, but at least Bernard could then call on Ian Woosnam as a replacement pick, because Woosie had initially been the unlucky one to miss out from the three stand-out players who did not make the team through the points list.

Woosnam had finished in 13th position in the Ryder Cup qualifying list, just behind Olazábal, and so there were no dissenters when the feisty little Welshman was called up for his seventh consecutive appearance.

Europe's team once again centred on a core of world-class players – Faldo, Langer, Ballesteros, Woosnam and Montgomerie, who had not won a major but who was now fully established as a world star – plus a knot of tough, experienced campaigners in Torrance, Clark and James.

Rocca and Gilford had endured unhappy experiences in their previous Ryder Cups, in 1993 and 1991 respectively, but at least they also knew what the event was all about and were in excellent form. Rocca had only lost out in that summer's Open to John Daly after a play-off at St Andrews.

The two rookies were Johansson – who was following Joakim Haeggman from 1993 in showing that Sweden were a coming force as a country of significant future Ryder Cup potential – and Ireland's Walton. It was a well-balanced, confident team.

Lanny Wadkins, the United States captain, also had a few problems to contemplate as his team gathered at Oak Hill. First, of course, he himself was not playing – having been the heart and soul of American teams for so long – and also retired from Ryder Cup combat was Ray Floyd, his fellow veteran and scrapper.

Neither Tom Kite nor Payne Stewart had made the team, as they had not played well enough, while Paul Azinger was absent, fighting the cancer that had been diagnosed shortly after the 1993 match. Ben Crenshaw, though winning the 1995 Masters to qualify for the team, had suffered an alarming drop in form since then, and Peter Jacobsen had not played in a Ryder Cup since the 1985 match.

Wadkins also had five rookies to assimilate into his team – Tom Lehman, Jeff Maggert, Brad Faxon, Loren Roberts and Phil Mickelson – and for established Ryder Cup 'big-hitters' he could only look at Fred Couples, Davis Love III, Corey Pavin and Curtis Strange, whom he picked alongside Couples for his vast experience rather than his current form.

We did not fear the Americans, but, away from home, we always knew it would be a tough job to beat them. Oak Hill is a difficult course, with tree-lined fairways that put a premium on accuracy and consistency of ball-striking. Mistakes are punished there, and its par of 70 was also very tough, not that this is of prime importance in matchplay. Seve's form was the main concern we had, as his game had really fallen away during the latter half of 1995 – after a fine start to the year – and he was struggling to keep the ball in play off the tee. But, otherwise, we were as confident as we could be as we practised in preparation for the start of hostilities on Friday morning.

Gallacher had a surprise in store for Torrance, however, when he finally settled on his first team selections for the opening foursomes. Originally, he had wanted to pair Torrance with Walton, who knew each other well, and also Langer with Woosnam for the foursomes matches, given that the German and the Welshman had combined to stunning effect at The Belfry two years earlier and had delivered two wins out of two in that format.

Then he had Faldo and Montgomerie, the other proven Ryder Cup partnership, and the Clark–James combination that had performed so well at The Belfry in 1989 and was another obvious pairing of good friends who had absorbed a lot of previous experience and would not be fazed by the unique pressure of the first morning of the match.

During practice, it was clear that Bernard wanted to go with these four pairings for the opening foursomes, but on the Thursday both Philip Walton and Woosie informed him that they did not feel that their games were right – and especially for foursomes. That was when, with just a couple of hours of practice left, I was paired with Rocca and Johansson was brought in to partner Langer. To this day, I don't know why Costantino and I were put together, and I don't think Bernard could tell you either. He had wanted me to act as a senior partner for Philip, especially as we were both coached by my dad, Bob, and got on very well, and I suppose he saw the other three pairings as tried and trusted ones. But then he was forced into this late switch – which, funnily enough, is exactly the same thing that I had to do during my own captaincy, when I threw García and Westwood together – and, like me seven years later, Bernard decided to go with a hunch, a gut feeling. The fact that both Rocca and I, and Langer and Johansson, then won our matches the following morning would have been brilliant for him.

Torrance and Rocca, playing in the second foursomes match behind Faldo and Montgomerie, beat Jay Haas and Fred Couples 3&2 and immediately clicked as a pairing. And, in the anchor foursomes, Langer and Johansson also gelled so well that, with five holes left, they were three up against Crenshaw and Strange and seemingly coasting to victory.

Costantino was always something of a loner on tour. He would most often eat by himself, and he seemed to be more comfortable keeping himself to himself, and, for that reason alone, he was more difficult to get to know than others. Obviously he had played in the 1993 Ryder Cup, but that was an unhappy experience for him, and when he lost his singles against Davis Love after being one up with two to play he was inconsolable, because he felt he had cost Europe the Ryder Cup. He came to Oak Hill determined to atone for that, and I found him to be the most wonderful of partners: passionate, totally committed and also good fun to be around.

My relationship now with Costantino, whenever we meet, is such that we will always give each other a big hug and we always have this special bond between us. Without the Ryder Cup, that would just never have happened, and, even then, it was really just sheer chance that our playing partnership came about in the first place. Of all the great things that have happened to me in the Ryder Cup, I count my friendship with Costantino as one of the best. And it's just another reason why the Ryder Cup itself is so special for every European golfer who is fortunate enough to play in it.

Gallacher's delight at the success of the Torrance–Rocca pairing was soon more than tempered, however, by the news that Faldo and Montgomerie had lost a tight contest against Corey Pavin and Tom Lehman by one hole, and then by the 4&3 defeat suffered by Clark and James against Love and Maggert.

Also, by this time, heavy rain was beginning to fall and the Langer–Johansson partnership suddenly began to falter as Crenshaw and Strange began to grind out some winning holes in the worsening weather.

In the end, they managed to hold on for a one-hole victory, squaring up the first series of matches 2–2, but by then Gallacher had decided to commit them to an afternoon fourballs together too. And, with their game finishing on the final hole and not sooner, as the European captain had expected when he put in his pairings an hour earlier, it left Langer and Johansson with just 30 minutes to get dry and changed and have a quick snack lunch before they were expected back on the first tee.

Gallacher said after the opening day that this had been an error, because Langer and Johansson were not given the best chance to play to their full ability against Pavin and Mickelson in the fourballs, soon going down to a crushing 6&4 defeat.

I would defend Bernard on that count, because he is only speaking with the benefit of hindsight. Ryder Cup captaincy is all about going with your instincts in terms of your pairings, and especially in the middle of the day when you often have to put in your afternoon pairings before the morning matches have all finished. There is often no time to think – you just have to make a call.

In this instance how was Bernard to know that it was going to rain and that Langer and Johansson were suddenly going to struggle because of it? They had played superbly up until that point, they were winning their match – and they still ended up winning it, remember – and I reckon Bernard was absolutely right to keep backing the hunch that had actually put them together in the first instance. OK, it didn't work out in the afternoon, but it was still a risk worth taking at the time he had to make the decision. That's what you have to do as a Ryder Cup captain.

The afternoon session also went extremely badly for Torrance and Rocca, who were brought back down to earth after their foursomes win by losing 6&5 to Maggert and Loren Roberts, one of the best putters in the American team. And, with the crack pairing of Faldo and Montgomerie going down for the second time in the day, with Couples and Love beating them 3&2, the European challenge desperately needed the inspiration it received from an unlikely source.

It was an inspirational move by Bernard Gallacher to pair David Gilford with Seve. You couldn't create two more different characters, but the Ryder Cup has often been the place for two contrasting golfers to come together in either foursomes or fourballs and seem to take something extra from each other. What Seve did with Gilford was really special. He was nowhere near being in control of his own game, but he gives so much to his partner in those situations and he ended up bringing the very best out of David. The shy Englishman, getting caught up in the passion and the excitement of being around Seve, suddenly started to play golf of the highest class, and, all the time, he seemed to have Seve grinning and grabbing him in celebration after yet another great shot, or great putt. The two of them just clicked, and the result was a 4&3 victory against Faxon and Jacobsen. And it was such a vital point for us.

At 5–3 down, though, after the opening day, the Europeans knew they had it all to do when the match resumed on the Saturday morning with the second round of foursomes. Gallacher also had some serious thinking to do, and the result of his deliberations was to stick with Faldo and Montgomerie and send out his number-one pairing for a third time in the hope, and expectation, that they were too good to lose a third match on the trot.

Torrance and Rocca, despite their heavy fourballs defeat, were also retained on the strength of their previous foursomes performance, but Gallacher had a big decision to make when it came to his third and fourth pairings of the morning.

The temptation was simply to bring out the Langer–Woosnam pairing of 1993, now that Ian felt back in the groove after a day of added practice on the Friday and felt ready for two matches on the second day. But, instead, Bernard split them and gave Woosie the job of looking after Walton in his first Ryder Cup match and Langer the company of Gilford, who was now on something of a high following his exploits alongside Seve the previous afternoon. And the result was that we nearly had a clean sweep. It was a mark of Bernard's cool captaincy style that he was prepared to react to circumstances as well as keep faith with certain partnerships. He was flexible, and that is again a very good characteristic of any successful Ryder Cup captain.

Out first, Faldo and Montgomerie defeated Haas and Strange 4&2, but not before Torrance and Rocca had obliterated Love and Maggert by a thumping 6&5 margin in the second game.

Woosnam and Walton were only just edged out, by one hole, by Roberts and Jacobsen, but Langer and Gilford proved to be the steadiest of partnerships as they engineered a highly impressive 4&3 victory against the fancied American pair of Pavin and Lehman in the anchor match. A superb morning's golf had brought Europe back to 6–6.

That match with Rocca on the second morning of 1995 gave me one of my greatest memories as a Ryder Cup player. And it was nothing to do with me. Costantino's hole-in-one early in our victory against Love and Maggert was one of those unforgettable Ryder Cup moments, and it is difficult for me to forget it, because I still have the bruises. He jumped into my arms in celebration, whooping and hollering, and then began to squeeze me. My chest felt as if it was about to cave in – he's a bull of a man and so strong. But it was worth the pain. It was a wonderful moment, although I had to work hard with Rocca after that to keep him calm and to make sure we did not waste the three-hole advantage that his great shot helped to give us.

Europe's stirring fightback, however, did not last into the afternoon, as the Oak Hill match took another of its dramatic twists. Again, Gallacher decided to mix up his pairings, in the search for a better fourballs result than the previous afternoon. He split Torrance and Rocca, and Faldo and Montgomerie, which were two big calls.

Indeed, the only fourballs partnership he left alone was the unlikely Ballesteros–Gilford combination. But, he felt, they had earned another outing after their great win of 24 hours earlier.

The second afternoon was incredibly frustrating for us. We felt ready to turn the match around, after the success of the foursomes, and again I don't think Bernard Gallacher's selection process can be criticised. Well, only in hindsight. Colin Montgomerie and myself had been badgering him to play us together. We got on very well, we were both playing extremely well and we fancied ourselves to beat anyone put in front of us. Colin's partnership with Nick Faldo had not produced the spark of two years previously, and despite their morning victory it was clear that it had run its course. So putting Colin and me together was an excellent move, and we were very happy to be playing together.

Rocca had to play again, of course, after his hole-in-one and our tremendous victory that morning, so pairing him with Woosie also made huge sense. You could argue that putting out Seve and Gilford again was a gamble, on the basis that lightning doesn't strike twice, but why not go with it? And then that left Faldo and Langer as two of our very best players. They had played together before in Ryder Cups, most successfully in 1983, and they were more than happy to be paired up again. When we all set off that afternoon, we were in high spirits.

As it turned out, only the Woosnam–Rocca pairing prevailed, beating Love and Crenshaw 3&2 in the second match out. But, by the time their point was secured, Torrance and Montgomerie had gone down 4&2 to Couples and Faxon, and, coming up in the third game, Ballesteros and

Gilford failed to find the same magic as before as they were beaten 3&2 by Haas and Mickelson.

Both Colin and I shot under par, or par at the very worst, but I don't reckon that either Couples or Faxon would have come in under 78 or 79 if they had been forced to hole out on those holes they picked up on. We were both very efficient, matching each other shot for shot almost, but the Americans simply hung on in there against us by finding birdie after birdie in amongst all their dross. And, what is more, they seemed to find those birdies just when they needed them most. It was extraordinary how they 'ham and egged' it around that day, and it is the perfect example of how different and how exciting a format matchplay is.

The moment that Freddie Couples chipped in from off the front of the par-five 13th green, for a birdie four, with Faxon out of the hole and both myself and Colin right next to the flag in three, was typical. My third shot, a pitch, had all but gone in the hole too, but, when Fred's chip and run hit the hole and dropped, the roar from the American gallery was probably the loudest I ever heard in a Ryder Cup. The topography of that hole made it like an amphitheatre, and as no one could get up in two it was normally the case that all the players were hitting wedges in for their third shots, and that just added to the drama of it all.

It was in the anchor match, though, that the most dramatic moment of the day – and, indeed, the whole contest up to that point – was to take place. With the other three matches now decided, and America leading 8–7, much seemingly depended on the outcome of the game in which Faldo and Langer were taking on Pavin and Roberts.

The Europeans both played extremely well, but they just could not build any sort of advantage against the tigerish play of Pavin and Roberts. Again, it was a case of the two Americans dovetailing perfectly at times to stay in touch with the relentless and mistake-free golf of Faldo and Langer.

For 17 holes, however, it looked like a match that would be going Europe's way. A half would be the very least that Gallacher could expect. Then, all square playing the 18th, came a dagger to the European heart delivered by Pavin.

Faldo and Langer were both on the green in two, which was in itself something of a triumph on that tough last hole at Oak Hill, and were facing long but possible birdie putts. Roberts was also on the putting surface but right on the other side of the green, and he had a difficult two-putt. Pavin's second shot had missed the green to the right, and, although he was reasonably close to the hole, it was downhill all the way to the pin, and there was a significant right-to-left swing on it too. Importantly for Pavin, his partner, Roberts, got his long putt stone dead, to make sure of the par four, and then he chipped in for an improbable three. Neither Faldo nor Langer could make their putt, and so we had lost that match by one hole, right at the death. That made it 9–7 to them, and we knew we were now very much second favourites, especially with Seve in no sort of shape for the singles. It was a substantial lead for America to take into the last day, and we knew that it was soon likely to become 10–7 to them with Seve being sent out first in the singles to get his point over and done with.

But should Ballesteros have been sent out first by Gallacher? Would it not have been better for him to go out last, therefore minimising the effect that his probable lost point would have on the rest of the singles matches? Indeed, had he gone out at the foot of the field, the overall match might have been decided by then.

Bernard gave Seve the option of going out first or last. And, knowing his game was all over the place, Seve could not bear the thought of everything coming down to him at the end. He didn't feel his game was up to that responsibility. Also, Bernard knew that Lanny Wadkins would put some of his strongest players out at the front of his line-up, in the hope of building quickly on their significant 9–7 lead, and so in that sense Seve could be used as a sort of wild card against one of their better players. Bernard also knew that Lanny would hold back a number of his best players until the last few games, as a sort of insurance policy on things not going as he would have hoped early on. So, whatever the situation, Seve was going to draw one of their better guys.

And, because Bernard wanted to concentrate most of his strength in the middle order – on the basis that he felt that was his best chance of getting the 7½ points out of 12 that we needed to win back the Cup – then he was, in the end, more than willing to get Seve out there early in the hope that he could produce something miraculous to, at least, hold up the American effort. What he did was extraordinary, and his exploits on the first seven or eight holes in particular held us spellbound as those of us going out later prepared on the range for our own games. We thought that if he could do what he was doing, when he was not even on the same planet as his opponent on some holes, then we should also go out and fight.

It was, in fact, exactly what happened. Ballesteros, dredging up his last reserves of magic, was still all square with an astonished Tom Lehman after ten holes of their singles match. Not that Lehman had seen much of Seve, so often was he off line and trying to conjure up yet another remarkable escape from amongst the trees or deep in some other hazard or two.

Gallacher said afterwards that, even though Ballesteros was finally beaten 4&3, his early efforts at matching Lehman and prolonging the match well into the back nine acted as a real inspiration to his fellow players, who were all setting out on their own matches with one eye on the progress of the charismatic Spaniard at the head of the team.

Ballesteros's manic progress around Oak Hill's front nine also took much of the attention away, initially, from what was happening immediately behind him – and that, increasingly, was very good news indeed from a European perspective.

Neither Howard Clark nor Mark James had played since their defeat together in the opening foursomes, but they had worked very hard to get themselves ready for the singles and Bernard had put them out in the key number-two and number-three slots. They drew decent but beatable opponents in Peter Jacobsen and Jeff Maggert, and they soon began to get into their games. Howard, of course, was considerably helped by his hole-in-one at the 11th, but then Jacobsen fought back just as Jesse [James] was pulling away to a fine 4&3 win.

Clark's match then became the first of several all-important matches to come down to the 18th. But, as on the 17th, he nervelessly holed from four feet to maintain his one-hole advantage over Jacobsen and, with James's point, to pull Europe back to 10–9.

It could easily have been 10–10, too, but in the fourth match Ian Woosnam saw his birdie putt for a win against Couples on the final hole shave the front and side of the hole as it died down the slope. Woosnam had a half to add to the European cause, but his agony at a great putt that just didn't drop was clear for all to see.

Rocca, who, like Woosnam, had drawn the same singles opponent for the second match running, also suffered the same result when Davis Love beat him 3&2, and Gallacher knew that Europe could now not afford to drop many more points. The Americans had 11½, Europe had 9½ and there were now just seven matches left out on the course.

Monty looked in control against Crenshaw in match seven, but Faldo was down against Strange, and, although I felt in control of my own game against Loren Roberts, I knew that the overall result was going to be tight. There were still a lot of games that you could not call, and the atmosphere out on the course was electric. Obviously, at the time, I was just concentrating everything on my own match, but looking back it is easy to see just how pivotal the Gilford v Faxon match became. It was, without doubt, the turning point.

Gilford was one up playing the last and found the fairway. Faxon hit his second shot into the bunker to the left and in front of the green after David, who is not the longest of hitters and still had more than 200 yards to the green, nailed it but also pulled it slightly over the green to the left, beyond some fluffy rough. Now, David is not the best chipper of a golf ball in the world, and it is a shot he tries to avoid. He tried to bump and run the ball through the rough and onto the downslope of the green. It would have required a miracle shot to get it close, but, even worse, the ball stopped in the tangle of long grass around the green.

Now Gilford was faced with having to chip it out of that lie, and, with his fourth shot, he ran it about 12 feet past the pin. It was a magnificent shot, really, but he was still facing a difficult putt for a bogey five, and Faxon, having splashed out to around eight feet but above the hole, was suddenly looking odds-on to win the hole and halve the match. That would have felt like a win for America, but Gilford somehow found the skill and determination to hole his putt and Faxon missed his. After they had played three shots each, it had to be Faxon's hole, but

Gilford had nevertheless managed to win his point, and, with Monty closing out Crenshaw 3&1, the overall match score was now tied at 11½ each.

The next match to come up the 18th was that of Faldo and Strange. Neither man had set the course alight, but Faldo had battled back to win the 17th hole and take the match up the last all square.

Faldo's tee shot, however, was hooked slightly into the left rough, and, from three, he could only play out with a short iron and leave himself a ninety-yard pitch into the green for his third shot. Strange, who had driven well, could only put his second shot onto the bank in front of the green to the left, and, from there, he chipped out well wide of the hole.

Nick said afterwards that he was delighted that his second shot ran just into the first cut off the fairway to the right. It meant that his pitch would not have the same amount of spin on it as well as giving him the perfect angle to attack the flag. It was a fantastic shot in, leaving the ball below the cup to the left and only about five feet from the hole. Strange, meanwhile, left his approach putt about seven feet short and then missed. Nick holed for a brilliant par, and we had won another vital point. Seve was one of the first to grab him, and he was already in tears at the drama of it all. Seve told Nick that he was a great champion, and that started Faldo off as well. I'm not sure that little scene would have happened the other way around, but it is yet another example of Seve's huge passion for the Ryder Cup. It was, in truth, starting to get very easy to become emotional.

Out on the course, Torrance had just finished off his match with Roberts, and so Europe now had 13½ points to the United States's 12½, which they reached when Pavin closed out Langer 3&2 in the tenth match. It was all coming down to the last two matches: Philip Walton against Jay Haas in match eleven, and Per-Ulrik Johansson in the anchor game.

I had actually finished my own match in time to run up and see Nick Faldo hit in his third shot to the 18th. And I was on a tremendous high because of all the adrenalin that had flowed during my match with Roberts. He was a tough opponent, because at that time he was one of the most consistent players on the American Tour as well as being probably their best putter. But I was in form, I was confident in my ability and I was utterly determined to win my point and do my bit. I also always felt in control, despite his best efforts, and when we came to the 15th tee I was one up.

A par three, it had the pin set back right and there was water all the way down the right of the green. A big slope right to left meant that I was looking to aim for the left half of the putting surface and then fade the ball in towards the flag. But, coming down into the ball, I felt myself trying to block my full turn and I was fighting to stop it and to commit fully to the shot that I had visualised. As the ball flew from the clubhead, I must admit I was thinking 'Water,' but, thankfully, I had managed to hang on to the intended stroke just long enough, and I looked up to see the ball going directly at the pin rather than to the left of it. Also, it stayed on that line and the ball came down maybe about eight feet from the pin. It was a fluke, really, but I was a happy man walking up to my ball. Roberts got his three, and I had a putt to go two up with three to play. I missed. But I had hit a good putt, and I was still pleased enough with the three considering how I had felt when the club was about to strike the ball back on the tee. That's the margins you are talking about at that level.

Standing on the 16th tee, Torrance found himself in that rare territory even for the elite sportsman: the zone. In what was to prove to be the final half-hour of his Ryder Cup playing career, he had the satisfaction of reaching a level of personal performance that still gives him enormous pride.

I hit a good drive, right up to the spot on the fairway I wanted, and Loren also drove well. I was one up, there were just three holes left to play and I was really in the zone that sportspeople talk about. In my own career I suppose I have only felt what I felt then at Oak Hill a few times. It was extraordinary. To this day I still can't fathom out why I did it, but as Roberts was preparing to hit his second shot I spotted Suzanne in the crowd and so I walked maybe 30 yards to the ropes and said to her, 'Watch this.' I just felt so absolutely ready for what I had to do. He was just off the green, but I was just so sure that I could hit it close. And my eight iron never left the flag. It pitched just over the right collar of rough and ran up to about eight feet from the pin. I then sank the birdie putt, and, although Loren's chip and run had almost gone in, the hole was mine and I was now dormie two up.

I then hit a three wood up the 17th, opting not to take a driver because I was just concentrating on making sure of the four in the knowledge that he would then have to make a birdie three simply to extend the match down the last. By now, all my thoughts and all my energy were focused on not messing up. I had come too far, and I wanted that victory too much. I hit a perfect five iron to the middle of the green, and the ball ended up perhaps thirty feet past. He made his four, again from off the putting surface, and I had to two-putt for the match. It was a very fast, downhill putt, and after striking the ball I watched it rolling on and on. I hoped it would get close enough for it to be conceded, and that was what happened. I had won 2&1. Loren and I shook hands, and the feeling inside was simply unbeatable. It was just fantastic, glorious.

With the glow of his vital winning point inside him, Torrance was then able to watch the remarkable conclusion to Faldo's match against Strange up ahead before going back down the course with many of the other European players to see Walton come home.

By then, of course, we also knew that Bernhard Langer had lost, and so Philip Walton was our best hope for the full point that would clinch the whole match for us. In the final game, Johansson had been up on Mickelson, but Phil was now coming back strongly and it was increasingly obvious that it had to be a win from Walton if we were to make sure of regaining the Ryder Cup. Philip was also three up with three to play and so had a half-point guaranteed, but his opponent, Jay Haas, was fighting grimly to deny him any more than that. On the 16th, Walton putted up stone dead for his par four, but Haas, in a greenside bunker, hit the flag itself with a slightly thinned splash-out and saw the ball dive into the hole. That was a hammer blow to Philip, but he still found himself with a shortish putt of around four or five feet to win the match at the 17th – but missed.

It was getting unbearable, and Philip was clearly devastated by his failure to finish things off at the 17th. As he walked past me to the 18th tee, I slapped him on the arse and said, 'You are still one up!' Haas was in all sorts of trouble off the tee, and he had to chop it out of the trees and was well short in two. Walton drove well but into the rough down the right side of the narrow fairway. He decided to hit a wood, and I reckon he did well to get it up to the side of the green. Indeed, if he was going to miss the putting surface with his second shot, he ended up in about as good a place as he could be, just short and in the rough on the bank guarding the elevated green to the front and left. Philip's ball, actually, was set well down in the clinging and thick rough, and, if you watch the television replays, his ball only just cleared the rough as he hacked it out and up to within about 15 feet below the hole.

Haas never looked like making better than five, and so Philip had two putts to win the Ryder Cup for Europe. I am not sure if he really allowed himself to understand everything that now depended on him, but he knew what he had to do and told his caddie, Bryan McLauchlan, that if he had two putts for it he thought he would take them. With that, rather sheepishly, he rolled his ball gently up the slope to within nine inches of the cup – the perfect lag putt – and the Cup was ours. I think Bernard Gallacher's leap into the air, as he rushed onto the green to congratulate his then favourite Irishman, said everything else that needs to be said.

For the first time in Ryder Cup history, the United States had lost the singles on home soil. For the first time since 1981, on Torrance's own debut, the United States had managed to lead the match going into the singles. But they had still lost, by 14½ points to 13½, and Oak Hill would go down as one of Europe's greatest triumphs.

Six of that European side of 1995, indeed, would never play in a Ryder Cup again. But it wasn't the end of an era. Gallacher's deserved third-time-lucky victory was but the reaffirmation that the golden era of nip-and-tuck Ryder Cup confrontation was back on track.

Since 1983, when Jacklin's captaincy and the determination of Europe's new modern breed of players had transformed the event, the score now read seven matches, three wins each, one tie. In terms of points scored during those seven matches, it was Europe 100, US 96.

It was – whichever way you looked at it – becoming almost too close to call, every time. For players and fans alike, the Ryder Cup had thrillingly evolved into an exhilarating sporting spectacle.

1995 RYDER CUP RESULTS: 22–24 SEPTEMBER, OAK HILL
Captains: Bernard Gallacher (Europe), Lanny Wadkins (US)

Europe		US	
Morning foursomes			
Nick Faldo/Colin Montgomerie		Corey Pavin/Tom Lehman (1 hole)	1
Sam Torrance/Costantino Rocca (3&2)	1	Jay Haas/Fred Couples	
Howard Clark/Mark James		Davis Love III/Jeff Maggert (4&3)	1
Bernhard Langer/Per-Ulrik Johansson (1 hole)	1	Ben Crenshaw/Curtis Strange	
Afternoon fourballs			
David Gilford/Seve Ballesteros (4&3)	1	Brad Faxon/Peter Jacobsen	
Sam Torrance/Costantino Rocca		Jeff Maggert/Loren Roberts (6&5)	1
Nick Faldo/Colin Montgomerie		Fred Couples/Davis Love III (3&2)	1
Bernhard Langer/Per-Ulrik Johansson		Corey Pavin/Phil Mickelson (6&4)	1
Morning foursomes			
Nick Faldo/Colin Montgomerie (4&2)	1	Curtis Strange/Jay Haas	
Sam Torrance/Costantino Rocca (6&5)	1	Davis Love III/Jeff Maggert	
Ian Woosnam/Philip Walton		Loren Roberts/Peter Jacobsen (1 hole)	1
Bernhard Langer/David Gilford (4&3)	1	Corey Pavin/Tom Lehman	
Afternoon fourballs			
Sam Torrance/Colin Montgomerie		Brad Faxon/Fred Couples (4&2)	1
Ian Woosnam/Costantino Rocca (3&2)	1	Davis Love III/Ben Crenshaw	
Seve Ballesteros/David Gilford		Jay Haas/Phil Mickelson (3&2)	1
Nick Faldo/Bernhard Langer		Corey Pavin/Loren Roberts (1 hole)	1
Singles			
Seve Ballesteros		Tom Lehman (4&3)	1
Howard Clark (1 hole)	1	Peter Jacobsen	
Mark James (4&3)	1	Jeff Maggert	
Ian Woosnam (halved)	½	Fred Couples (halved)	½
Costantino Rocca		Davis Love III (3&2)	1
David Gilford (1 hole)	1	Brad Faxon	
Colin Montgomerie (3&1)	1	Ben Crenshaw	
Nick Faldo (1 hole)	1	Curtis Strange	
Sam Torrance (2&1)	1	Loren Roberts	
Bernhard Langer		Corey Pavin (3&2)	1
Philip Walton (1 hole)	1	Jay Haas	
Per-Ulrik Johansson		Phil Mickelson (2&1)	1
Europe	**14½**	**US**	**13½**

Sam's Analysis: 1995

Europe

Seve Ballesteros	His last act as Europe's greatest Ryder Cup golfer, in terms of his leadership on the course and his personality, was his almost comical attempt to hang on to Tom Lehman in the singles despite hardly hitting a fairway. And, for ten holes at least, he succeeded. His last great tangible achievement, though, was inspiring David Gilford to a wonderful fourballs point.
Howard Clark	A sixth and final Ryder Cup appearance ended with a brilliant singles win against Peter Jacobsen. Howard only played in the opening foursomes before his singles but dug deep over the closing holes to make sure of the victory with some gutsy putting.
Mark James	The veteran of seven Ryder Cups also made his final bow with a tremendous singles win, this time by 4&3 over Jeff Maggert. Lost in his only other match, one of the opening foursomes alongside Clark, but as ever he was a valued and valuable member of the team.
Ian Woosnam	Proved, as we knew he would, to be a more than capable last-minute replacement for the injured José María Olazábal. His seventh Cup brought a fourballs win with Costantino Rocca, a narrow foursomes defeat, and a halved singles battle with Fred Couples that could so easily have rewarded him with a full point.
Costantino Rocca	Played in all four sessions on the first two days and won three of those matches, two with myself and one with Woosnam. After his poor showing at The Belfry two years earlier, he really came of age as a Ryder Cup player. But he still couldn't beat Davis Love in the singles!
David Gilford	Like Rocca, he was able to wipe away the bad memories of his only previous Ryder Cup appearance, which for him had been at Kiawah Island in 1991. Inspired by playing with Seve on the first afternoon, he was then also played in the second round of foursomes, alongside another European legend, Bernhard Langer, and came away with another point. But it was his heart-stopping singles win against Brad Faxon that, in the end, did the most to bring the Cup back to Europe.

Colin Montgomerie	His partnership with Faldo cooled, with only one win from their three outings together, and Monty needed to win his singles point against Ben Crenshaw to feel that he had made a solid contribution to the cause after also losing a fourballs match with myself.
Nick Faldo	Nerveless up the 18th in the crucial singles against Curtis Strange, and his pitch into that last green – and then the five-footer to win the point – will long remain in Ryder Cup lore. But he mainly found only frustration during the first two days, when he enjoyed just one victory from his four outings on his tenth successive appearance.
Sam Torrance	I did not know it was to be my last Ryder Cup as a player, and nor did I want it to be, but looking back I could not be more happy to have bowed out with perhaps my best sustained performance in my eighth appearance. I won 3 points out of 5, and it was enough to help us to win. And that's what has always mattered most to me.
Bernhard Langer	One of five players to feature in all five sessions, and he enjoyed foursomes wins with both Per-Ulrik Johansson and David Gilford. But the fourballs and his singles were far more of a struggle. Another sound overall performance, however, from someone who was making his eighth consecutive appearance.
Philip Walton	Ireland's rookie goes down in history as one of the men who 'sank the putt to win the Ryder Cup', although in his case it was a tension-filled lag up to the side of the final hole and then a concession from his opponent, Jay Haas. His singles victory gained him the only point of his Ryder Cup career, as he lost a foursomes with Ian Woosnam the previous day, but what a point it was.
Per-Ulrik Johansson	The Swedish rookie played brilliantly on the first morning to win a foursomes victory alongside Langer, but the pair then lost in the afternoon fourballs and Per-Ulrik did not appear again until his anchor singles against Phil Mickelson. Up with 12 holes played, he then failed to withstand a fierce Mickelson rally and eventually lost 2&1. The Cup, by then, though, had been secured.

171

Bernard Gallacher (captain)

He played eight times in a row from 1969, and, as a member of the 1983 side that narrowly lost in Florida under Tony Jacklin, he neatly straddled the two eras of the post-war Ryder Cup: complete American domination and then the rise of the European challenge. After three Cups acting as Jacklin's assistant, he was ready for the captaincy himself, and, after the agonising defeats of 1991 and 1993, he was more than ready for a taste of victory. We were all so delighted that we could give it to him at Oak Hill. Once again, Bernard handled his team with great skill and understanding. He also demonstrated his ability to think on his feet, being rewarded especially by his gut decisions to pair me with Rocca, to put Gilford alongside Seve and then also to give David an unplanned extra outing in foursomes with Langer. His singles order was also clever tactically.

United States

Tom Lehman

He was restricted to just two foursomes outings before the singles, winning one point in partnership with Corey Pavin, but Lehman also had the pleasure in his debut Ryder Cup appearance of watching the escapology skills of Seve Ballesteros up close and personal during their singles match. It may have been a Ballesteros very far from his pomp that he beat, but it was a famous victory all the same.

Peter Jacobsen

One win and one defeat in his two outings before the singles, but it was his narrow one-hole defeat against Howard Clark that revealed the first cracks in the last-day American structure. A lovely man, and one of my best friends in the States.

Jeff Maggert

Like Jacobsen, he was not an American player who we feared, and he also lost his singles early on the final day, this time by 4&3 to Mark James. But, by then, he had also contributed to two fine American wins on the opening day, alongside first Love and then Roberts, and emerged with credit from his debut appearance.

Fred Couples

Two fourballs wins, with Love and Faxon, but a foursomes defeat to kick off with and also fortunate to escape with a half from his singles with Ian Woosnam, although he did hole a good putt for his par four after Woosie's birdie effort had somehow stayed out. One of America's senior men, in his fourth appearance, and justified his captain's pick.

Davis Love III

One of only two Americans to play in all five matches, he won 3 points overall and showed in his second appearance that he was someone the United States could depend upon for many future Ryder Cups. Huge natural talent.

Brad Faxon

Famed as one of the best putters in the world game, he nevertheless cracked under the pressure of his singles match against David Gilford, missing a crucial putt on the final green that would have gained him a critical half. In two fourball outings he had one win and one loss.

Ben Crenshaw

The 1995 Masters champion was far from his best in this match, which was the last of his four appearances. Played three, lost three says it all, and he was no match for Monty in the singles, although he hung on until the 17th.

Curtis Strange

One of Lanny Wadkins's picks, he let his captain down, and I know that Curtis was absolutely gutted by his performance on the course on which he had won the 1989 US Open. Lost both his foursomes matches and then the dramatic singles with Faldo, in which he had a bogey five at each of the last three holes.

Loren Roberts

He had a highly impressive debut, winning both his fourball matches and also his foursomes outing – with three different partners – and I was absolutely delighted to be able to play well enough to beat him in the singles. A silky putter, he also hit most fairways and most greens in regulation, which made for a tough opponent in matchplay.

Corey Pavin	He and Love were the only Americans to feature in every match, and Pavin emerged as his team's best and most successful player, with 4 points. His holed chip at the 18th in the Saturday fourballs win against Faldo and Langer will rightly go down as one of the great shots of the Ryder Cup, and it was typical of this tenacious little bugger.
Jay Haas	Won just 1 point from his four matches, gaining it alongside Mickelson in the second round of fourballs. In the end, the whole contest came down to the outcome of his singles match against Philip Walton, but he was down all the way around and could never put the rookie Irishman under any real pressure until it was virtually too late.
Phil Mickelson	His Ryder Cup debut saw him emerge with a 100 per cent record, with two fourballs wins alongside Pavin and then Haas and a third point gained from his 2&1 singles victory over Per-Ulrik Johansson. The shape of things to come.
Lanny Wadkins (captain)	He juggled his resources constantly in an effort to wrong-foot Gallacher, and for the first two days he was the happier captain. His faith in Curtis Strange, however, proved misplaced as one of his picks failed to win even a half-point, and he also played Ben Crenshaw twice on the opening two days when he did not need to do so. In the end, though, all his hopes came down to the way five of his golfers – including Strange, of course – dealt with the unique pressure of coming up the 18th hole with the destiny of the Cup itself at stake. Of those five, there were one-hole defeats for Jacobsen, Faxon, Strange and Haas and just a scrambled half from Couples.

Chapter Nine

1999 Brookline

I was so disappointed at not making the 1997 Ryder Cup team, after playing so well in 1995, that I decided to give up drinking for a year and a half in a bid to win selection for the 1999 team at Brookline. That's how much it meant to me! Even now, it is a great regret to me that I did not get to play in another Ryder Cup team after Oak Hill, which was my eighth consecutive appearance. And certainly, at the time, I was sure I was going to get another chance to take on the Americans. Throughout the late '90s it was what I expected to do, and, indeed, I won the French Open in 1998. That proved to be my last European Tour victory, but, again, at the time I felt it was just a stepping stone to getting back into Ryder Cup contention.

In a very private conversation, after Valderrama, both Mark James and I were told by Ken Schofield, the executive director of the European Tour, that the Ryder Cup committee wanted us to captain the next two Ryder Cup teams, in 1999 and 2001. Because of my own determination to make the 1999 team as a player, I said to Jesse [James] that I thought he should go ahead and be captain for 1999. As it turned out, he was closer to making his own team than I was, and Ken Brown, who was an assistant to Mark at Brookline alongside myself and Ian Woosnam, was on standby to take over the captaincy itself if Mark had actually done enough to qualify.

With the benefit of hindsight, however, Torrance now sees his failure at making either the 1997 or 1999 teams as being crucial to the way he carried out his own captaincy in 2002.

I wasn't very happy at the time at not being asked to join up with the European team in some capacity at Valderrama, but what that meant was that I was able to sit in my armchair at home and watch every single shot played. And I mean every single shot. Like many golf fans, I suppose, I settled back and decided to watch every minute of the television coverage of the match, and I must say I really enjoyed the experience. I know it sounds obvious to say it, because before I had actually been involved in playing the matches, but getting the overview from the television coverage and being able to follow the entire match from beginning to end was quite an eye-opener for me. I was caught up in the match as a fan, and as a supporter of the European cause, but because I knew all the players so well I saw quite a lot from watching it so closely that gave me a tremendous insight into the event. It gave me a different perspective on things, and a valuable one too.

Before 1997, the only coverage I'd watched of a Ryder Cup was the highlights packages that were put together by the television company covering it and the commemorative videos released afterwards. But to watch it all unfold live, from minute to minute and from hour to hour, was fascinating, and, mentally, I suppose I spent all those long three days pegged out in front of my television taking notes about what I was observing. And, to give but one example of the impressions I got from watching every minute of it, I felt that the shot of the week was the putt Lee Westwood hit on the 16th green to clinch a foursomes point. Rain the previous day meant that the end of that match had to be played out very early the following morning, and Westwood, partnering Nick Faldo in his debut Ryder Cup, had marked the European ball on the green when play was called off the previous evening.

Now, I know just how difficult it is, mentally more than anything, to go to bed thinking about the shot you have to play when you get up the next morning. The pressure on Lee, especially in his first Cup, would have been very draining even though he and Faldo were two up at the time and expected to win their match against Justin Leonard and Jeff Maggert. But Lee was equal to it, knocking it in from about 12 feet to clinch their match 3&2. I thought it spoke volumes for his temperament as well as his ability, and it was a big clue to me about how good a Ryder Cup performer Westwood was going to become.

There was one other moment from Valderrama that made a significant impression on Torrance, and that was very much to do with the captaincy of Seve Ballesteros, who led Europe to their 14½ to 13½ triumph in a manner that could only be described – generously – as 'inimitable'.

Seve, as captain, charged around the course in his buggy, and I think if he could have played every shot for every player he would have done. His pairings were excellent, especially his inspired decision to put Westwood with Faldo, and he built a remarkable five-point lead going into the singles. In the end, however, it all came down to Colin Montgomerie's match against Scott Hoch, with Monty working so hard to turn things around. First, he got back level and moved in front of Hoch with pars at the 14th and 16th. But, with the overall match suddenly looking incredibly tense, as Olazábal lost the last three holes to Lee Janzen, a loss at the 17th had put Monty back to all square. But he summoned up all his resolve to play the tough final hole at Valderrama in exemplary style, whereas Hoch was in the trees off the tee and only made the green in three.

As it happened, Colin would have most probably got a full point if Hoch had been made to finish the hole, because he was still thirty feet or so away in three when Colin putted up stone dead for his par four. Seve went onto the green to congratulate Colin, and to celebrate the overall victory gained by his guaranteed halved match and, as a result of that, in effect he conceded Hoch his four, and a half point. All Seve was interested in was the team getting to 14½ points. It seemed the only thing that mattered to him was winning the Ryder Cup itself.

But while Torrance was absorbing these lessons, and adding the conclusions and insights he drew from watching intently from afar to those stored up inside him from his eight appearances as a player, he knew that helping his great friend James at Brookline would bring far, far more knowledge about what it would take to be a good captain himself when the time came.

Brookline was where I really started to learn about Ryder Cup captaincy and when I truly began to understand just how much work goes on behind the scenes to get everyone and everything right. Compared with what I knew after that match, and that experience, what I knew about leading Europe into battle was virtually nothing. But, of course, everything that had happened to me – as a player during eight matches, as a professional for three decades and as a television fan for one match – had also given me layers of experience and understanding that I brought with me into the job of being an assistant to Mark James in 1999. I loved every minute of it, and I only wish we could have got over the line at the end of it. Jesse [James] did a wonderful job as captain, and it hurts me so much to think that he will always go down in history as a losing captain.

The Country Club at Brookline, in the state of Massachusetts, was a magnificent and historic venue for what, by now, had become one of the most eagerly anticipated sporting contests in the world. But it was just half an hour out of Boston, and, with a boom in that great financial centre and in the wider United States going on in the late 1990s, the demand for corporate hospitality was enormous.

As a result of this, and the demand for tickets generally, the 1999 match was attended by far more people than could sensibly be accommodated by the grand old Country Club. It is estimated that crowds of 30,000 to 35,000 attended the first two days of the match, plus a ludicrous 40,000 on the Sunday.

By comparison, only 25,000 spectators per day were ever allowed in at The Belfry, which is a venue that features more space both for viewing the golf and for corporate or public facilities than is available at Brookline. In that respect, it was a powder keg in terms of overcrowding and the subsequent frenzied atmosphere that that produced.

There was indeed a very intimidating atmosphere all week, and I do not need to go into all the details again of the horrible treatment that Colin Montgomerie, in particular, received from the American crowds. Obviously, the one big thing that the 1999 Cup will be remembered for will be the incident on the 17th green in the singles match between José María Olazábal and Justin Leonard, but there were several other very unsavoury moments in a week that will for ever remind everyone in golf about what can happen if things are allowed to get out of control in a contest as intense as a Ryder Cup. But I believe we have moved on from 1999, and let's hope we never see its like again.

There was some controversy, however, before the actual match began – and not just with the American players making voluble noises about being paid for their participation before settling, correctly, for a sum of $100,000 per player being given to the chosen charities of each member of the team.

For some time before the Europe team was finalised, it was assumed that both Sergio García and Jesper Parnevik – who both played largely in the United States – would be in need of James's two captain's picks if they were to appear at Brookline.

Parnevik had played with some distinction at Valderrama and was viewed as a certain selection, while the flamboyantly talented García was widely viewed as the next European superstar – and natural successor to his Spanish compatriot Ballesteros – and a must for a Ryder Cup debut at the age of 19.

García had won the Irish Open after turning professional earlier in the year, but it was only when he almost pipped Tiger Woods to the US PGA championship title, finishing runner-up, that he gathered enough Ryder Cup qualification points to play his way into the team in seventh position.

There was a lot of discussion and speculation in the media about who Mark's second wild-card pick was going to be once Sergio had made the top ten automatic qualifiers. The most experienced candidate was Bernhard Langer, who, though not in the best of form that year, had outperformed his fellow veteran Faldo. But then there were the claims of both Robert Karlsson of Sweden and Scotland's Andrew Coltart, who had finished in 11th and 12th places respectively in the qualification table. In the end – and this was Mark's decision, and he had every right to make it – he went with Coltart and got some criticism for that. His reasoning was that Coltart was the golfer in the better form over the two months going into the match, and you couldn't really argue with that.

Coltart, however, was a seventh rookie in the European line-up, alongside García, Paul Lawrie, Miguel Ángel Jiménez, Pádraig Harrington, Jarmo Sandelin and Jean Van de Velde. Would not Langer's vast experience have brought a better balance to the team? The Americans, by contrast, had just one rookie, David Duval, but he had been runner-up at the Masters the year before and was one of the game's hottest new properties.

In Europe's favour was the fact that Olazábal and Lawrie were the reigning Masters and Open champions respectively in 1999, but it was the United States who seemed to have much greater depth in heavy-hitters against the first European Ryder Cup team since 1975 not to feature any of the original 'big five' of Faldo, Ballesteros, Lyle, Woosnam and Langer.

Woods had won the 1999 US PGA to add to his 1997 Masters title, and Payne Stewart had claimed the 1999 US Open, just one shot ahead of Phil Mickelson, after being runner-up the previous year. Leonard had narrowly been pipped in a play-off by Lawrie in the Carnoustie Open, after winning at Royal Troon two summers earlier, and Mark O'Meara had won both the Open and the Masters in 1998.

In that American line-up at the time was a collective total of eleven major wins, while the Europeans could boast just Olazábal's two Masters green jackets and Lawrie's Open Championship triumph at Carnoustie two months earlier.

I think that is also a mark of just how well the European team performed over the first two days in the foursomes and fourballs. To go into the final day at 10–6 up was the stuff of dreams, to be honest. All the pairings that Jesse [James] put together worked well. Monty and Lawrie playing together was an early call of ours. It was an obvious partnership, to be fair, in that they are both Scots and also because it was time for Monty to assume the role of true elder statesman in the team and of leader on the course. In the 1997 match he had performed that role in one of the fourballs with Darren Clarke, who was making his debut at Valderrama, but he had still played with Langer in all the other three team matches. Now James asked Colin to go out first in the first three rounds, too, and he responded magnificently.

I also remember how Paul Lawrie, teeing off first in the opening foursomes on the Friday morning in their match against Duval and Mickelson, absolutely ripped it 320 yards down the middle of the fairway. They were a very good new team, while, for me, Clarke and Lee Westwood were also a really strong pairing. They were just gold: great friends but also two players who worked so well together. They were another early call. As for Parnevik and García, and also Jiménez and Harrington, they were both Mark's decisions – and pretty good ones. For the fourballs, Olazábal was brought in to partner Jiménez, and that worked out very well too. After two days' play, we could not have been more delighted.

Parnevik and García, indeed, were the only one of the three European pairs to go out twice on the first day and win both their matches. In the foursomes they beat Woods and Tom Lehman 2&1, and then in the afternoon fourballs they defeated Mickelson and Jim Furyk by one hole.

Montgomerie and Lawrie were also unbeaten, however, beating Duval and Mickelson 3&2 in the foursomes and then halving a tremendous battle against Leonard and Davis Love in fourballs play.

Jiménez, like Lawrie, enjoyed a memorable first day as a Ryder Cup player by halving alongside his fellow rookie Harrington against Love and Stewart in the morning foursomes and then teaming up with Olazábal to beat Hal Sutton and Maggert 2&1 in the fourballs.

Clarke and Westwood, meanwhile, may have lost 3&2 against the Sutton and Maggert partnership in the foursomes but bounced back after lunch with a quite superb one-hole victory against the Americans' marquee fourballs pairing of Duval and Woods.

After an unbelievable day's golf we were leading 6–2, and the Americans looked shell-shocked. As assistants to Mark, we had been responsible for feeding him bits of information about how everyone was playing – especially in the practice rounds. We were there to be as honest as possible, and brutally honest at times, but the truth after that first day of competition was that everyone was playing beautifully and that all Mark's plans could not have gone better. And we went to bed that night knowing, and daring to believe, that if we could do the same again on the Saturday then the match would be all but over before the singles could even begin.

For part of Saturday morning, indeed, it looked as if Europe could stretch their 4-point lead. Clarke and Westwood, in the second foursomes match, and the revelation that was the Parnevik–García pairing in the anchor game, both took control and romped to 3&2 wins.

But Montgomerie and Lawrie, against the dogged duo of Sutton and Maggert, and Jiménez and Harrington, who were up against Woods and Steve Pate, could not quite get anything from their matches. Both European pairs lost out by just one hole, meaning that the overall score now stood at 8–4.

The Saturday afternoon fourballs were clearly going to be absolutely crucial, and to me Mark James was utterly right to stick rigidly to his strategy of the previous day. Also, a rain delay of half an hour that second morning meant that, when the afternoon pairings had to be given in, just before noon, the foursomes matches had still not developed as much as they would have done if there had been no hold-up. And, when Mark had to put his pairings in, we were not just up in two matches but all square in the other two. The first day had been sensational, and the second day could have been the same. Europe was on a roll, and Mark was totally correct to go with it. A big lead after two days would be job done, and so in came Olazábal for Harrington, to partner Jiménez, and off they went again.

There was talk of Parnevik possibly wanting to play in just three of the first four rounds, but he won three out of three with García. After that, who would have split them up? I know there are a lot of people who feel that Mark could have given a run-out to two of his unplayed rookies that afternoon – possibly Sandelin and Van de Velde playing together or by giving each of them Olazábal or Clarke or Westwood as a senior partner to play with – but my view is that the captain's most important job in any Ryder Cup is, apart from determining the singles order, getting as many points on the board from the first two days. And that, over all my time being involved in the event, has been the basis of so many European successes. It was what Tony Jacklin believed, and indeed it is my belief that using just the minimum of eight players over

the first four sessions would be the right tactic if it gained you the maximum
number of Friday and Saturday points.

As it was, in another desperately close and fiercely fought round of
matches, Europe could do no better than another 2–2 result, even
though they lost just one of the four games.

Leading off the Europeans for the first time, Clarke and Westwood
were beaten 2&1 by Mickelson and Lehman. There were halves,
though, for both Parnevik and García, and for Jiménez and Olazábal,
while Montgomerie and Lawrie shook off the disappointment of their
morning defeat by toppling Woods and Pate 2&1.

Just look how close so many of those second-day matches were. Four out of
eight went to the 18th hole, but we only got the two halves from them. And
in the two matches we lost in the foursomes on the second morning it was a
case of the Americans getting birdies and not of our players throwing it away.
It could so easily have been 11–5 or even 12–4 at the end of Saturday. But, at
10–6, we were still more than happy – and even more so when we saw how
the singles draw had come out.

Ben Crenshaw, the United States captain, used the Saturday evening
press conference to utter his memorable – and ultimately prophetic
– phrase, 'Mark my words, I have a feeling about this thing.' Whether
he genuinely had a vision of the extraordinary events of the following
day, or was simply trying a psychological trick to pump up the flagging
confidence of his players, must remain part of Ryder Cup legend.

What is absolute fact is that the immediate reaction in the European
team room, following the announcement by the two captains of their
singles running order, was unanimously positive.

We were more than pleased, and when we passed the singles draw around
the players it was incredible how we all felt it had come out just as we hoped.
There has been quite a bit of debate, and criticism, of the fact that Mark put
all three of his unplayed rookies together in the order – and near the top of the
draw. But just look who they were drawn to play against: Mickelson, Love and

Woods. That was possibly their three best players, and so that was fantastic for us. We only needed 4 points to retain the Cup and 4½ to win it again outright, and so we were delighted that three of their gun players had drawn our so-called lesser players. It meant that three of their biggest players would not take out any of ours. In that respect, it worked out very well for us, and I'd challenge anyone to deny that.

We knew that the Americans would send out six of their best and most experienced players in the top half of the draw because they had no option at 10–6 down other than that. But Mark put Westwood and Clarke out in our top two, and he reckoned he would get at least a point – or a half at worst – out of those two games. When they drew Lehman and Sutton, too, he was doubly sure of that. Then, even accounting for the fact that the next three singles games might be lost, we were extremely confident that the bottom seven matches would yield a decent harvest of European points. And, even sat here now, I think that it looks a wonderful match-up from a European perspective. I know it didn't turn out like that, which is part of the delicious unpredictability of the Ryder Cup, but tell me which of the last seven games looks like it would have been a runaway American point? Not one of them. Indeed, at the time, we had ourselves down for at least five out of seven points at the bottom of the draw.

The reality, however, was something so different that no one could have foreseen anything like it. Brookline's vast crowds were whipped up into almost demented excitement as America's first six players out all moved swiftly into commanding leads.

Suddenly, Europe's 10–6 lead looked like becoming a 10–12 deficit – and quickly – as Lehman, Sutton, Mickelson, Love, Woods and Duval led the charge. The expected early point from either Westwood or Clarke disappeared as they were beaten by 3&2 and 4&2 respectively.

Sandelin and an unhappy Van de Velde went down 4&3 and 6&5 to Mickelson and Love, and although Coltart fought bravely he, too, was soon overwhelmed 3&2 by Woods. And, with Parnevik being crushed 5&4 by Duval, all Europe's worst fears were being realised.

It was as much the huge margins of all those six defeats that got the crowds going as the wins themselves. The United States team were on a massive high, as all six of the first six matches were being won with a lot to spare, and that helped to create the atmosphere that it did. None of them got much beyond the turn as contests. There were also a couple of unfortunate incidents, in both the Sandelin and Coltart matches, which did not help our cause.

First, on the second hole, Jarmo – who had been an incredibly supportive member of the team that week – hit in a brilliant tee shot on that par three to just a few feet, but when he went to mark his ball near the flag he discovered to his horror that there was a hole in his pocket and his marker had fallen through it. His caddie didn't have a marker on him either and went to rummage around in their bag to try to find one, but the crowd thought that Jarmo's delay in marking his ball was because he was waiting for his opponent, Mickelson, to concede the putt. And so they began to boo and jeer him, and, concentration ruined, he eventually missed the birdie putt and with it the opportunity to get into what was always going to be a difficult match against one of America's best players.

Coltart, meanwhile, could have been all square with Woods after nine but found himself two down when Woods holed an improbable chip. Then, after pulling his tee shot slightly at the par-five 10th, he lost his ball. As it happened, I was on the 10th tee giving out sandwiches and drinks to any of the European players who wanted them, and so I immediately jumped into a buggy, because the last thing you want to do in any Ryder Cup match is lose a ball. When I got down to the area which I felt the ball would be in, I couldn't see it anywhere, and two marshals there said it had hit a tree and flown fifty yards away. We looked but could not see it anywhere. When the permitted five minutes were up, I then had to drive a distraught Coltart back to the tee so that he could hit again – three off the tee. Only when that ball was in play, and I drove back down the side of the fairway, did the marshals tell me that they had found the original ball plugged in the ground. Balls that hit trees do not usually plug. Woods went on to win the hole and go three up.

From 12–10 down, though, the Europeans at last began to rally. Not all was yet lost, and perhaps James's strategy would win the day at the death. At this stage, the only player seemingly out of contention was a spent García in the 11th match, against Furyk.

Lawrie, in the anchor match, had established a sizeable lead, against Maggert – as had Olazábal, who was four up against Leonard. And the matches involving Harrington, Jiménez and Montgomerie looked as if they could all go Europe's way. If Lawrie and Olazábal could close out their games then that would mean that just 2 points from the other three matches would keep the Cup in European hands.

It was truly remarkable what happened in the Olazábal–Leonard match, with Leonard suddenly holing just about everything to turn the match right around. After nine holes, Ollie was four up, but he lost four holes out of six despite not dropping a single shot, and when Leonard sank another long putt across the 16th green their match was level. It was obvious by now, too, with Jiménez losing to Pate, that both Olazábal and Monty had to win their singles so that those 2 points, with Harrington's win against O'Meara and Lawrie's against Maggert, would get us to 14 and the retention of the Cup. Both Olazábal and Leonard found the 17th green in two, with Olazábal marginally closer but both of them a long way away from the hole. Ollie actually had to move his ball marker, so that's how much he was on Leonard's line. And then it happened. Leonard holed his huge birdie putt right up the green. It was 50 feet or more. And the whole world erupted.

Torrance, together with most of the rest of the European and American teams, and their wives, was crouched beside that 17th green when Leonard's putt hit the hole and dropped. Bedlam ensued, with American players and their partners reacting with sheer ecstasy to Leonard's miracle stroke.

I've called it the most disgusting and disgraceful day in the history of professional golf, and so that's on the record. So much else has been written and said about those scenes that I don't need to go into all the exact detail of it again. Suffice to say that it was 15 minutes or so before the situation had calmed down enough for Olazábal to be able to attempt his own putt. In those crazy ten or fifteen minutes, Ollie had been totally forgotten about. I had to restrain Suzanne at one point because she wanted to leap up and remonstrate with one of the American wives.

Tom Lehman, of course, ran fully 50 yards from where he was crouched by the 17th green, back down the fairway, fist-pumping and helping to raise the crowd's reaction to Leonard's great putt into something akin to a frenzy. It was behaviour I just can't condone. I can understand why it happened, because we're all human, and in the intensity of a situation like that it is only natural to celebrate it fairly unrestrainedly. But it went on for far too long, and the manner of it was just wrong. I actually saw a cameraman walk across Ollie's line. No American players or wives or caddies stood on his line, as they cavorted around and beside the green, but the cameraman did because he too was reacting to what was happening in front of him.

But, for me, the worst aspect of it all was to celebrate like that when Olazábal had still to putt. And how important was his putt? Well, it might only have won the Ryder Cup for us had he followed Leonard in. It was a putt to keep our Ryder Cup hopes alive. He had already had a good read of the putt, too, from the line of Leonard's ball, but so much time elapsed before he could actually settle over his own putt that it was difficult – impossible really – for Olazábal to remember exactly how the ball had travelled across that green. If he had holed it, their match would have still been all square going up the last. As it was, Ollie won the 18th, to halve their singles game, but because he missed on the 17th it meant that Europe could only finish on a maximum of 13½ points – which we duly did when Payne Stewart lost by one hole to Monty on the 18th and Lawrie also won.

As I look back on the incident now, I feel more and more strongly that Crenshaw, as the United States captain, should have stepped in and conceded Olazábal's putt. That would still have given Leonard the chance to halve the final hole and thus confirm America's victory, but it would also have been the best possible response to what happened on that 17th green. It would have been a concession of even greater symbolic power than that of Nicklaus to Jacklin in 1969. It would also have underlined forever what the Ryder Cup should be all about, but instead we got at Brookline what it should never be about:

1999 RYDER CUP RESULTS: 24–26 SEPTEMBER, BROOKLINE
Captains: Mark James (Europe), Ben Crenshaw (US)

Europe		US	
Morning foursomes			
Colin Montgomerie/Paul Lawrie (3&2)	1	David Duval/Phil Mickelson	
Jesper Parnevik/Sergio García (2&1)	1	Tom Lehman/Tiger Woods	
Miguel Ángel Jiménez/Pádraig Harrington (halved)	½	Davis Love III/Payne Stewart (halved)	½
Darren Clarke/Lee Westwood		Hal Sutton/Jeff Maggert (3&2)	1
Afternoon fourballs			
Colin Montgomerie/Paul Lawrie (halved)	½	Davis Love III/Justin Leonard (halved)	½
Jesper Parnevik/Sergio García (1 hole)	1	Phil Mickelson/Jim Furyk	
Miguel Ángel Jiménez/José María Olazábal (2&1)	1	Hal Sutton/Jeff Maggert	
Darren Clarke/Lee Westwood (1 hole)	1	David Duval/Tiger Woods	
Morning foursomes			
Colin Montgomerie/Paul Lawrie		Hal Sutton/Jeff Maggert (1 hole)	1
Darren Clarke/Lee Westwood (3&2)	1	Jim Furyk/Mark O'Meara	
Miguel Ángel Jiménez/Pádraig Harrington		Steve Pate/Tiger Woods (1 hole)	1
Jesper Parnevik/Sergio García (3&2)	1	Payne Stewart/Justin Leonard	
Afternoon fourballs			
Darren Clarke/Lee Westwood		Phil Mickelson/Tom Lehman (2&1)	1
Jesper Parnevik/Sergio García (halved)	½	Davis Love III/David Duval (halved)	½
Miguel Ángel Jiménez/José María Olazábal (halved)	½	Justin Leonard/Hal Sutton (halved)	½
Colin Montgomerie/Paul Lawrie (2&1)	1	Steve Pate/Tiger Woods	
Singles			
Lee Westwood		Tom Lehman (3&2)	1
Darren Clarke		Hal Sutton (4&2)	1
Jarmo Sandelin		Phil Mickelson (4&3)	1
Jean Van de Velde		Davis Love III (6&5)	1
Andrew Coltart		Tiger Woods (3&2)	1
Jesper Parnevik		David Duval (5&4)	1
Pádraig Harrington (1 hole)	1	Mark O'Meara	
Miguel Ángel Jiménez		Steve Pate (2&1)	1
José María Olazábal (halved)	½	Justin Leonard (halved)	½
Colin Montgomerie (1 hole)	1	Payne Stewart	
Sergio García		Jim Furyk (4&3)	1
Paul Lawrie (4&3)	1	Jeff Maggert	
Europe	**13½**	**US**	**14½**

SAM'S ANALYSIS: 1999

Europe

Lee Westwood

Won 2 points out of 4 in the company of his great pal Darren Clarke but no point or half-point in the singles when he was sent out first by his captain to lead off the European effort. But, overall, built solidly on his fine debut at Valderrama and was clearly one of Europe's leaders on the course. One of the best drivers of a golf ball I have ever seen.

Darren Clarke

I would have to give him a very similar report to Westwood's, and before the last day I would have backed him to get something out of Sutton in the singles if Lee didn't get anything out of his match against Tom Lehman. The fact that both he and Westwood got nothing was the start of Europe's problems.

Jarmo Sandelin

The big Swede earned my undying respect for the way he threw his heart and soul into the European effort. He did not get a game on either of the first two days, but you would not have known it in Europe's team room. He was so full of life and enthusiasm, and he was a real member of our team that week.

Jean Van de Velde

My one big personal regret of the week was the fact that I didn't press Jean to say more to me when I found him sitting alone near our team room soon after play had started in the Saturday afternoon fourballs. He was clearly upset at not being asked to play on either of the first two days, but he answered my query by saying he was OK. I should have spent time with him then, but I walked away.

Andrew Coltart

It might have been especially difficult for Coltart not to play on the first two days, simply because he had been a captain's pick. But he was just genuinely proud to be a Ryder Cup player, and he, like Sandelin, did everything he could to be a helpful and willing member of the team.

Jesper Parnevik	He had already shown his worth under intense Ryder Cup pressure at Valderrama, where he had recorded a win and two fiercely fought halves in his three team outings, but here he surpassed himself by forming an unexpected but superb partnership with Sergio García. With 3½ points out of 4, they were at the heart of Europe's challenge.
Pádraig Harrington	One half from his two foursomes matches alongside fellow rookie Miguel Ángel Jiménez, but then a superb fighting singles win against Mark O'Meara, clinched by one hole when he held his nerve to win the 18th against the 1998 Open and Masters champion. An excellent debut.
Miguel Ángel Jiménez	He had a taste of what the Ryder Cup was all about as one of Seve's assistants at Valderrama, but it was still a lot to ask of him on his playing debut to appear in all five rounds of matches and to play with two partners. But he was unbeaten in the fourballs, with a win and a half alongside Olazábal, and also gained a valuable half in the opening foursomes with Harrington. But just couldn't get into his singles match against Steve Pate, which many of us thought he would win.
José María Olazábal	His sixth Ryder Cup appearance saw him add to his magnificent overall record by remaining unbeaten in his three matches. Though sometimes erratic with his driver at this stage of his career, and therefore not played in the foursomes, he was still one of Europe's greats, as he had showed earlier in 1999 with his second Masters title. Also, his diplomacy when interviewed after the shameful episode on the 17th green during his singles half against Leonard was in direct contrast to my own reaction!
Colin Montgomerie	No golfer should ever have to endure the verbal abuse he received from the Brookline spectators, but once again Monty rose above it all to show in his fifth Ryder Cup appearance that he was now the leader of the European team out on the course. Won 2½ points out of 4 alongside Paul Lawrie, and a singles point too.

Sergio García

A quite brilliant debut, with his unbridled enthusiasm and flair bonding magically with the eccentricity and unflappability of Jesper Parnevik to create a new European Ryder Cup pairing of wonderful power. Nothing seemed beyond their ability and imagination as they won 3½ points out of a possible 4. But Sergio's energy levels, at still only 19, burned out finally on the last day when he was well beaten in his singles.

Paul Lawrie

In his undemonstrative way, he enjoyed almost as brilliant a debut as García. He played in all four team rounds, winning 2½ points alongside Montgomerie, and then also won his anchor singles convincingly. It could easily have been the point that retained the Cup for Europe, too. Totally justified his status as the 1999 Open champion.

Mark James (captain)

I thought he was magnificent as captain, and he should be remembered not as the leader who lost to that incredible American last-day fightback but as someone who came agonisingly close to pulling off a sporting miracle. The United States team in 1999 was a very powerful one – arguably one of their best in modern times – but for two days the sheer brilliance of Europe's golf was too much for them to handle. Brookline could, and perhaps should, have been one of Europe's greatest Ryder Cup victories, especially as it was on US soil, and it was so close to being exactly that. For me, that is how Mark James's team should be remembered.

He was also an absolute scream in his press conferences. His bone-dry humour had us in stitches, especially as the American media simply couldn't understand what he was saying, and the team spirit he fostered was fantastic. He was also unafraid to make the toughest of decisions, like leaving three of his players on the sidelines until the Sunday because that was the best way of trying to win the match. He didn't hedge his bets or sit on the fence. He was a strong captain, and if you'd offered him 10–6 going into the singles before the match, he would have ripped your arm off in shaking on the deal.

United States

Tom Lehman

Won an important fourballs point alongside Phil Mickelson on the Saturday afternoon, against Clarke and Westwood, and his lead-off singles against Westwood, but it will be for what he did in celebration of Leonard's great Ryder Cup winning putt that will unfortunately outlive that in the memory.

Hal Sutton

One of the strongmen of Ben Crenshaw's team, winning 2 points alongside Jeff Maggert in the foursomes and also grabbing a vital fourballs half in the company of Leonard in the Saturday fourballs. Played in all five matches, as only he and Woods did for the US team, and his singles win over Clarke was part of America's great Sunday charge.

Phil Mickelson

Two defeats on the opening day saw him withdrawn from the Saturday morning foursomes, but he then bounced back by winning in that afternoon's fourballs and also gaining a vital singles point.

Davis Love III

Unbeaten in his fourth Ryder Cup appearance, he somewhat unusually gained three halves from his three outings in foursomes and fourballs, with three separate partners, but then followed that up with a thumping singles win.

Tiger Woods

Added to his poor overall Cup record by losing three matches out of four on the first two days; his only win was a narrow one-hole victory in foursomes alongside Steve Pate. But while Crenshaw would have been puzzled over Woods's lack of fourballs success, he was happy enough to see his star player overcome Coltart in the singles after being sent out fifth in the order.

David Duval

Another American to suffer two defeats on his nightmare opening day, but he then recovered some composure with a halved fourballs match alongside Love, against the previously all-conquering Parnevik and García, and finished strongly on Sunday with a singles demolition of Parnevik.

Mark O'Meara	In poor form, he was only played once on the first two days, losing a foursomes alongside Jim Furyk, and his personal misery was complete when he was beaten in the singles by Harrington.
Steve Pate	The man at the centre of the Kiawah Island brown-envelope controversy eight years earlier now found himself caught up in the most controversial Ryder Cup of them all. Nowhere to be seen again on day one, he then emerged unexpectedly as Tiger Woods's partner on day two and began by winning a foursomes point. But it was his singles point, won against Jiménez, that was the deadliest dagger to Europe's heart.
Justin Leonard	He will for ever be remembered as the man who sank the putt on Brookline's 17th green, kicking off the biggest controversy the event has known and also winning the Cup itself for his country. But he was not to blame for anything. His own reaction was more than understandable, and acceptable, and he was soon trying in vain to get everyone else off the green so that his opponent, Olazábal, could have a go too.
Payne Stewart	Tragically killed in a plane crash a month after this Ryder Cup, he was a good friend to many European golfers, including myself, and he has been sorely missed indeed in the decade or so that has passed since. This was his fifth appearance, and, although it was not one of his best, his last gesture was typical of the man. With so much that was ugly going on in the scenes around him, as America celebrated the return of the Ryder Cup, he conceded his singles match to Colin Montgomerie on the 18th.
Jim Furyk	Luckless on the first two days, in the company of Mickelson and then O'Meara, he more than did his bit for the American cause by gunning down García 4&3 in the penultimate singles.
Jeff Maggert	Well beaten in the anchor singles by Paul Lawrie, but he had already contributed solidly to his team's hopes of winning back the Cup by partnering Hal Sutton to two victories in foursomes that did much to keep the American ship afloat in the first part of the match.

Ben Crenshaw
(captain)

A winning Ryder Cup captain, and, on the American side of the Atlantic, he goes down in the annals as the orchestrator of perhaps their most remarkable comeback victory. He did well to get his team back on track after the shock of going down 6–2 on the opening day, and his Saturday-night prediction of surprises in store will be remembered as one of the most famous of Ryder Cup quotes. You also have to say he got his singles order spot on, especially in terms of the first six. But what a Ryder Cup legend – and an even bigger golfing icon – 'Gentle Ben' Crenshaw would be if he had stepped back from all the nonsense that was going on in the aftermath of Leonard's astonishing putt at the 17th and walked onto that green to pick up Olazábal's marker and concede to him his birdie three. Perhaps that is asking too much, but I wish it had happened.

CHAPTER TEN

RYDER CUP CAPTAIN

The huge responsibility of being European Ryder Cup captain began for me, in effect, on the 17th green at Brookline and, because of the terrible events in New York and Washington on 11 September 2001, ended up spanning a three-year period. Golf, of course, like many other sports and pastimes, becomes something of an irrelevance when compared with something like the terrorist attacks on the World Trade Center and the Pentagon, which claimed so many innocent lives. But perhaps golf, and the Ryder Cup in particular, needed the reality check of being put in perspective following the 1999 match at Brookline and the discord it produced. At least, too, because of my comments in reaction to the incident on the 17th green, I had set out my stall very early about how I felt the Ryder Cup had got out of hand.

In the immediate aftermath of the Justin Leonard putt that, as it transpired, won the Cup back for the United States, a livid Torrance told viewers of Sky Sports television, 'The US should be ashamed. It's about the most disgusting thing I've seen, and this is not sour grapes. The way they ran across the green was disgraceful. Tom Lehman calls himself a man of God, but his behaviour today has been disgusting.'

They were words that, obviously, hit the headlines on both sides of the Atlantic and also provoked a heartfelt response – and apology – from Lehman himself. Barely 24 hours after the 1999 match had finished, moreover, Lehman sent a lengthy letter to Torrance.

Clearly Tom did not understand what I meant when I said what I did. When we spoke later on the telephone I made sure he knew that I was not doubting his Christian beliefs. I just reiterated my own belief that his actions – running back down the fairway and inciting the crowd with his own fist-pumping reaction to Leonard's putt – were not the actions I would expect from a man of God. When he replied that he understood what I was saying, and apologised from the bottom of his heart, I immediately accepted it. I wanted to draw a line under the incident. I wanted to move on. I wanted to concentrate completely on the next Ryder Cup, scheduled for late September 2001, and happily I found that my rival captain, Curtis Strange, felt exactly the way I did.

When my appointment as Europe's captain was officially confirmed two months after Brookline, I immediately rang Curtis, and we said what needed to be said in little more than a few seconds of conversation. We both agreed then and there that the Ryder Cup needed to be put back on track when the two teams met each other at The Belfry, and that was all we needed to say. I knew, trusted and liked Curtis. And I'm also happy to say that what happened at Brookline has not even come close to being repeated since. There has been no trouble in the four Ryder Cups that have taken place since, and long may that continue to be the case.

One of the first decisions that Torrance took, concerning his captaincy reign, was that he wanted Mark James and Ian Woosnam to be his vice captains, or assistants. It was a decision he made before leaving Brookline, where the pain of defeat had been sharpened even more when the European players returned from the closing ceremony to find that all their lockers had been opened and ransacked, with scores of personal items and signed mementos stolen.

I had learned more about the Ryder Cup from being a vice captain under Mark James than I learned from being a player in eight successive matches. And, throughout the week at Brookline, I also knew that the responsibility of being captain next time out was going to be mine. After all the controversy and upset, of course, I knew too that it was a vital part of my job in 2001 – or 2002 as it turned out – to put things right again. But, despite that massive requirement, I can honestly say that the only thought I had in my own head about doing the job was the desire to win. I only had to look at Mark James and all the players afterwards at Brookline. I knew that a lot of other people would be working towards getting the event back to the standards of behaviour required, besides Curtis and me taking the necessary lead, and so I wanted to devote all my energies to the one single most important factor. And that was our belief: that the Americans had stolen the Ryder Cup from us. We wanted it back so badly, and that was my motivation. I also felt strongly that my time had come. I was ready to be Ryder Cup captain.

What Torrance was not ready to do, however, was to tell Mark James that he had to resign as his official vice captain, but that was the sorry state of affairs that came to pass in the summer of 2000, following the publication of James's book about the Brookline match, *Into the Bear Pit*, and in particular the jokey revelation that a good-luck note sent to the European team by Nick Faldo had been binned.

A newspaper serialisation of the book did not help, and the eventual upshot was that James's position in the 2001 team hierarchy became untenable. Torrance tried everything he could to keep his lifelong friend as his vice captain, but to no avail.

I was kind of forced into making the decision to ask Mark to resign as official vice captain, and I was very upset, because the whole situation – and especially the bit about the Faldo good-luck message – was blown so far out of proportion it is scary. The original incident was totally a joke – a flippant episode, and no more than that – but the story just grew and grew, and, in the end, the politics of it all dictated to me what had to be done. My friendship with Jesse [James] did suffer a bit as a result of it, but I also think it is a wonderful pointer to the depth and strength of that friendship that he was willing to continue in a role of unofficial helper and assistant at The Belfry even though his official title had been taken away. I had said to him all along that I still wanted him to be there with me, in an unofficial if not official capacity, and I am just so glad that Jesse was able to experience the joy of winning the 2002 match and to be part of everything – he was, after all, still wearing all the team gear and appeared in many of the official photographs – after enduring the pain of Brookline.

Ian Woosnam stepped in as Torrance's official vice captain, following James's enforced resignation, and Joakim Haeggman later joined a back-room team also featuring long-serving tour pro Derrick Cooper when it became clear that three Swedes – Jesper Parnevik, Pierre Fulke and Niclas Fasth – were to line up in Europe's twelve for the delayed thirty-fourth Ryder Cup.

I wanted four assistants – call them what you will – because during practice rounds and during the first two days, when there are four matches going on at any one time, you need at least that number of pairs of eyes. As captain, I didn't want to be trying to dash here, there and everywhere. I wanted to be able to watch who I wanted, when I wanted, and to be able to keep an overview. But, to do that, I needed trusted lieutenants with every single match who could then report back to me what I might need to know. And, of course, they had to be people I knew would give me the right information – accurate, informed and to the point. And it is amazing, over the years, how much input the vice captains or assistants or helpers – they've always been there, but only in recent times have the vice captain or vice captains been made official – have had. There are so many jobs to do in and around the team, of course, but I remember as a player being handed raw carrots to eat during one Ryder Cup because someone had decided that they were good for your nerves!

Most of the decisions Torrance had to make in terms of the nitty-gritty of being Ryder Cup captain were all in place by the late summer of 2001. Together with his wife, Suzanne, and with various other supportive European Tour and Ryder Cup staff, such as Mark MacDiarmid, the director of special projects, he sorted out all the necessary accommodation at The Belfry, designed the team uniforms and golfing wear, worked on course set-up and put particular thought and care into the gifts that would be given to the players and officials of both the European and American teams.

He also liaised with his opposite number, Curtis Strange, and his wife, Sarah, and in an overall sense attempted to leave no stone unturned. And, while attending to all the many organisational matters that needed doing, he watched and pondered while his 12-man team came together.

The most difficult decision I had to make during my captaincy was over the second of my two picks. I had actually made a tentative enquiry of the Ryder Cup committee about whether I could have a third pick, as it was becoming pretty obvious that Sergio García – despite being then ranked in the top five in the world – was not playing enough on the European Tour to qualify by right as one of the top ten points-scorers. I thought it was crazy that I had to waste one of my two permitted selections on García, and I was very glad when the qualification criteria were changed in 2003 to allow in the top five world-ranked European players automatically, and irrespective of where they played. But, in 2001, I had to abide by the then agreed method of selection, and so, quite early on that summer, I told García in confidence that he would be one of my two picks even if he didn't manage to play his way into the team through his finishes in the major championships and in the few other European tour events to which he was committed.

That left, in the end, a choice between Jesper Parnevik and José María Olazábal, after I had been very relieved to see Bernhard Langer make sure of his own automatic qualification by winning the TNT Open, his first tour victory for four years. I wish I could have had both Jesper and Ollie, but there are only twelve places and I had only two selections. After much soul-searching, and a massive amount of thought, I went with Parnevik, and telling Olazábal that he had not made it was one of the worst experiences of my life. It still hurts me to think about it now. As a Ryder Cup captain, though, those are sometimes the hard and tough decisions you have to face. It is not easy.

Then, however, came 11 September. And suddenly, as the world tried to come to terms with the aftermath of perhaps the most terrible and far-reaching terrorist attack of modern times, the thought of playing a golf event of such huge profile brought only one sensible answer.

I had just arrived at the Sunningdale Golf Club and was parking when I heard the news of the tragedy. The rest of that day, and much of the next, was spent sitting in front of the television trying to take in the enormity of the terrible images being beamed right across the world. I spoke several times with Curtis over the next few days, and, soon, the decision was made to postpone the match for 12 months. It was absolutely the right decision, and all my players were totally supportive of it as well as being relieved that they would still get to play as a team in 2002.

For the rest of that winter, neither Torrance nor Strange – nor the 24 selected players – thought too much more about the Ryder Cup. The events of 11 September cast a long shadow, but by the time 2002 came around – and golfers began to emerge from their short end-of-season holidays over Christmas and New Year – the momentum of what was now the first even-numbered Ryder Cup year again began to grow.

It was difficult in certain ways for Curtis and I to pick up where we had left off, but mainly I saw the 12-month delay as being something that I could make advantageous to my team and the way I performed my captaincy. There was the huge minus of some players not playing as well as they had been when the team was finalised in 2001 – Jesper Parnevik for example, whose game had really suffered – but that was something that both teams had to contend with, to be honest, and so I decided not to get too worked up about that. What I felt most strongly was that the extra time I had been given could be put to great use in terms of bonding the team and getting them to gel even stronger. Plus, I could also spend more time looking at the Brabazon course at The Belfry and tailoring it even more to what I considered to be Europe's advantage. And I did well there.

Torrance summoned ten of his twelve players – only Parnevik and García were absent, playing in America – for a special get-together at The Belfry during the summer of 2002. The group, including vice captains, socialised and played, and it was an important exercise.

The four rookies in the European line-up were especially grateful for the chance to get themselves into Ryder Cup mode, mentally as much as anything given the extra stress they were feeling because they had all been forced to wait a further 12 months than is usual before hitting their first Ryder Cup shot.

Playing together as a group at The Belfry also enabled me to give both Pierre Fulke and Phillip Price a little kick in terms of trying to lift their games up to the level where I thought they needed to be. It worked well, and Fulke came up to me later and thanked me for doing it. We had other informal meetings too, during other tour events, and by the time late September 2002 came around we were so much stronger a team unit than we could have been the previous year.

The gathering at The Belfry had also enabled me to give an awful lot more thought to the set-up of the course. Because the Americans, on average, were much longer hitters than us, I decided to put in some extra bunkers to try to nullify that length advantage and also created a couple of little dog-legs. I narrowed the fairways more at the 290- to 320-yard mark and made sure the rough was a lot thicker at those distances from the tee. I wanted the greens to be a bit slower than we were used to, which would make them a lot slower than the ones the Americans normally played on, and I took out all the rough from around the greens so that our players could play the little chip and runs that we are brought up on and so the Americans could not get to play the floppy chips they all seem adept at and which certain players, like Phil Mickelson for instance, are absolute geniuses at. I also made sure that the tee on the iconic short par-four 10th was up at around 275 to 280 yards so that we would all go for it with three-wood or driver. I knew the Americans were less inclined to take that risk, believing, even in fourballs, that one of their pairings would make a three from laying up and then wedging in. We were looking for eagle twos!

Torrance made one other golfing and one other non-golfing decision during the lead-up to the 2002 match, which, he believes, helped him enormously in his job as an effective leader of the European team.

I decided that, no matter what, I wasn't going to concern myself with what the American players were doing. I didn't want to watch them in practice. I didn't want to know who was likely to play with whom on their side. I didn't want to watch them hit one single shot ahead of the match. To be frank, I didn't care less what they were up to or what they were thinking. I wanted to concentrate fully on making my own decisions and getting those decisions right. For instance, my job was to make sure I got my very best four teams out onto the course for the first round of matches on the Friday morning. After that, whoever they played was fine by me. There was simply no point in trying to second-guess what Curtis and the Americans were planning. I wanted to keep my mind clear and focused on what we were doing.

The other decision involved conquering his irrational fear of public speaking, and during 2001, in what he believed at the time to be the final months before his appearance as captain, Torrance had also set about that task with the obsessive attention to detail that was to characterise his leadership.

When I accepted the job as captain, the only thing I was worried about was the public-speaking side of it. It terrified me. Everything else about being captain I relished, but to stand up and speak in front of a live audience – plus millions watching on television, remember – was a thought that made me feel ill. I had sat as a player and watched the great captains I had played under, like Tony Jacklin, making their speeches at the opening and closing ceremonies – and at the other official functions during the week – and marvelled at how well they did them. I can remember, even then, thinking that this was something I would never be able to do myself. I wasn't a bad heckler, but I was no speaker. Nevertheless, it was not something I was going to turn down being Ryder Cup captain over, so I had to find a way to make myself do that side of the job properly, and in the end I learned a lesson that I wish I'd fully appreciated when I was 16: in short, if you work hard enough at something, you can do it.

The person who made it all possible for me was a chap called David Purdie, a gynaecologist who was a renowned after-dinner speaker and whom I heard for myself at the Sunningdale club's centenary dinner just after Christmas 2000. I asked him for his help, which he generously agreed to give, and we met up around half a dozen times in all over the next few months and put together all the speeches I had to make. Then I went home and practised them, using all the tips about when to pause and how to deliver them that David had given me, and I also had the actual lectern that would be used for the opening and closing ceremonies at The Belfry delivered to my home *so that I could practise those speeches as near to the reality of doing them on the day as I could. I desperately wanted to do those speeches well because I knew from personal experience how important they were for the team. I wanted to maximise how proud and inspired they would feel going into the match.*

The American team that Strange eventually brought to The Belfry was a powerful one, however. Tiger Woods, who had used the extra year to add both the Masters and the US Open titles to a growing collection of majors that now stood at eight, was unrivalled as the world's number-one golfer.

Mickelson, meanwhile, was ranked at number two and had finished as runner-up to Woods at that year's US Open as well as to David Toms in the 2001 US PGA. David Duval had won the 2001 Open at Royal Lytham, and there were, in total, seven major winners in that American line-up. The Europeans had only one, Langer.

Torrance, though, had by now engendered such a tight feeling in his own team that he and they feared no one. Again, he preferred to look at the strengths of his own players, although in the days leading up to the first matches he was also flexible enough in his thinking, despite all the rigorous preparations he had put in, to make the highly significant late changes that were to have a massive impact on the eventual result.

I'd arrived at The Belfry with all my pairings for all the foursomes and fourballs all written down, and that was a mistake. What I found, as the week went on, was that you get a gut instinct about things. My singles order, funnily enough, was not to change at all – remarkably, it was exactly what I had written down back in 2001 when I was contemplating the match being played then. But, in the team matches, most of it changed. There were some decisions that I was soon happy with – like splitting up Darren Clarke and Westwood, and putting Monty and Langer back together, as they were for one fourballs match at Kiawah and both foursomes at Valderrama. Yet that decision was only taken quite late during practice, because originally I had liked the look of Monty partnering Westwood.

I also planned to use Fulke and Price together in foursomes if I got the chance, but I was certainly not going to give all my four rookies a guaranteed run-out before the singles if I felt I had a better chance of winning the thing by playing others more. Also, Parnevik turned up saying he would not be offended if he did not play at all until the singles because his game was not where he wanted it. But he also pledged to work day and night to get it as right as he could, which is exactly what he did, and, in the end, I decided to give him an outing in the second fourballs session after all.

It was early in practice that Torrance decided, having split up the successful Clarke and Westwood pairing from Brookline, to partner Clarke with Thomas Bjørn. They were great friends, and both were intimidating players when in full sail. He also knew he could pair up Pádraig Harrington with anyone, and was fully expecting to play the Irishman in all four team rounds. It was another part of his pre-planning that proved, in reality, to be awry.

My decision on the Clarke and Westwood partnership was based on two things: first, that Lee was not that happy with his form and, second, that I didn't want to put too much expectation on them as a pairing. Yes, they'd done superbly at Brookline together, but I knew that because of that the Americans would probably be expecting them to go out there again and that the European supporters would be seeing them as guaranteed points. I felt I could get more out of them playing with different partners, and I knew that Clarke and Bjørn would love to play together. Their games were similar, and they would not be overawed by anyone or anything. I wanted them on the first tee together in the first match. They would relish that challenge.

As the week of practice and preparation went on, however, with certain other pairings being looked at out on the course by Torrance and his assistants, Torrance found that he was thinking ever more deeply about who was to partner García and Harrington. He now had the Montgomerie–Langer and Clarke–Bjørn pairings inked in, but which two other pairings would make up the eight with the responsibility of firing the first European shots in anger?

Niclas Fasth was playing well, and he is the sort of player who can come up with a lot of birdies, and so I started to lean towards him for the opening matches, which I had also decided would be fourballs rather than the traditional foursomes. Seve had done the same when he was captain in 1997, and for the same reasons as me. I felt that the European players were more relaxed playing the fourballs format, and, first up, I wanted to play to our own strengths. That's why I began and ended the team element of the 2002 match with fourballs and put the two foursomes sessions in the middle. As I said before, I wanted my eight strongest players in those first four matches, because I wanted, if at all possible, to get a fast start.

But Harrington got paired with Fasth in the end, because, right at the tail end of practice, I suddenly had a bit of a eureka moment about what to do with Westwood. I had told him I wanted him in the fourballs even though his game was not as he would have liked coming into the week. I told him not to worry about any poor shots and to be positive. He was a class player, and I told him class was permanent and form only temporary. And then, even though he hadn't really played with him in practice, it hit me like a lightning bolt that García would be ideal for Westwood, with his aggression and passion for the battle. To this day, I don't know where that thought came from, because that pairing had just not been in my mind at all. Goodness knows why I didn't see it before, but I'm glad I finally saw the sense in it. What a pairing they were that week! I had this sudden feeling that they would revel in each other's games, and that is what happened right from the off. It is amazing in Ryder Cups how a brand-new thought can hit you like that, and that particular late decision was probably the best I made all week. They won their first three matches, bouncing and feeding off each other, and they should have had a half in their fourth game too.

There was still the opening ceremony speech to get through, now that the decision about the four pairings for the opening matches had finally been made, but an exhaustively rehearsed Torrance sailed through it, showing to his twelve players the feeling of confidence and control as their captain that he sought to give them at that moment.

Later that Thursday evening, though, as he finally relaxed in his room watching and enjoying the television highlights of the opening ceremony, Torrance received a phone call from Bernhard Langer.

I couldn't believe it when Bernhard told me that he was worried about a problem with his neck. I was even more stunned when he admitted that he had first felt the soreness the previous day! If I had been in possession of that information I might have decided to leave him out of the opening fourballs. But now his name had gone in alongside Monty's, and they were due to tee off against Scott Hoch and Jim Furyk very early the following morning. So I decided I had to get to grips with the problem suddenly at hand and asked Bernhard what he needed. The answer was his physio, Dale Richardson, but the additional problem was that he was not staying in The Belfry hotel. After a fairly frantic round of phone calls, however, we did manage to track him down and to get him to our team room to give Bernhard the treatment he required. Ian Woosnam, my vice captain, was asleep by the time of this drama so I decided not to wake him and, with Mark James as my sounding board, decided that Pierre Fulke would step in to partner Monty if Bernhard did not feel better the next morning. Thankfully, Langer was fit, but it was yet another example of how in a Ryder Cup a captain has to be ready for anything . . . anything!

CHAPTER ELEVEN

2002 THE BELFRY

The 34th Ryder Cup could hardly have begun better for the captain of the European team. After the opening morning fourballs, Europe led 3–1, giving Torrance a vital early lead to show for his decisions regarding his four pairings and also for actually kicking off the match with the fourballs format for only the third time in the event's history.

In the lead-off match there was a tremendous one-hole win for Darren Clarke and Thomas Bjørn against Tiger Woods and Paul Azinger – despite nine birdies in total from the Americans – and, by the time that match was completed in front of huge crowds at The Belfry's famous 18th hole, there had also been European victories for Lee Westwood and Sergio García and the Colin Montgomerie–Bernhard Langer partnership – both by commanding 4&3 margins.

I was absolutely delighted to go 3–0 up initially and to see those first three pairings all playing as well together as I'd hoped and envisaged. It was especially thrilling for me, of course, to see Sergio and Lee hit it off so instantly. And it could so easily have been 4–0 or, at the very least, 3½ to a half. Pádraig Harrington and Niclas Fasth also played superbly but were eventually beaten by one hole by the excellent American partnership of Phil Mickelson and David Toms when Harrington saw a twenty-footer at the last horseshoe out.

I'd picked fourballs as the opening session because I wanted each of my chosen eight players to feel as relaxed as possible and to be able to get into their golf as soon as they could, which is far easier when you are playing your own ball and not alternate shots. I believed strongly that this format first up would suit my team better, and it worked. How you set up the match, in terms of how the first two days of competition are ordered, is very much part of the home captain's role in my view. It's his party! And you want to maximise your own side's advantage. That's why Paul Azinger went back to foursomes first in the 2008 match, simply because he knew by then that the Europeans would have rather had fourballs.

The success of his initial pairings, chemistry-wise as much as results-wise, also meant that Torrance soon knew that all he had to do for the afternoon foursomes was to wind up his three winning teams and send them out again, in exactly the same order.

Paul McGinley was brought in alongside his great friend and compatriot Harrington for the final foursomes match, in place of Fasth, while Curtis Strange reacted to being 3–1 down by immediately mixing up his own pairings.

Mickelson and Toms, his only morning winners, were sent out again – this time in the third match, against Montgomerie and Langer – but both Woods and Furyk were given fresh partners, and a completely new pairing, that of Hal Sutton and Scott Verplank, was brought in.

David Duval and Davis Love, who had lost to García and Westwood, were both rested, while Scott Hoch and Azinger were the other two players sidelined as Strange opted to give all twelve of his team a first day run-out.

And the American changes worked well, with only Tiger Woods and Mark Calcavecchia tasting defeat. That their conquerors were the buoyant partnership of García and Westwood only added to Torrance's sense of high satisfaction that he had followed his instincts and paired them up.

But Europe's captain was also left grateful for the half that a tiring Montgomerie and Langer got against Mickelson and Toms. They disappointingly lost three of the last four holes, but at least, with that half, Torrance was able to reach the end of a magnificent day's golf still with an overall one-point lead following the defeats suffered by Clarke and Bjørn, to the new Sutton–Verplank pairing, and by Harrington and McGinley, who went down 3&2 to Furyk and Stewart Cink.

I walked down from the practice putting green to the first tee with all my pairings on the first two days, and I did exactly the same thing in the singles on the Sunday. It was something I felt was important to do. The atmosphere was electric, but besides it being a thrill for me to accompany all my players through the crowds to that first tee, it also gave me the chance to say something appropriate to them and to check for myself that they were ready for the challenge ahead. And, in every case, I could see in their eyes that they were relaxed but exhilarated by the experience. It was all very different from the first time I made that walk, from the Walton Heath clubhouse to the first tee in 1981 alongside my partner Howard Clark, but it was still unique. As captain in 2002, I made that special walk 28 times from the putting green in front of The Belfry's hotel to the first tee. It was fantastic, and it made me realise even more strongly – if I didn't already know it – that the Ryder Cup gave you goosebumps all over.

There was some hard thinking to do for Torrance towards the end of the first day of competition. Clarke and Bjørn, despite being two up with six holes to play, had lost their foursomes match against Sutton and Verplank, while the fancied Harrington–McGinley foursomes partnership had also struggled on the inward half.

Also, despite the bonus of the García–Westwood partnership winning both their matches, the pairing of Montgomerie and the veteran Langer looked as if it had found the strain of playing twice in the day a tough task.

The second morning's pairings have to be submitted to the match referee soon after the end of play on the first day, and so some decisions had to be made ahead of the second set of foursomes. Again, I had deliberately chosen to end the team element of the match with fourballs, because I wanted my players to be as relaxed as possible – playing their own ball – going into the singles. I had already earmarked Fulke and Price to make their debuts together in the Saturday-morning foursomes, and to lead us off, and so I saw no reason to change my mind on that, especially as both players had spent much of Friday working towards getting their games ready for that challenge. But, looking at the results of the opening day, the conclusion that I quickly came to was that

Pádraig Harrington would have to be stood down from the third round of matches, even though at the start of the week I had fully intended to play him in all four team sessions.

But that is yet another example of how flexible you need to be as a Ryder Cup captain. You have to be ready to react to what you see in front of your eyes, and the evidence was that Pádraig was not playing to his full capability. He needed some time to work on a few things on the range, with my father, and so I decided to give both Pádraig and his coach the following morning off to do just that. I also knew that Bernhard Langer would only be playing in three of the four team rounds, and so it made sense to keep him going into the second foursomes and then rest him for the Saturday-afternoon fourballs. Jesper Parnevik, too, if I wanted to play him before the singles, would only be considered for the fourballs format. So, in the end, and with an all-new rookie partnership included in my line-up, it was once more a fairly straightforward decision to continue to trust in my three other experienced teams. I kept García and Westwood at two in the order, and Monty and Langer at three, and switched Clarke and Bjørn into the anchor match.

What Torrance was also pleased about, as Harrington opted for a quick session on the driving range in semi-darkness while his teammates relaxed and swapped banter in the team room, was that all his players still seemed tight as a group and confident about their prospects.

He also knew that there was likely to be a backlash from Tiger Woods, who had lost both his matches on that opening day to add yet more misery to the struggles he had experienced in his first two Ryder Cup appearances, in 1997 and 1999. Indeed, after that Friday at The Belfry, Woods's personal record stood at P12 W3 L8 H1.

The world number one would, in fact, remain unbeaten for the rest of the match, but, despite the Woods factor, Torrance announced on the Friday evening that he was seeking an improved lead the next day to take into the singles.

I felt really relaxed. I was careful to say that I did not think we needed to be more ahead in order to go on and win the Cup on the Sunday, but I did feel that any sort of lead would be invaluable. I was very aware of how powerful a team the United States were, and there was still a feeling that they had probably the stronger depth. But I was happy enough with where I was on that Friday night, even though we had looked at one stage during the afternoon foursomes as if it could have been as much as a 6–2 lead for us at the end of the day.

Torrance's mood of cautious optimism remained throughout the first half of the second day, with a 2–2 result in the foursomes maintaining the European one-point advantage.

Fulke and Price had drawn the top-performing American pair of Mickelson and Toms and lost 2&1 after a valiant battle, but there were further wins for García and Westwood, against Cink and Furyk, and for Montgomerie and Langer, who beat Verplank and Hoch by one hole.

Clarke and Bjørn, however, were well beaten 4&3 by a resurgent Woods and his new partner, the highly experienced Davis Love. It was time for another tough decision from the European captain.

As the morning went on, I became convinced that the afternoon fourballs was the right time to get Parnevik into the action. Although he had made it clear, like the brilliant team man that he is, that he would have gladly sat it out until the singles, he had worked furiously on his game and I felt he was getting back to the sort of form where a run-out before the final day would do him, and the team, a lot of good. Niclas Fasth also deserved another fourballs outing, and so putting those two Swedes together and sending them off first in the afternoon – as a fresh pair, eager for the fray – seemed a solid decision. I also had García and Westwood to go out there for a fourth time.

The main problem with regard to the rest of my afternoon line-up was Thomas Bjørn. It was becoming obvious, as he and Clarke struggled against Woods and Love, that Thomas was getting more and more frustrated with his golf. And so again I made an instinctive call. Bjørn was originally going to play in all four team sessions, but I decided to pull him out of the afternoon competition and give McGinley a first fourballs match alongside Clarke. That left Harrington, who I knew would be coming back in after his morning off, to partner Monty while Langer rested up. I particularly liked the look of the Monty–Harrington pairing. When I informed Monty of this, as he was playing the 15th, he said he'd like to play with McGinley. My reply was short and to the point: 'No, you can't. You're playing with Harrington. He's perfect for you. Go out there and win.' My view is that, whomever it involves, the captain makes the final decision. If you feel strongly about putting certain players together, you have the final say.

It was during the Saturday morning foursomes, however, that Torrance felt he had made the one big mistake of his captaincy. Price and Fulke had slipped from one up after ten to two down with two holes to play when Torrance, following them up the long 17th, failed to step in when he should have offered the rookie pair the correct advice.

Phillip was going with a five wood from a fairway bunker in an effort to get over the burn that runs across the fairway about a hundred and sixty yards or so short of the green. But the Americans had driven in the longish rough themselves, and there was no way they could have got their ball up near the green in two either. So I knew the right play for us was to play up short of the burn and then gamble on getting up and down from there with a good third shot in to the green. Price and Fulke knew they had to make a four somehow, because they could not depend on the Americans making more than the par five. But it was the wrong call to try to force things at that point, and I should have been stronger and stepped in – I was right there. Instead, I let Price hit his shot, which he nailed pretty well considering its difficulty, and then watched as it failed to carry the burn.

Much now depended, though, on the outcome of the afternoon fourballs, and there was a tense time in store for both captains, plus the thousands watching the live action in front of them and the millions more glued to television screens on both sides of the Atlantic.

Fasth and Parnevik were doing well early on and played excellent golf throughout their match to justify Torrance's faith in them. But Duval and Calcavecchia, their opponents, then shot seven birdies between them on the back nine to nick the match by one hole on the 18th.

Montgomerie and Harrington, however, playing as brilliantly together as their captain had anticipated, beat Mickelson and Toms

2&1 – the American partnership's only defeat in four matches – and with García and Westwood one up playing the 17th, and Clarke and McGinley all square with Hoch and Furyk in the final game, it looked odds-on that Torrance would secure the overall lead he desired at the end of day two.

It was a travesty of justice that Sergio and Lee lost their match against Woods and Love, and heartbreaking at the time. Sergio was the only player of the four to reach the par-five 17th in two, and it looked as if the American pair would have to find a birdie simply to take the match down the last. But, with Woods just three feet away in three, Love chipped in for the four and then Sergio three-putted. With Lee also not getting a four, it meant that suddenly the match was all square with everything to play for. And worse was to come when both Sergio and Lee three-putted the 18th green for bogey fives, with Lee missing his par putt from four feet. That gifted the Americans a win with their par four, and in fourballs it is an absolute no-no to lose any hole to a par. It was gut-wrenching, and García was extremely upset. It was also upsetting for all the European support, because they had seen just how magnificently those two had played right through the first two days. They deserved to keep their unbeaten record and get at least a half out of their final fourballs match, but it was not to be.

The American point had swung the whole momentum of the match away from Europe, especially as in the last game out on the course it had been Furyk and Hoch who had won the 17th to go one up. Crisis time, indeed.

That lost Westwood-and-García point, or half-point, was the first time in the whole first two days that something really important had slipped away from us. The huge success of their partnership had been central to our overall performance and meant that I never even considered going back to the Parnevik–García pairing that had been so successful at Brookline. That fall-back option had just not been needed. But their loss to Woods and Love hit us hard, and now we needed Clarke and McGinley to win the 18th and squeeze a half out of their match.

And that was when Bernhard Langer's great experience and capability to think well under pressure came to the fore. It was when he showed just what a great captain he would also become in the Ryder Cup. After all the players had driven at the last, and with all eyes now fixed on what was going to happen in this last game of the day, Bernhard came up to me and suggested that I tell McGinley to play his second shot first from the fairway, even though Clarke was technically the furthest from the hole. Indeed, according to the rules of fourball play, and as Clarke was further away than both Americans, Europe had the option of using McGinley to hit his second shot first instead. If he went first, and hit it close, the pressure would be piled right up on the two Americans. It was absolutely the right call, and, unlike earlier in the day with the Price shot, I had a word with the two players when they walked up to their drives. And McGinley hit a wonderful shot in with a four iron.

Then, as I walked up to the green, McGinley asked me to find Harrington and ask him if the putt he had left was the same one they had talked about in practice. Harrington, who was watching from back down the fairway, told me it was, and I relayed this nugget of information to his fellow Irishman. Apparently, the putt swung more than it looked as if it would and was also faster. McGinley hit it stone dead, Hoch missed his 12-footer for par and we had scrambled a half out of this crucial game. It was now 8–8 going into the singles.

Little did he know it at that time, amid the tension around the great natural arena of the 18th green, but Torrance was just about to produce the masterstroke of his whole captaincy.

There is no way to overstate the impact that the revelation of the singles draw made on both teams, and on the watching golfing world, that Saturday evening. And it would not be unfair to record that it was greeted with absolute glee in the European team room.

In short, Torrance had front-loaded his singles order to the extent that, from one to twelve, it could be argued that he had simply decided to send them out according to their Ryder Cup stature and current playing ability, from Colin Montgomerie and Sergio García in the first and second spots to the out-of-form Jesper Parnevik in the anchor role.

American captain Strange, by contrast, had decided to leave his greatest experience and strength – Azinger, Furyk, Love, Mickelson and Woods – until the final five places in his line-up. The contrast in thinking between the two captains was shocking in its starkness, and it left many observers – and unsurprisingly most of them American – totally stunned.

At 8–8, the destiny of the Ryder Cup was balanced on a knife-edge. But, as the singles draw and the subsequent match-ups were digested and analysed, it soon became clear that the momentum of the contest, which had already twisted this way and that in the dramatic last hour of the afternoon fourballs, had been shifted forcibly towards Europe by the straightforward brilliance of Torrance's order.

I think that Curtis was trying to second-guess me a bit with his decision to put Mickelson and Woods right at the end of his line-up. That was something I never did all week. I wasn't concerned about what the Americans were thinking. I was just trying to give my own team their best chance of expressing themselves. And, at 8–8, I felt we had to attempt to seize the initiative on the final day. I had also given my singles strategy a huge amount of thought in the previous 18 months. My singles order would have been exactly the same – and I mean exactly – if the match had been played in 2001. But that is not such an extraordinary fact when you consider how my thinking had gone. At the same Sunningdale Golf Club dinner at which I had met David Purdie, I was sat next to a fellow club member called David Holland, and he had told me that night that, to him, a Ryder Cup captain could do worse than simply send out his singles players in an order dictated by best first and worst last.

Now, I wouldn't rank any Ryder Cup player 'best' or 'worst' – at that level they are all magnificent players – but I knew what he was saying and it did stick with me throughout 2001 and then into 2002 when the original match was postponed. And, the more I thought about it, I couldn't come up with any situation on a Saturday night when that method of selecting your line-up would not work. If you were four points down then obviously you wanted your strength up top in the singles, and if you were four points up then there was also much to commend a strategy in which you tried to wrap everything up early by again putting your leading players out in front. If you were tied . . .

well, you wanted to seize the initiative. That was my thinking. Of course, if every Ryder Cup captain started to do what I did as an automatic action then the opposition would soon know what you were doing and could plan their strategy accordingly. Indeed, if I'd known in advance what Curtis's line-up was, then perhaps I would have changed my own a hair, but, on that Saturday evening, the roar that greeted the announcement of the singles matches told me everything.

Torrance had not told his players in advance about where they would be placed in his order. He had merely informed them that he had 'a plan' and had asked each in turn if they had any preferences about where they were played. When they all replied that they didn't mind, he had the final all-clear to implement his long-held idea.

In running order, the singles draw was Montgomerie v Hoch, García v Toms, Clarke v Duval, Langer v Sutton, Harrington v Calcavecchia, Bjørn v Cink, Westwood v Verplank, Fasth v Azinger, McGinley v Furyk, Fulke v Love, Price v Mickelson, Parnevik v Woods.

Asked in the Saturday-evening press conference about what might happen on the tumultuous final day, Torrance replied that he was still very confident. 'They've got one Tiger, but we've got twelve lions,' he said, displaying another skill of Ryder Cup captaincy in the modern era: that of the perfect soundbite.

Another part of my thinking was my belief that, in the heat of a Ryder Cup, and in the cauldron of a last day when everything is on the line, it doesn't really matter who you have in your final four singles places. I don't care if it is Woods or Nicklaus or Ballesteros at his peak, or Faldo. In those last matches, with the pressure on, anything can happen, and in Ryder Cups it often has. I myself have played in many different places in the singles order, and so I know something about how it feels to be in the mixer in those different areas of the order. And, to me, the bottom line in 2002 was that I had no fear about exposing any of my so-called lesser players to what they might face in the bottom part of the draw. I have a phrase for it: out of the shadows can come heroes. In 2002, they certainly did.

Strange, meanwhile, underwent a distinctly uncomfortable press conference following the announcement of the singles draw, with many inquisitors suggesting to him that the whole contest could be effectively over before his biggest guns, Mickelson and Woods, came into the picture.

Clearly rattled, he admitted that it could indeed be the case. Strange, however, insisted that his team were still confident, although the next day, when they were on the putting green still waiting for their matches to begin – and with Montgomerie's match already all but won and with European leads elsewhere filling up most of the scoreboard – the body language of both Woods and Mickelson suggested the exact opposite.

There have been so few Cups when the whole thing has come down to the last match or last two matches. In 1991, obviously, and in 1969, but it is a rare occurrence even in the recent history of the event, when so many matches have been so close. Therefore, even starting out the last day at 8–8, it was remarkable for us to see both Mickelson and Woods down at numbers 11 and 12. They were ranked one and two in the world, and I would have wanted them both to have a big impact on how the last day went. Perhaps you would put them in at numbers four and five in your order, or perhaps you would split them and place them at, say, four and seven. But I would want them somewhere having an influence!

Montgomerie, Torrance's leader on the course in the same way that Ballesteros had been the talisman for Tony Jacklin's teams, relished the opportunity he had been given at the head of the European field. He won the opening hole against Hoch with a majestic birdie three, and soon there was a sea of blue on the giant scoreboards dotted around the Brabazon course as Europe's leading players threw everything at their American opponents.

Monty's opening tee shot, a three wood that flew well over three hundred yards down the middle of the first fairway, was one of the great moments of that Ryder Cup. The atmosphere around the first tee and down that hole was utterly incredible, and Colin was revelling in it. He is big enough as a character and as a player to take all that pressure and thrive on it. Hoch was actually closer to the hole than Monty after they had both played two shots, but then Monty holed a wonderful putt for birdie and the roar that greeted that was enormous. We were on our way. At one stage, as I surveyed the scoreboard, we were up in every single one of the first eight matches.

As captain, the whole experience was exhilarating, and all I concentrated on for the first couple of hours was being with each one of my players as they walked to the first tee. I chatted to them on the putting green and then went down through the crowds with them. I also tried to make sure the European players were on the tee after the Americans, so that they knew that the last roar that rang in their ears was for them. And, of course, so that the American knew that it was not a roar for him! I also said the same to every European player: that it was the greatest day of their lives, that they would remember it forever and that they should enjoy it and embrace it.

Langer and Harrington, in particular, were soon in commanding positions in their singles matches, against Sutton and Calcavecchia respectively, and Montgomerie was four up at the turn.

Torrance, who had just seen Fulke off against Love in the tenth singles game, then decided – with Europe in such ascendancy – to permit himself a piece of psychological fun at the expense of Hoch, who had not endeared himself to the European team hierarchy with a remark he had made about the short par-four 10th hole at the start of the week.

He is a tricky customer to say the least, but he had also said to me during the practice rounds that the 10th hole, set up as a classic risk-and-reward matchplay hole for the event, was 'a great hole for your stats'. What he meant was that, with a seven or eight iron off the tee to a generous fairway and then a wedge in over the water for your second shot – that is, if you passed up the opportunity to go for the green off the tee with your driver or three wood – it was an easy fairways-and-greens-in-regulation hole. It was a heavily sarcastic remark, revealing that most of the Americans didn't like the hole and were not prepared to take on the tough tee shot, which also had to be faded in through a narrow gap in the trees surrounding the green to make the putting surface safely. All week, it had been the Europeans taking it on, and now we were winning the event.

I wanted, now, to look Hoch in the eye, and I wanted him to see me and to know why I was looking at him. So I sprinted over to the 10th tee, from the putting green, and leapt a barrier as Monty was striding up from the 9th green with Hoch walking up after him. I didn't say anything. I just made sure Hoch saw me. And then I ran back to the putting green, just in time to accompany Phillip Price down to the tee for the start of his match against Mickelson. There was also a wonderful comment from Parnevik, who was on the putting green alongside Woods waiting for their anchor singles to start. 'Nice leaderboard, Tiger!' said Jesper, in a reference to a scoreboard that, by that stage, showed Europe up in virtually all the matches out on the course. 'Let's just see if it comes down to our match,' was Tiger's reply.

Montgomerie was soon to overwhelm Hoch 5&4, achieving his and Torrance's aim to get an early European singles point up on the board, and although García was beaten by a resilient Toms on the final green, there was also good news for Europe in every other match in the top six.

Clarke halved with Duval, who holed a superb 15-footer on the last, before Langer, Harrington and Bjørn all posted emphatic victories. Europe now had 12½ points, America 9½. Two points from the last six matches was all that it would take for the Ryder Cup to be back in European hands. But that became 2 points from the last five matches when Westwood was beaten 2&1 by the steady Verplank, who had impressed all week.

I had spent at least two hours, once the last match had gone off, sitting at the back of the 9th green, where I could watch most of the field coming through and also keep an eye on what was happening elsewhere on the big screen. My son Daniel was with me, and we had a great time just sitting there and watching everything develop. I was always confident that we would win. By the time the bottom half of the singles order was starting to come in, I was out on the course, and I joined the Fasth–Azinger match as it came up the 17th behind Lee Westwood's match, which had finished on the penultimate hole. Niclas was one up and hit an enormous drive, but his second shot was blocked by a tree. He chipped out but still only needed a six iron to reach the par-five's green. I watched as Fasth tried for the 12-foot birdie putt that would have won the hole and also given him a 2&1 win. But it slipped past, and Azinger then sank an eight-footer to match Niclas's par and take their match down the 18th.

By now, Price was two up with three to play against Mickelson, having played superbly and, at the sixth hole, hit one of the greatest shots in Ryder Cup history – which is some statement – to get inside Phil's ball, which was already close to the flag, from a hanging lie and with one foot in a hazard. And Price then ended up winning that hole when Mickelson missed his putt and the Welshman holed his. Instead of being four down there, he was only two down and on the way back towards an eventual victory to enter Ryder Cup legend. And so, with Price looking like he could close out his match on the 16th, I decided to follow Fasth up the last. If he also won his match, that would be the Cup.

Niclas hit the most wonderful drive down that difficult hole, and it filled me with pride – on his behalf – to see how well he was handling such a situation. Then, as I was walking onto the fairway, there was a massive roar from the direction of the 16th green. The radio in my ear told me that Price had holed brilliantly for birdie. Moments later, another roar and sustained cheering: Mickelson's birdie attempt had failed, and Price had won 3&2. Filling up with emotion, and desperate for Suzanne to make it through the milling crowds to get to me, I then saw Azinger hit his long approach to the 18th into a greenside bunker. Fasth, wonderfully composed, struck his second shot onto the putting surface – and onto the correct, second, tier, where the flag was located. This was it. I blurted out that we had won, but Thomas Bjørn, suddenly appearing beside me, immediately chastised me. And, of course, it never pays to get ahead of yourself in the Ryder Cup.

What followed was another of the remarkable, barely believable moments that have become the special preserve of the Ryder Cup, and particularly over the past three decades.

Azinger, summoning up his last reserves of skill and sheer defiance, holed his bunker shot with a stroke that was both miraculous and stunning in its execution under the most intense of pressure. Fasth was shattered. Now he had to hole his tricky downhill putt to match Azinger's three and thus gain the full point that would clinch the Cup.

Torrance himself could hardly look. The massed ranks of spectators, many craning for a view of this astonishing drama, fell silent as Fasth hit his putt. It did not drop. The courageous Swede had played his heart out, and he had secured a precious half. At worst, Europe would now tie the match, as they had 14 points on the board. But, to regain the Cup, another half was needed.

On the fairway behind us, waiting for the green to clear, was the slight figure of Paul McGinley. He and Furyk were all square. If he could halve this hole, at the very least, then the celebrations could begin. But it was so tense. It became tenser when Furyk hit his second into the same bunker as Azinger had just been in and McGinley pulled his second a bit wider and the ball settled in the semi-rough to the left of the sand. As Paul came over the little bridge to begin his walk up to the green, I went to meet him and said, 'If you don't want to do it for yourself, or for your country, then do it for me.' Paul later said he thought it was a funny thing for me to say. I just wanted him to do it – I didn't care how!

I think by now it was all becoming almost too much to bear. But Paul played his difficult little pitch with great nerve and was a bit unlucky that the ball didn't release further towards the hole. It was ten feet short. Furyk then nearly gave every European supporter a heart attack by all but holing his splash-out from Azinger's bunker. It was another truly unbelievable shot, but thankfully for us it didn't go in this time. And then McGinley, who remembered he had faced a very similar putt on the same green in one of the Benson & Hedges International Opens that had been staged at The Belfry, rolled in his putt for the four, for the half and for the Cup. 'McGinty,' I call him. I will love him for ever.

The noise that greeted McGinley's winning putt was extraordinary. It was pent-up emotion and tension released, as much as celebration. McGinley himself, seeing his teammates by the side of the green jumping up and down for joy, simply jumped up and down on the spot himself. He later said it felt like he was a bottle of champagne and that he was jumping up and down in an effort to let all the bubbles out. *Willie Aitchison, my caddie when I turned pro all those years before, in 1970,* grabbed me first. Then it was Lee Westwood. I was momentarily paralysed, as if I still couldn't quite believe what I had seen, and I remember that I couldn't seem to move as everything and everyone erupted around me. Then Suzanne and I were able to have a hug, and then the celebrations began. McGinley clearly didn't know what he was doing either and isn't it wonderful how, in moments like that, people react in such an unplanned, crazily natural way? I'd had my own moment of holing the putt that won the Ryder Cup, of course, on that very green 17 years before, and my own reaction then had been something similarly unique to the occasion. Now it was Paul's turn to take the acclaim, and, after all the other matches had finished – with Pierre Fulke and Jesper Parnevik also coming in with well-deserved halves – McGinley found himself in the lake beside that wonderful 18th green, soaked from head to foot and with an Irish flag wrapped around him.

What a setting it is there, what a great finishing hole. Does anywhere else come close to it? The 18th at Pebble Beach, perhaps, or the last at Loch Lomond? But above and beyond all else, what a result – and on the most beautiful and glorious of autumn days too. It is my greatest moment in golf and will never be bettered. I was just so pleased for the players, for my backroom staff, for my family, for the European Tour and our supporters. For everyone. And I still haven't watched a video of it. We've got loads of photographs, of course, and one day I will probably put the video on. But, then again, I don't really need to. Everything that matters, and all the memories, are there inside my head. They will be there for ever.

2002 Ryder Cup Results: 27–29 September, The Belfry
Captains: Sam Torrance (Europe), Curtis Strange (US)

Europe		US	
Morning fourballs			
Darren Clarke/Thomas Bjørn (1 hole)	1	Tiger Woods/Paul Azinger	
Sergio García/Lee Westwood (4&3)	1	David Duval/Davis Love III	
Colin Montgomerie/Bernhard Langer (4&3)	1	Scott Hoch/Jim Furyk	
Pádraig Harrington/Niclas Fasth		Phil Michelson/David Toms (1 hole)	1
Afternoon foursomes			
Darren Clarke/Thomas Bjørn		Hal Sutton/Scott Verplank (2&1)	1
Sergio García/Lee Westwood (2&1)	1	Tiger Woods/Mark Calcavecchia	
Colin Montgomerie/Bernhard Langer (halved)	½	Phil Mickelson/David Toms (halved)	½
Pádraig Harrington/Paul McGinley		Stewart Cink/Jim Furyk (3&2)	1
Morning foursomes			
Pierre Fulke/Phillip Price		Phil Mickelson/David Toms (2&1)	1
Lee Westwood/Sergio García (2&1)	1	Stewart Cink/Jim Furyk	
Colin Montgomerie/Bernhard Langer (1 hole)	1	Scott Verplank/Scott Hoch	
Darren Clarke/Thomas Bjørn		Tiger Woods/Davis Love III (4&3)	1
Afternoon fourballs			
Niclas Fasth/Jesper Parnevik		Mark Calcavecchia/David Duval (1 hole)	1
Colin Montgomerie/Pádraig Harrington (2&1)	1	Phil Mickelson/David Toms	
Sergio García/Lee Westwood		Tiger Woods/Davis Love III (1 hole)	1
Darren Clarke/Paul McGinley (halved)	½	Scott Hoch/Jim Furyk (halved)	½
Singles			
Colin Montgomerie (5&4)	1	Scott Hoch	
Sergio García		David Toms (1 hole)	1
Darren Clarke (halved)	½	David Duval (halved)	½
Bernhard Langer (4&3)	1	Hal Sutton	
Pádraig Harrington (5&4)	1	Mark Calcavecchia	
Thomas Bjørn (2&1)	1	Stewart Cink	
Lee Westwood		Scott Verplank (2&1)	1
Niclas Fasth (halved)	½	Paul Azinger (halved)	½
Paul McGinley (halved)	½	Jim Furyk (halved)	½
Pierre Fulke (halved)	½	Davis Love III (halved)	½
Phillip Price (3&2)	1	Phil Mickelson	
Jesper Parnevik (halved)	½	Tiger Woods (halved)	½
Europe	**15½**	**US**	**12½**

SAM'S ANALYSIS: 2002

Europe

Colin Montgomerie Truly outstanding, with 4½ points out of 5 in a wonderful unbeaten performance across the three days. Led the singles charge majestically. My belief in Colin as a leader out on the course was fully justified.

Sergio García The most exciting thing to hit European golf since Seve Ballesteros also had a fine match, winning his first three matches in the company of Westwood. After 2006, his fourth Ryder Cup, Sergio's overall record was fourteen wins and two halves from his twenty matches up to that point: remarkable. He may have then suffered two halves and two defeats in the 2008 match at Valhalla, but this boy could well go on to claim the most prolific Ryder Cup record of all, from both sides.

Darren Clarke What a great chip on the 18th, and what a solid contribution. Big Darren's opening fourballs win with Thomas Bjørn was one of the biggest points of the week, and his two halves, in foursomes and singles, were both vital moments too. One of four Europeans to play in all five matches.

Bernhard Langer What a way to go out as a Ryder Cup player. His overall record, with twenty-one wins and six halves from the forty-two matches he played in his ten Cup appearances, puts him up with the elite performers. Here it was 2½ points from 3 alongside Monty and then a superb singles victory to cap it all off. And he still had his 2004 captaincy to look forward to – and a stunning victory at Oakland Hills.

Pádraig Harrington Came back strongly after two defeats on the opening day, and I was delighted that all his hard work came to fruition with a final fourballs win alongside Monty and then a crushing singles victory. Eh!

Thomas Bjørn	A great singles win over Stewart Cink was the highlight of his superb overall contribution both on and off the course. When it was asked for, he gave. And his opening fourballs win alongside Clarke, against Woods and Azinger, wasn't too bad either.
Lee Westwood	Everything about his performance during five draining matches told me that I was right to say to him at the start of the week that form is current, class is for ever. Gave everything when not at the top of his game to gain 3 crucial points alongside García and reaped the ultimate reward.
Niclas Fasth	He played magnificently throughout all his three matches and was desperately unfortunate to emerge with only a half to show for it. Lost both his fourballs on the final green and then saw Azinger hole his amazing bunker shot just when he was contemplating a singles victory to clinch the Cup itself. The man we call 'Robocop' was a rookie who performed like a seasoned veteran, and I was delighted to have him on my team.
Paul McGinley	The man who holed the putt that won the Ryder Cup also showed a lot of character, as well as golfing ability, after losing his opening foursomes match alongside his great friend Harrington. Vital fourballs half with Clarke on the second evening, and then that final putt and the winning half it secured. Thank you, McGinty.
Pierre Fulke	Another rookie who performed superbly, and I was delighted he and Davis Love agreed their half on the 18th fairway. He deserved that after narrowly missing out in his other outing, a foursomes with Phillip Price.
Phillip Price	'Tell 'em who I beat – go on, tell 'em who I beat!' The answer, of course, to the question that the Welshman kept asking all and sundry in the magnificent Sunday-night celebrations that followed our victory is Phil Mickelson. He was three down after five holes and still won 3&2. Astounding.

Jesper Parnevik	Came to The Belfry with no form at all but worked so hard to get something going. In the end he emerged with huge credit for his brave fourballs performance on the Saturday afternoon and for a spirited display to earn an agreed singles half with Tiger Woods when the match was all over. Proved to be a great captain's pick.
Sam Torrance (captain)	I was just so privileged to be the captain of such a committed and highly talented European team. I loved every single minute of it and felt such pride at the end. Overall, I just tried to do what Tony Jacklin did when he was Ryder Cup captain, which was to do everything I could to make the players feel special and to help them to perform to the very best of their ability.

United States

Scott Hoch	In his second Ryder Cup he was played in four matches by Curtis Strange but managed just half a point, from the second set of fourballs. Blown away by Monty in the singles. Good hole, the 10th, don't you think, Scott?
David Toms	You had to pinch yourself to remember that this was Toms's Ryder Cup debut. The 2001 US PGA champion played magnificently throughout his five matches, earning 2½ points in his excellent partnership with Mickelson and then collecting the prized scalp of García in the singles. America's best player in this match.
David Duval	Emerged with credit with his fourballs win on Saturday and a gutsy half in his singles against Darren Clarke. Also impressed off the course; he was the last American at our Sunday-night – and Monday-morning – celebrations and showed just what a classy individual he is.

Hal Sutton	Remarkably, he won his opening foursomes alongside Scott Verplank but then did not appear again in the second set of foursomes on the Saturday morning. Was well beaten by Langer in the singles, which in itself was an eerie forerunner of how they were to fare as opposing captains two years later at Oakland Hills. A much better bloke than he looks!
Mark Calcavecchia	A fun-loving character who was another of the Americans to greet defeat with grace, he lost an opening foursomes alongside Woods but then partnered David Duval to victory in the following day's fourballs. Swept aside by Harrington, however, in the singles.
Stewart Cink	The man who was to go on to become Open champion in 2009 won once in two foursomes outings alongside Jim Furyk but was then beaten by Thomas Bjørn in the singles. A quiet Ryder Cup debut.
Scott Verplank	Impressive on the course, especially with his singles win against Westwood, and probably should have played at least once more than his two foursomes outings on the first two days. He was also a perfect gentleman off the course, and was immediately well liked by the Europeans.
Paul Azinger	No one will ever forget his very last shot as a Ryder Cup player, let alone poor Niclas Fasth. But apart from that remarkable bunker shot and the typically gutsy singles half that it won him, there was little else from 'Zinger', as his only other outing was a defeat alongside Woods in the opening fourballs match. I loved his manic high-fiving with his caddie after that sand shot, though!
Jim Furyk	What might have happened if Jim's brilliant bunker shot at the 18th, ten minutes or so after Azinger had holed his, had also gone in? I don't want to think about it too much. Two points in all in this match from one of the toughest Americans.
Davis Love III	Partnered Tiger Woods to two wins on the second day and then added a singles half when he and Fulke agreed to share their point once the overall result was known. A fine gentleman of golf.

Phil Mickelson	Who was it that Price beat? It was a sad end to a fine Ryder Cup for Mickelson, who had won 2½ points out of a possible 4 alongside David Toms during the first two days but clearly could not then comprehend what he was doing playing in the eleventh singles match.
Tiger Woods	Like world number two Mickelson, the best golfer on the planet was plainly perplexed by the decision to send him out last in the singles. A bad opening day was avenged in some style on day two, alongside his new partner Love, and he agreed a half with Parnevik as the victory celebrations started up ahead at the 18th. Didn't need to set his alarm on that Sunday morning!
Curtis Strange (captain)	I could not have wished for a finer opposite number. Curtis and I had known each other since the early 1970s, and we had always liked each other and got on as people. He and I were determined to get the Ryder Cup back on track as a sporting contest of the highest quality following the brouhaha at Brookline, and he more than played his part in that. His choice of singles order caused huge comment, but it might have worked for him on another day, and I also admired the dignified and gracious way he dealt with the pain of defeat. A tough competitor and a classy man.

Afterword

Ryder Cup in the Blood

Only minutes after the 2002 Ryder Cup was won, a Spanish golf writer pushed through the scrum of people milling around the 18th green at The Belfry and handed me a mobile. It was Seve Ballesteros on the end of the phone. He had rung through to his Spanish journalist friend asking if he could speak with me to offer his congratulations.

It was a wonderful moment for me, with my team beginning to celebrate all around that iconic green, to be able to speak briefly with Seve, the man who for so long had been the heart and soul of the European team in the event's modern era.

The previous eleven chapters, mixing my recollections and thoughts with Mark Baldwin's narrative, have chronicled my eight Ryder Cups as a player – in which all but my first, in 1981, featured Seve as the most inspirational of teammates – plus my experiences as a vice captain, at Brookline in 1999, and then as the proudest of captains in 2002. In them, I have tried not just to recount some of my memories of those times but also to analyse the tactical and practical approaches of all ten Ryder Cup teams I was involved in.

You will have read already how much we were all in awe of Seve's ability and sheer force of personality – including the other truly great players, like Nick Faldo, Bernhard Langer and Ian Woosnam, who also formed the basis of so many great Ryder Cup performances by Europe in the 1980s and 1990s.

Seve had also led Europe to triumph at Valderrama, five years before we had won back the trophy lost in such controversial circumstances at

Brookline, and now he just wanted to tell me, 'Fantastic. You did a great job. Fantastic.' He had also sent the whole team a pre-match message saying he would be watching every shot on television at his home in Pedrena and that he believed we could beat the Americans.

Just speaking with him at that moment was another privilege I felt as a winning European Ryder Cup captain. I also could not help myself as I held up the mobile to the cheering spectators nearest to me. 'Look,' I shouted above the din, pointing to the mobile in my hand, 'It's Seve . . . Seve!'

Soon, it was time for me to leave all the players, the caddies and the rest of my backroom staff as they posed for yet more photographs and did more interviews on and around a green that had seen such drama in the previous hour.

Our eventual 3-point victory may have looked comfortable for much of the final day, as Colin Montgomerie gave us a lead in the singles that we never looked like surrendering, but it had got more than a little tense before Paul McGinley rolled in the ten-foot putt across that 18th green that meant that the Ryder Cup was Europe's again.

With my wife, Suzanne, who had done so much herself to help in the preparation of that European team and who had also supported me so brilliantly all week, I walked back up to The Belfry hotel through huge crowds of our celebrating supporters. It was an amazing experience for us both to share, and the tears that had flowed again for me after McGinley had sunk his winning putt began to well up once more.

Back in the sanctity of our hotel room, I headed for the shower. I wanted to freshen up and change for the closing ceremony, which would demand another speech from me, but I also wanted just a little bit of time to myself. I felt so emotional, and, as I stood under the shower, I cried uncontrollably at the sheer happiness of it all.

I have always been someone who shows emotion, and I have probably shed more tears at the 18th green at The Belfry – and in the Ryder Cup generally – than any other player! But passion is a big part of the Ryder Cup, and I suppose that is just another reason why it has played such a massive part in my professional career. The Ryder Cup is, simply, in my blood.

Even when we had won the 2002 Cup, I still knew it was important that I finished off my captaincy in the correct manner. I felt the closing ceremony was every bit a part of my responsibility, to do the job well, as it was at the opening ceremony. As with all my public-speaking commitments that week, I had prepared exhaustively with the help of David Purdie. One thing David had told me, to help me settle my nerves, was to have one drink – just one, and anything I wanted – and before walking out to the opening ceremony I had downed a Scotch whisky.

Now, as Suzanne and I paused at the hotel bar before the wonderful walk down with the team to the closing ceremony, I had three whiskies! I was so emotional and on such a high I knew that one would just not be enough to settle me down. Thankfully, too, I had my winner's speech in my top pocket.

I had prepared for both results, and here – having dug it out of my desk at home for the benefit of this book, having not seen it for eight years – is the speech that I had entitled 'The Speech I Will Not Learn'. It reads:

> Curtis, members of the US Ryder Cup team, I congratulate you
> on a victory gained in hard but fair competition and in the
> true spirit of the game we all serve. A great feature of golf is the
> acceptance, with good grace, of the defeats which fortune hands
> down. Yours is the Cup, until our next meeting. Guard it well. We
> will be paying you a visit in two years' time.

I'm glad to say that speech never saw the light of day. Instead, as we all experienced the wonderful feeling of being the winning team at a closing ceremony, and after Curtis Strange had graciously mentioned my parents, Bob and June, in his own congratulatory speech, I was able to read out the following words:

> Curtis, I accept the Ryder Cup into our safekeeping, and I accept
> it from an outstanding captain of a fine US team. We will cherish
> it for two years, until we meet again. On behalf of the European
> team and myself, I thank Curtis and his men for the way the

Ryder Cup has been contested – with passion and intensity but also with the tradition and courtesy and sportsmanship which are the bedrock of our great game.

Throughout my professional life, the Ryder Cup has formed and strengthened friendships with many of my fellow players, both European and American. I could also give you countless examples of how it has done the same for others. My friendship with Curtis Strange was strengthened just by going head to head with him that week, and my relationship with all 12 of the players in my own team will always be special as a result of what happened at The Belfry – however well I knew some of them before the match began.

It is the sheer intensity of the Ryder Cup, and therefore of the emotions it stirs within you, that makes it such an unforgettable experience. I hate to say it, for obvious reasons, but it really is a bit like what people feel when they go to war together, because in a golfing sense you are experiencing things out there in the battle that you have never experienced before. Whatever you have achieved in your own individual career, it is a whole new world.

Tom Watson once said to Davis Love, in describing the Ryder Cup, that it was the only event that would make his knees shake. This was Watson talking, one of the very greatest players golf has seen. And, of course, as Davis later admitted, Tom was right.

It is the ultimate team event, comparable to anything else in sport, and you form the most tremendous bonds with people as a result of being involved in it. You get to see the bare bones of people in the way that elite sport truly exposes you in terms of both your character and your ability to play under its unique pressures. And you also see certain people, in an arena like the Ryder Cup, grow visibly in stature and become better people as well as better players. Yet, of course, it can also break people.

My own relationship with Howard Clark, for instance, was made so much stronger as a result of our Ryder Cup partnerships. He was so strong, and he always seemed to be there for me. He made such a big impression on me. But then there are guys like José Maria Cañizares and Costantino Rocca, whom I would never have got to know like I do if it weren't for the Ryder Cup. And Sergio García. I love him, as a person and for the way he plays the game, and my relationship with him works even across the generations because of the Ryder Cup.

Americans such as Lee Trevino, Ray Floyd and Hale Irwin, who are legends of the game, have become wonderful friends to me simply because of this great event and the chance it gave to get to know them as people. To be able to go into the American team room and chat with players like that, even after a defeat, was always an enormous privilege for me.

I could go on, and the list would stretch to dozens. Suffice to say that the Ryder Cup also gave me the opportunity of playing with one of my greatest friends, David Feherty, in a Ryder Cup match. It was a dream made reality, and the same might be said about what Darren Clarke and Lee Westwood felt when they played together, for instance. And could there be any bond stronger, or greater, than that which exists between Severiano Ballesteros and José María Olazábal?

Looking back now, as a former player and captain, I also see how hugely privileged I am to have had ten Ryder Cup experiences in my life. For many players over the years – including the likes of Phillip Price and Pierre Fulke in my own team – memories of being a Ryder Cup golfer were distilled into just one match. But what an amazing honour it was for them to have a winning experience too.

As for the influence on the match of the captain, it is interesting to see how the Americans reacted to their terrible beating at The K Club in 2006 by immediately giving their future captains – starting with Paul Azinger at Valhalla in 2008 – no fewer than four picks.

Europe, by contrast, allowed only two captain's selections from 1995 until 2008, although Colin Montgomerie will have three selections available to him for the 2010 match. Three picks were also the case from 1985 until 1993. In 1983, in Florida, Tony Jacklin had none – which didn't please him tremendously – while in 1979 and 1981 there were two wild cards permitted.

My own view is that Europe have now got it about right, with the top four world-ranked players being joined by the top five others from the European points list and then the three captain's picks.

With the vagaries of Europeans playing far more around the world, there is an argument for us going to three picks – in 2008, for instance, it was ridiculous that Nick Faldo could not find room in his team for Darren Clarke, who had won twice late in the year – but, in the American system, I think that it is almost as if they don't need as many as four picks.

To my mind, the captain's picks are there for the players who may have had an injury earlier in that year or who have made a dramatic late run of form, or for the odd case of those who do not play on their home tour but who combine very impressive results with not being ranked high enough in the world to make the team that way.

I think American captains now have a very difficult task, because they must have very good reasons not to pick those players who finish at nine and ten on their qualification list. If they don't pick them, and go for someone who finishes in eleventh or twelfth spot instead, or go for four players well outside those positions, it is putting a lot of unnecessary pressure on those players.

To me, four picks makes decisions even more difficult for a captain and has the effect of taking options away rather than increasing them. Also, I like a system in which the large majority of players have to play themselves onto their team. Someone who busts a gut to get that last place, for instance, is bringing an awful lot of desire and commitment to the party.

Ryder Cup captaincy should never be like being a football manager, with the power to pick every member of your team. Every Ryder Cup captain wants a balance to his team, especially in terms of a mix of younger and older players, and his own selections give him the opportunity to achieve that. Earning your own place on the team is, however, a vital part of what makes the event so great, and I speak as someone who played my way into all of my eight appearances!

From those I played with, and if I had the chance of captaining another Ryder Cup team on some fantasy island where everyone is at the peak of their powers, a highly personal selection would be Ballesteros, Olazábal, Westwood, Clarke, Faldo, García, Lyle, Woosnam, Langer, James, Montgomerie and Gallacher. Clark and Oosterhuis would be my vice captains and playing reserves.

And if I were given the chance of watching just one fantasy Ryder Cup fourball, again with those involved at their absolute best, it would be Ballesteros and Olazábal versus Nicklaus and Woods.

It is the future that is more important than such idle make-believe, though, and I hope the event maintains its current format and doesn't tinker with trying to fit in five foursomes and fourballs on each of the first two days. In fact, I don't think there would be the daylight available to do that.

I hope, from a European perspective, that the Ryder Cup is taken around mainland Europe – into Sweden, France, Germany and Italy as well as Spain again – and that golf on this side of the Atlantic continues to grow as a game as a result of that. I also hope that the event will never die, nor lose its style, and that the Americans win, on average, once every ten years or so!

Writing this, as the 2010 Ryder Cup approaches, it is wonderful for me to observe the genuine excitement of the new generation of golfing stars as they contemplate the chance to play in their first matches. Some from this new generation, of course, including the likes of Rory McIlroy and Ross Fisher from the European side, can look forward to many matches in the future if they maintain their form, their health and their desire.

Others, such as García and Westwood, are the new veterans of our team. It is now down to them to bear the leadership load that, for so long, the likes of Seve and Faldo and Langer and Monty carried so well. European golf, largely as a result of the Ryder Cup successes of the past three decades, has improved so much in terms of strength in depth that perhaps we now do not need to put out the same partnerships time and again on the first two days in the way that Ballesteros and Olazábal, Faldo and Woosnam, and Montgomerie and Langer were needed.

But any successful Ryder Cup team will always need leaders out on the course, and it is now time for García, Westwood and Pádraig Harrington to take on the mantle of their great predecessors.

García, indeed, could yet become the best Ryder Cup player ever seen. Why not? He has already won 16 points from his five matches to date – despite a poor 2008 match – and at his age could play in another five Ryder Cups at least. Some players, like Sergio, seem to raise their game during Ryder Cup competition, and I think that is because they love matchplay golf so much – plus the chance to represent their countries in such a magnificent event. It simply inspires them to reach greater heights.

I find myself wondering about what great new pairings might be formed in the future: what about García and McIlroy, for instance. How good might that pair be? And what about the two Molinari brothers, Francesco and Eduardo, who won the 2009 World Cup together for Italy? If they qualify to play together in a Ryder Cup team, how could you not pair them up?

But then there are likes of Ian Poulter, Paul Casey, Justin Rose, Luke Donald and Graeme McDowell. There are players such as Simon Dyson, who, in my opinion, would be a magnificent addition to the European team if he made the final 12. Martin Laird, the Scot who is doing so well on the US tour, is another intriguing character. And there are even younger guns than the remarkable McIlroy out there, such as the Italian Matteo Manassero and England's Oliver Fisher.

There are other names, too, and future European captains look as if they are going to have some incredibly difficult decisions to make when it comes to their two picks. It was hard enough for me when I had to choose just one from Olazábal and Jesper Parnevik, but future captains are likely to face having to pick their two choices from a whole clutch of highly worthy candidates.

I also like to imagine who some of our future European captains will be, and it's great fun for me to think about how they might do the job. Olazábal, in my opinion, will be one of the very greatest of Ryder Cup captains – you only have to remember his diplomacy at Brookline, after his singles match against Justin Leonard, and the passion he showed during his own magnificent Cup-playing career to know that he will be a huge success.

Olazábal, too, has already had vital experience as a vice captain, to Nick Faldo at Valhalla in 2008, and by all accounts he was a major influence on all the European players in the team room. Ollie had the European players in tears in the Saturday-evening meeting just with his passion for the Ryder Cup and what it means to be chosen to represent your country and your continent. Indeed, I would go so far as to say he is a captain born and bred and that he could prove to be our best captain ever. That's how strongly I rate him.

But then there are other excellent candidates, like Paul McGinley, who made such a good impression as captain of the British and Irish team at the last Seve Trophy, and Thomas Bjørn, who impressed everyone behind the scenes as one of Bernhard Langer's assistants at the 2004 Ryder Cup and has the respect of everyone in the European game.

Pádraig Harrington, too, will one day be a great captain, as I've no doubt Colin Montgomerie will be this year at Celtic Manor. And I wonder how Lee Westwood or Darren Clarke would do the job, and, one day well into the future, Sergio García? The main requirement, in my opinion and from my experience, is that any captain should still be playing on the main tour and can therefore have the best chance of a close working relationship with his team.

On the American side, I would think both Jim Furyk, a fighter, and Phil Mickelson, who is very affable and easy with people but has a lot of steel inside, would make great captains. Someone like Fred Couples, however, might not have the killer instinct of someone like Azinger. Fred might be a bit like Tom Kite as captain.

It is also fascinating to imagine Tiger Woods as a Ryder Cup captain one day. He would be a tough captain to play under simply because he is so good a player that it might be difficult to impress him. But perhaps he would be inspirational for his players in the way I remember Jack Nicklaus once inspiring me during the 1987 match when he arrived at our game, when he was American captain, and I hit a fantastic mid iron, which was always the weaker part of my golf. Jack's presence on the tee didn't put me off – it made me want to hit an even better stroke.

The answer to the question about what all these great current players will be like as Ryder Cup captains, when it gets to be their turn, is that they will all do it slightly differently – reflecting their characters as much as their ideas on how best to do the job in their particular year – and that's exactly how it should be.

There is no absolute blueprint on how to be a great Ryder Cup captain, but, as I did, you can take bits from other captains. What I got from Tony Jacklin, for instance, among other things, was the desire to make sure my players felt special and that I, as captain, had done everything in my power to give each of them the best chance of success.

The bottom line, though, is that you have to pour your own personality into the job, and that's why, after my own captaincy in 2002, it was totally right that none of Langer, Woosnam nor Faldo – nor, indeed, Monty this year – came to me asking specific questions about how to do it. Like me, they will have picked up bits and pieces over the years, as highly experienced Ryder Cup golfers, but they will all have had their own vision of how the job should be done, and quite right too.

During the lead-up to my captaincy, the only people I spoke to about specific aspects of the job were a number of sportspeople outside of golf, like Manchester United manager Sir Alex Ferguson, for instance – who told me a successful team could have no one who was treated or acted like a superstar – and Sven-Göran Eriksson, then the England football manager.

As a player, I found the sense of pride you had when you walked to the first tee to start a Ryder Cup match, or when you were introduced at the opening ceremony, was second to none.

As a vice captain, and then as captain, that sense of pride was multiplied by the feelings you got for your team. And for me, someone from the Seve Ballesteros generation of players, becoming Ryder Cup captain was all about continuing the legacy of Tony Jacklin.

For the next instalment of this magnificent sporting contest, we have two captains in Colin Montgomerie and Corey Pavin who, in their very different ways, both sum up the very essence of the Ryder Cup and why it has captured the imagination of so many. As someone who has lived and breathed the Ryder Cup, and for whom it is very dear, I believe it remains in very good hands.